THE PSYCHOLOGY
OF SOCIETY

THE PSYCHOLOGY
OF SOCIETY

AN ANTHOLOGY

SELECTED AND EDITED BY

Richard Sennett

VINTAGE BOOKS
A Division of Random House
NEW YORK

A VINTAGE ORIGINAL APRIL 1977
First Edition

Copyright © 1977 by Richard Sennett

All rights reserved under International and Pan-American
Copyright Conventions. Published in the United States by
Random House, Inc., New York, and simultaneously in
Canada by Random House of Canada Limited, Toronto.

Library of Congress Cataloging in Publication Data
Main entry under title:
The psychology of society.
1. Social psychology—Addresses, essays, lec-
tures. I. Sennett, Richard, 1943-
HM251.P844   301.1   76-62488
ISBN 0-394-72234-5

Manufactured in the United States of America

*Grateful acknowledgment is made to the following for permission to
reprint previously published material:*

George Allen & Unwin Ltd.: Specified excerpts from *The Genealogy of
Morals,* by Friedrich Nietzsche, translated by Horace B. Samuel.

The American Sociological Association: Specified excerpts from "On
Social Regression," by Philip E. Slater. Reprinted from *American Sociological Review,* Vol. 28, June 1963, pages 339–364, 340–353 and
359–363.

Basic Books, Inc.: Specified excerpts from *Metamorphosis: On the De-
velopment of Affect, Perception, Attention and Memory,* by Ernest G.
Schachtel. Copyright © 1959 by Basic Books, Inc., Publishers, New
York.

Beacon Press: Chapter 4, "The Dialectic of Civilization" by Herbert
Marcuse. Reprinted from *Eros and Civilization,* by Herbert Marcuse.
Copyright © 1955, 1966 by The Beacon Press.

The Bobbs-Merrill Co., Inc.: Quotations from "Role Distance," by
Erving Goffman. Reprinted from *Encounters* by Erving Goffman. Copyright © 1961 by Erving Goffman.

Dr. Elias Canetti: Specified excerpts from *Crowds and Power,* by Elias
Canetti, translated from the German by Carol Stewart (The Viking Press,
Inc. 1963).

For Herbert

CONTENTS

**Part Four   The Psychology of Power:
Five Classic Propositions**

Part Five   Marxian Psychology:
What It Can and Cannot Be

Part Six   Psychoanalytic Sociology: Four Directions

INTRODUCTION

Social psychology can best be defined as the study of the relationship between people's emotional life and the social conditions they experience. Up until a few decades ago this relationship had no formal or academic name. A nineteenth-century historian like Lord Acton would easily discuss what desires for power people have innately, in the course of writing diplomatic history. Writers of a more theoretical cast of mind like Machiavelli or Vico would analyze, with no sense of crossing boundaries or jumping disciplines, the effects of political tyranny upon the family or the effects of biological instincts upon politics.

In the past few generations those disciplinary boundaries have grown up, both in the schools and in the general categories we use in our thinking. Social psychology now lies uneasily between sociology and psychology. It ought to be what unifies these two subjects; it ought to correct the distortions which arise when, for whatever gains that may arise in analytic rigor, psyche and society have to be studied as though they were isolated from each other. But, in fact, the academic discipline of social psychology has sought to become a specialized subject of its own. It treats such themes as personal interchanges in small groups, the acquisition of language among children, or marital relations; it is less comfortable with, and often shuns as "unscientific," problems such as the family conceived as a political system, or the relationship between psychological processes of consciousness and forms of group awareness like class consciousness.

The purpose of *Psychology of Society* is to provide some sense of the larger, unifying dimensions of the subject. The book is aimed not only at college students taking a course in social psychology but also at the general reader who wants to understand something about the emotional conditions of society. The book attempts to realize its purpose in two ways. It poses questions which bridge the domains of psychology and sociology; it relates current thinking about these questions to thinking about them in the past, before the discipline of social psychology as such existed, but when the subject matter of social psychology appealed to a broad, diverse group of writers. Thus, the *Psychology of Society* attempts to place the subject in the context of Western intellectual history, as a way of reviving interest in the larger questions of the subject itself.

The purpose of the book dictates its form; this is a book of readings. The essays are classic works in social thought, from ancient Greece down to the present day. I have sought out in each writer chapters or passages which give his views on specific issues in the relationship between psyche and society. Because before the era of academic specialization these views appeared unselfconsciously in a writer's discussion of a wide variety of subjects, I have also tried to make clear in each case the context in which the writer presents his ideas. Moreover, when a writer presents a mass of evidence to support a particular point of view, I have not sought, either in my own commentary or in the textual selection, to summarize it all, but rather to present a representative example of the kind of evidence the writer uses in making his argument.

Since this book is meant to be read through, the editorial commentary on the essays is woven into each part rather than lumped together in a single introduction. My editorial interventions aim at two things. One is to orient the reader, by giving a sense of how a particular essay or group of essays relates to other essays or themes in the book. The other is to indicate what connection these essays have to current research of high quality in social psychology. I have tried to keep my own opinions out of this editorial matter as much as possible, although the very act of selecting something as worth reading is rendering an opinion on it.

Each of the six parts of this book concern a unifying theme in the relationship between emotional and social life. As the book progresses, the themes become those which particular schools of thought make use of in constructing this unifying relationship; for instance, at the opening of the book we look at the basic premise of St. Augustine's that different kinds of societies produce different psychological conditions within them—i.e., that the "psyche" is not a universal principle; by the end of the book we look at the particular interpretation modern Marxist writers give to this general idea.

The book opens with a presentation of the basic issues involved in thinking social-psychologically. This thinking involves two assumptions: that the psyche and the mind are not identical, and that social conditions can influence emotional experience. On the basis of these assumptions, two broad areas of inquiry open up: what kinds of images groups can form of themselves (the problem of what today is called collective personality) and what other kinds of symbols and values groups share because of their social interchanges (the problem, in modern terms, of collective consciousness). Collective behavior is involved in both these issues; in Part Two, general theories of collective behavior are presented as they arise in the description of two forms of collective activity: role-playing and crowd life.

In the first two parts of the book, the focus is on "society" as a general condition, rather than on the relationship of social and psychological change. This latter becomes the issue in Part Three; theories about changes in the modern family are presented, as are theories about life-cycle changes in the individual; these two are woven together in an opening section through an historian's argument about the hidden affinities between family and life-cycle evolution.

In Part Four the readings concentrate on the specific topic

of the psychology of power. Two of the writers in this section, Hobbes and Rousseau, have appeared before; now their general social-psychological ideas are applied to the question of the emotional motives for, and consequences of, the exercise of power. This part of the book is organized as a set of propositions about power which are largely anathema to the ideals of modern liberal democracy, but propositions which are also taken seriously by the liberal-democratic writers who are appalled by them.

In Part Five and Part Six we focus on two current schools of social-psychological thought which have grown out of the classic tradition. Among Marxian writers there is today strong debate about both the possibilities and the limits of a Marxian psychology; among Freudian writers there is today a search for ways of creating a psychoanalytic sociology which transcends a mechanical application of Freud's ideas to contemporary social conditions. Neither Marxian psychology nor psychoanalytic sociology is part of the social psychology taught in the academies, but by a perverse irony, both of these "outsider" approaches have kept more touch with the scholarship of the past than academic work in the field itself.

If we assume that writers in the past speak to present-day concerns, we cannot assume they speak as our contemporaries. Sometimes a simple chronological arrangement of writings can cope with this difficulty, so that the reader sees what is disputed, gained, or lost over time in the thinking about a specific issue; this chronological arrangement is used in the section on "roles" in this book, for instance. But chronology alone does not suffice to meet the problem. Apart from the question of whether any two persons mean the same thing when they use the same word, different cultures and different historical periods set up meanings for words which a particular writer will assume his audience understands, and therefore not explicate himself. A Roman writer would assume, for instance, that his audience understood that feeling an "emotion" and experiencing a change were a single phenomenon because in Latin *movere* means both to feel, in the sense of being moved, and movement itself. And conversely, when a writer like

Aristotle begins to probe consciously this equation of feeling and change, the modern reader in retrospect has trouble understanding why he makes the effort because he may not know that Aristotle is challenging an assumption which ruled classical thought.

If this problem is carried to its logical extreme, it leads to idiocy: nothing means anything to anyone outside a given time and place because everything is culturally and historically relative. Moreover, no one else in our own culture and time can really understand anyone else because, similarly, each does not know the context out of which the other speaks. The historical argument is in its extreme form the glorification of absolute subjectivity. In a less extreme form, the historical problem is real, and it requires acts of judgment and discrimination on the reader's part. A judgment that writers like Diderot or Hobbes do not speak our language may, of course, indicate as much what modern discourse has lost intellectually as it may "date" these writers in a pejorative sense. And the value of setting the issues of social psychology in the context of the Western intellectual tradition is therefore twofold: it may lie in reinstating meanings in contemporary issues which have been lost over time, and it may also lie in an act or recognition across the boundaries of time.

R.S.

PART ONE

BASIC ISSUES

I.
The Two Assumptions
of Social Psychology

Social psychology is based on two assumptions. Both are so sweeping that they can neither be falsified or proved; both are subject only to rational debate. Each idea was first introduced in antiquity. The first distinguished the psyche from the mind; the second separated different forms of social organization in terms of their psychic effects. It would be unreal to say that all writers in the Western tradition who have since dealt with issues of collective emotion accept both these distinctions, or even that writers who do believe both that psyche differs from mind and that society differs from society emotionally intend one and the same thing. But equally it is true that once these assumptions are made in one form or another, questions about the psychology of society can be raised in a coherent and logical way.

The distinction between mind and psyche originates in Greek thought. The Greek word *nous* meant "mind" in the sense of "that which is capable of receiving an impression," like a blank wax tablet which shows the clear impression of a stamp. The Greek word *psyche* by contrast meant "animating force" or "spirit." Thus Greek usage separated mind from movement, and allied the idea of movement in turn with what we would call today "the sphere of emotional experience." This latter connection was picked up in Latin; our word "emotion"

3

derives from the Latin *movere,* meaning "to move," a connection we directly express in English when in speaking of an emotional impact someone has upon us, we say we were "moved" by the other person.

These usages in antiquity are important clues to an enduring intellectual problem. The distinction between nous and psyche implies that feeling is exterior to thought, and moreover, that in some sense feeling governs thought; what animates is what makes an impress on the mind. Therefore, psychic energy, animation or force requires an explanation separated from a theory of cognition. But is it really correct to separate thinking from feeling?

Aristotle's *De Anima* is an attempt to answer this question by defining the principle of animation itself. In showing what is the nature of the "soul," by which he sometimes means the human psyche, sometimes the psyche (as animating principle) of all living things, Aristotle hopes then to move to broader questions like the relation of thinking and feeling, and of the mind to the body.

If an object or thing, Aristotle tells us, can both receive sensation and then react to the sensation in more than one way, so that the reaction is not a simple mechanical response, then the thing is alive. Sensitiveness and pliable react are the principles of animation; they define the psyche. The "mind" is the special process by which sensations received are reflected on, so that different kinds of responses are defined. Thus does Aristotle separate the mental, as the reflective, from sheer sensate impression—but both together are involved in the general process called "psyche." Because he thinks in this way, Aristotle speaks to a quite contemporary issue in the social sciences, the problem of stimulus and response; he argues that any living creature is alive only to the extent that it can formulate alternative responses to the sensations a given stimulus arouses. Mental reflection is therefore a *strategic* element in any form of human activity, even the activity of expressing the most violent emotions.

"Psyche" in Aristotle's work stands for a very general definition of life. How can it, in a more focused way, be related to concrete social conditions? This is the question St. Augustine takes up in *The City of God.* Augustine was influenced by Aristotle, as were all Roman and early Christian writers; Augustine accepts the notion that the psyche is a principle of animation, but he argues that the nature of this animation depends on the environment in which the living creature feels and reflects. If that environment is defective, the psychic processes at even the most minor and trivial level will always be defective; in a corrupt world, human beings can neither sensately feel nor reflect upon sensations fully. A defective environment always constricts human possibility, a constructive environment always expands it.

This seemingly simple idea in fact contains three complex elements. The first is that Augustine connects psychology to morality; how fully man realizes his psychological potential depends on the moral state of the society in which he lives. Second, society itself is taken to be variate—there are different kinds of societies—and the measure of these variations is ultimately how well or poorly a given society permits man to receive impressions and to reflect upon them. Third, the psyche is capable of improving or healing itself; we may all be born into sin, but we are also capable of redemption if we enter into a better life.

Thus, when the psyche is seen to be contingent on social conditions, it becomes plausible to imagine the psychic process as amenable to therapy and also, in its state of sickness or health, as a moral measure of the society.

Many cultures would find either the assumption of a psyche divorced from mind or a psychic process contingent on specific social conditions puzzling. A split between thought and feeling is alien to classical Buddhist thought, for example. In many so-called primitive societies, correlations between psychic principles and specific social conditions would be considered sacrilegious, since both the state of the soul and the conditions of material life are determined by the gods; to talk about the dependence of psyche upon society is to advance a false construct of thought which blinds one to their unifying Source. If these assumptions about psyche and society are not universal, they are on the other hand enormously broad within their own terms of reference. Some writers, like the Italian Enlightenment writer Vico, imagined psychic animation to be the life inherent in language, for language enables man to express the fact of feeling a sensation and then to reflect upon this feeling. Freud called the sensate part of the psychic process "blind instinctual energy," and introduced language only as the instrument of reflection. The theories advanced in this section by Aristotle and St. Augustine are basic to our subject in that they define a particular point of view, but a number of different, even conflicting theories can adopt this point of view.

1. Aristotle: *De Anima* [384–322 B.C.]

The soul is in some sense the principle of animal life. Our aim is to grasp and understand, first its essential nature, and secondly its properties; of these some are thought to be affections proper to the soul itself, while others are considered to attach to the animal owing to the presence within it of soul.

A further problem presented by the affections of soul is this: are they all affections of the complex of body and soul, or is there any one among them peculiar to the soul by itself? To determine this is indispensable but difficult. If we consider the majority of them, there seems to be no case in which the soul can act or be acted upon without involving the body; e.g. anger, courage, appetite, and sensation generally. Thinking seems the most probable exception; but if this too proves to be a form of imagination or to be impossible without imagination, it too requires a body as a condition of its existence. If there is any way of acting or being acted upon proper to soul, soul will be capable of separate existence; if there is none, its separate existence is impossible. In the latter case, it will be like what is straight, which has many properties arising from the straightness in it, e.g. that of touching a bronze sphere at a point, though straightness divorced from the other constituents of the straight thing cannot touch it in this way; it cannot be so divorced at all, since it is always found in a body. It therefore seems that all the affections of soul involve a body—passion, gentleness, fear, pity, courage, joy, loving, and hating; in all these there is a concurrent affection of the body. In support of this we may point to the fact that, while sometimes on the occasion of violent and striking occurrences there is no excitement or fear felt, on others faint and feeble stimulations produce these emotions, viz. when the body is already in a state of tension resembling its condition when we are angry. Here is a still clearer case: in the absence of any external cause of terror we find ourselves experiencing the feelings of a man in terror. From all this it is obvious that the affections of soul are enmattered formulable essences.

Consequently their definitions ought to correspond, e.g. anger should be defined as a certain mode of movement of such and such a body (or part or faculty of a body) by this or that cause and for this or that end. That is precisely why the study of the soul must fall within the science of Nature, at least so far as in its affections it manifests this double character. . . .

The movement of growth and decay, being found in all living things, must be attributed to the faculty of reproduction and nutrition, which is common to all: inspiration and expiration, sleep and waking, we must consider later: these too present much difficulty: at present we must consider local movement, asking what it is that originates forward movement in the animal.

If then Nature never makes anything without a purpose and never leaves out what is necessary (except in the case of mutilated or imperfect growths; and that here we have neither mutilation nor imperfection may be argued from the facts that such animals (a) can reproduce their species and (b) rise to completeness of nature and decay to an end), it follows that, had they been capable of originating forward movement, they would have possessed the organs necessary for that purpose. Further, neither can the calculative faculty or what is called 'mind' be the cause of such movement; for mind as speculative never thinks what is practicable, it never says anything about an object to be avoided or pursued, while this movement is always in something which is avoiding or pursuing an object. No, not even when it is aware of such an object does it at once enjoin pursuit or avoidance of it; e.g. the mind often thinks of something terrifying or pleasant without enjoining the emotion of fear. It is the heart that is moved (or in the case of a pleasant object some other part). Further, even when the mind does command and thought bids us pursue or avoid something, sometimes no movement is produced; we act in accordance with desire, as in the case of moral weakness. And, generally, we observe that the possessor of medical knowledge is not necessarily healing, which shows that something else is required to produce action in accordance with knowledge; the knowledge alone is not the cause. Lastly, appetite too is incompetent to account fully for movement; for those who successfully resist temptation have appetite and desire and yet follow mind and refuse to enact that for which they have appetite.

These two at all events appear to be sources of movement: appetite and mind (if one may venture to regard imagination as a kind of thinking; for many men follow their imaginations contrary to knowledge, and in all animals other than man there is no thinking or calculation but only imagination).

Both of these then are capable of originating local movement, mind and appetite: (1) mind, that is, which calculates means to an end, i.e. mind practical (it differs from mind speculative in the character of its end); while (2) appetite is in every form of it relative to an end: for that which is the object of appetite is the stimulant of mind practical; and that which is last in the process of thinking is the beginning of the action. It follows that there is a justification for regarding these two as the sources of movement, i.e. appetite and practical thought; for the object of appetite starts a movement and as a result of that thought gives rise to movement, the object of appetite being to it a source of stimulation. So too when imagination originates movement, it necessarily involves appetite. . . .

Appetites run counter to one another, when a principle of reason and a desire are contrary. This is possible only in beings with a sense of time, for while mind bids us hold back because of what is future, desire is influenced by what is just at hand: a pleasant object which is just at hand presents itself as both pleasant and good, without condition in either case, because of want of foresight into what is farther away in time. . . .

All movement involves three factors, (1) that which originates the movement, (2) that by means of which it originates it, and (3) that which is moved. The expression 'that which originates the movement' is ambiguous: it may mean either (*a*) something which itself is unmoved or (*b*) that which at once moves and is moved. Here that which moves without itself being moved is the realizable good, that which at once moves and is moved is the faculty of appetite (for that which is influenced by appetite so far as it is actually so influenced is set in movement, and appetite in the sense of actual appetite *is* a kind of movement), while that which is in motion is the animal. The instrument which appetite employs to produce movement is no longer psychical but bodily: hence the examination of it falls within the province of the functions common to body and soul. . . .

To sum up, then, and repeat what I have said, inasmuch as an animal is capable of appetite it is capable of self-movement; it is not capable of appetite without possessing imagination; and all imagination is either (1) calculative or (2) sensitive. In the latter all animals, and not only man, partake.

2. Augustine: *The City of God*   [d. 604?]

Now, the first man born of the two parents of the human race was Cain. He belonged to the city of man. The next born was Abel, and he was of the City of God. Notice here a parallel between the individual man and the whole race. We all experience as individuals what the Apostle says: 'It is not the spiritual that comes first, but the physical, and then the spiritual.' The fact is that every individual springs from a condemned stock and, because of Adam, must be first cankered and carnal, only later to become sound and spiritual by the process of rebirth in Christ. So, too, with the human race as a whole, as soon as human birth and death began the historical course of the two cities, the first to be born was a citizen of this world and only later came the one who was an alien in the city of men but at home in the City of God, a man predestined by grace and elected by grace. . . .

Now, it is recorded of Cain that he built a city, while Abel, as though he were merely a pilgrim on earth, built none. For, the true City of the saints is in heaven, though here on earth it produces citizens in whom it wanders as on a pilgrimage through time looking for the Kingdom of eternity. . . . When that day comes it will gather together all those who, rising in their bodies, shall have that Kingdom given to them in which, along with their Prince, the King of Eternity, they shall reign for ever and ever. . . . In the world community, then, we find two forms, one being the visible appearance of the earthly city and another whose presence serves as a shadow of the heavenly City. . . .

As for the city of this world, it is neither to last forever nor even to be a city, once the final doom of pain is upon it. Nevertheless, while history lasts, it has a finality of its own; it reaches such happiness by sharing a common good as is possible when there are no goods but the things of time to afford it happiness. This is not the kind of good that can give those who are content with it any freedom from fear. In fact, the city of man, for the most part, is a city of contention with opinions divided by foreign wars and domestic quarrels and by the demands for victories which either end in death or are merely momentary respites from further war. The reason is that whatever part of the city of the world raises the standard of war, it seeks to be lord of the world, when, in fact, it is enthralled in its own wickedness. Even when it conquers, its victory can be mortally poisoned by pride, and if, instead of taking pride in the success already achieved, it takes account of the nature and normal vicissitudes of life and is afraid of future failure, then the victory is merely momentary. The fact is that the power to reach domination by war is not the same as the power to remain in perpetual control.

Nevertheless, it is wrong to deny that the aims of human civilization are good, for this is the highest end that mankind of itself can achieve. For, however lowly the goods of earth, the aim, such as it is, is peace. The purpose even of war is peace! . . . The things of earth are not merely good; they are undoubtedly gifts from God. But, of course, if those who get such goods in the city of men are reckless about the better goods of the City of God, in which there is to be the ultimate victory of an eternal, supreme, and untroubled peace, if men so love the goods of earth as to believe that these are the only goods or if they love them more than the goods they know to be better, then the consequence is inevitable: misery and more misery.

Now, the city of man was first founded by a fratricide who was moved by envy to kill his brother, a man who, in his pilgrimage on earth, was a citizen of the City of God. It need not surprise us, then, that long afterwards, in the founding of that city which was to dominate so many peoples and become the capital of that earthly city with which I am dealing, the copy, so to speak, corresponded to the original—to what the Greeks call the archetype. For, in both cases, we have the same crime. As one of the poets puts it: 'With brother's blood the earliest walls were wet.' For Rome began, as Roman history records, when Remus was killed by Romulus, his brother. However, in this case, both men were citizens of the earthly city. It was the ambition of both of them to have the honor of founding the Roman republic, but that was an honor that could not be shared; it had to belong to one or the other. For, no one who had a passion to glory in domination could be fully the master if his power were diminished by a living co-regent. One of the two wanted to have the whole of the sovereignty; therefore, his associate was removed. Without the crime, his postiion would have had less power, but more prestige. However, the crime made everything worse than before.

What, then, is revealed in the quarrel between Remus and Romulus is the way in which the city of man is divided against itself, whereas, in the case of Cain and Abel, what we see is the enmity between the two cities, the city of man and the City of God. Thus, we have two wars, that of the wicked at war with the wicked and that of the wicked at war with the good. For, of course, once the good are perfectly good, there can be no war between them. This much is true, however, that while a good man is still on the way to perfection one part of him can be at war with another of his parts; because of this rebellious element, two good men can be at war with each other. The fact is that in everyone 'the flesh lusts against the spirit, and the spirit against the flesh.

The spiritual longing of one good man can be at war with the fleshly passion of another just as fleshly passion in one man can resist spiritual tendencies in another. And the war here is much like that between good and wicked men. So, too, a good deal like the war of the wicked against the wicked is the rivalry of fleshly desires in two good men, and this will continue until grace wins the ultimate victory of soundness over sickness in both of them. . . .

Man's will, then, is all-important. If it is badly directed, the emotions will be perverse; if it is rightly directed, the emotions will be not merely blameless but even praiseworthy. The will is in all of these affections; indeed, they are nothing else but inclinations of the will. For, what are desire and joy but the will in harmony with things we desire? And what are fear and sadness but the will in disagreement with things we abhor?

The consent of the will in the search for what we want is called desire; joy is the name of the will's consent to the enjoyment of what we desire. So, too, fear is aversion from what we do not wish to happen, as sadness is a disagreement of the will with something that happened against our will. Thus, according as the will of a man is attracted or repelled by the variety of things which he either seeks or shuns, so is it changed or converted into one or other of these different emotions.

It is clear, then, that the man who does not live according to man but according to God must be a lover of the good and, therefore, a hater of evil; since no man is wicked by nature but is wicked only by some defect, a man who lives according to God owes it to wicked men that his hatred be perfect, so that, neither hating the man because of his corruption nor loving the corruption because of the man, he should hate the sin but love the sinner. For, once the corruption has been cured, then all that is left should be loved and nothing remains to be hated. . . .

Now, since every home should be a beginning or fragmentary constituent of a civil community, and every beginning related to some specific end, and every part to the whole of which it is a part, it ought to follow that domestic peace has a relation to political peace. In other words, the ordered harmony of authority and obedience between those who live together has a relation to the ordered harmony of authority and obedience between those who live in a city. This explains why a father must apply certain regulations of civil law to the governance of his home, so as to make it accord with the peace of the whole community.

II.
Collective Personality

Two images govern much contemporary thinking about psychology and social life. One of these images is of collective personality, the other is of collective consciousness. It would be pleasing if we could simply define the differences between these two in terms of the premises we have already encountered. Collective personality would consist in the collective sensations people share in a society; collective consciousness would consist in the work of reflection and reaction people share in dealing with these common sensations. If the matter were divided up this way, we would neatly meet the Aristotelian criterion of psyche as sensation and reflexion, and the Augustinian criterion of sociability, by showing what sensations and reflexions were shared under given social conditions.

Unfortunately, this won't work. The word "personality" derives from *persona*, which means a creature with a recognizable shape or form. A collective personality must involve reflective activity, in that people recognize the common characteristics of this person who is the image they share as "an Arab" or "a worker" or "a woman." The word "consciousness" also pulls in another direction. Knowledge and consciousness are in many philosophical systems closely related, as for instance in the writings of Descartes. This means it would be possible to talk about collective consciousness simply as knowledge shared in common: if we work in this direction we soon erase the Aristotelian distinction between psyche and nous, anima and mind.

As a practical matter, a definition of collective personality has to run something as follows: it is the ability of people to interact with each other, to share sensations, to perform common actions, only because people believe they share an essential ilkeness; this likeness is expressed in images of a typical person. Collective consciousness involves the ability of people to interact without having to imagine this collective person of whom they all are part. Writers who work in terms of the first idea believe people cannot share without seeing themselves in other persons. For housewives to interact they must have an image of what "a housewife" is, an image each person relates to her own life; the fusion of self and other creates pictures of the person who "represents" a particular group. Writers who work in terms of the second idea think other collective symbols—like purity and impurity, sin and virtue—develop through interaction rather than just group self-representation. Furthermore, the writers on collective consciousness we are concerned with reject the notion that consciousness and knowledge are the same. These writers, and especially Karl Marx, are interested in the ways consciousness can falsely depict social reality. These writers on collective consciousness are concerned with questions such as how people come to share illusions or why false consciousness is pleasurable. While there is a difference between writers who use the idea of collective personality and those who don't in order to arrive at notions of how people feel related to each other, often this difference is a matter of emphasis, and that emphasis can change within the course of a writer's work.

In the present section, writers who believe in or emphasize the creation of a collective person are our subject. And here we do find a sharp analytic division. One group of writers who analyzes collective personality simply magnifies the characteristics of individuals, so that the sensations and reflectiveness of the group person is the same *in kind* as the sensations and reflectiveness of one person. The other group of writers believes that social conditions act upon the persons in a group such that a common image arises unlike the personality of any single human being. In the first approach, the human being is "writ large" in society; in the second, society creates its own cast of characters.

Among the theories of a person "writ large" we will focus on those of Thomas Hobbes and Sigmund Freud. Hobbes saw this collective person to be formed by the power of imagination; Freud saw this collective person to be formed by blind instinct. In the selections from *Leviathan* appearing in this section, Hobbes starts with a description of the faculties every human being possesses to define and shape experiences in individual life. These faculties lean heavily on what would be called today powers of fantasy and projection—one makes up of meanings for experience by the use of imagination for what is inadequately known in fact. From this starting point, Hobbes then analyzes how we imagine what other people are like; he shows how a sense of a common collective person is erected through this movement in fantasy from self to others. This collective person embodies the common good; he is, in Hobbes's words, the "commonwealth in person," and because of this collective fiction men have created for themselves, they become willing to surrender liberties which in isolation they would be loath to give up. Just as the commonwealth is a fictional person, the laws of the commonwealth have a fictional quality. Neither Nature nor Truth is their source, but rather man's imagination; laws cannot be challenged, because they offend nature or any outside standard of truth. For this reason, Hobbes's critics, like Rousseau, believed Hobbes used a psychological beginning to justify the political ends of tyranny. Hobbes's method, shorn of the politics, is the progenitor of a type of social-psychological analysis today called "the social construction of reality" approach, and whose major modern exponent is Peter Berger (see Berger and Luckmann, *The Social Construction of Reality*).

Hobbes might seem to have reversed the assumption with which St. Augustine began, for the starting point here is the reflective processes of the individual rather than social conditions. But in fact there is a unity between the two writers: in Hobbes, as in Augustine, if the commonwealth is by the accidents of history or circumstance imperfectly built, then the imaginative powers of all the person in it will subsequently be diminished, and the commonwealth will be in danger of becoming an empty police state.

Freud, however, might be read as a real challenge to the Augustinian idea, for in Freud's writing on society, composed in his life after the basic precepts of psychoanalysis had been developed, social forces are indeed portrayed as the forces of individual personality magnified. A thousand psychopaths are more dangerous than one, but "psychopathology" may be defined in a way that fits both cases. As appears in the selections from *Group Psychology and the Analysis of the Ego* and *Civilization and Its Discontents,* society is at war with itself because each man is psychologically at war with himself. This inner warfare, between the instincts of death and life, at the basic interpersonal level expresses itself as warfare between individuals in a family; the warfare in the family, resulting from the conflicting instincts within each of its members, is an image repeated in larger and larger social groups. The image can be infinitely magnified, because no matter what his circumstances, Freud argues, man can never escape the burden of the instinctual base.

Here then are two ways to conceive of a single person made into a collective figure. What difference does it make to think in this way? One answer to that is Tocqueville's; he uses this framework for analyzing the meaning of majority tyranny in a society, and justifying resistance to the will of the majority, as appears in the selection from Volume I of Tocqueville's *Democracy in America.*

Another way to conceive of collective personality is to imagine that social conditions so transform individuals that group images of personality are created which cannot be related to the images of single persons.

The classic version of this idea has been to contrast the individual human being in a state of nature to human beings living together in society. As individuals move from the natural state into the social state, an image of the group is formed, in terms of a man whose features express the features of their common life. Each person partakes of him, but this social creature can be known only by describing the material, legal, educational, and moral circumstances which define the particular society, not by describing the natural instincts, the abilities, or the tastes of any one person. He is "the Jew," "the Italian," or at a more general level, "the citizen." In Rousseau's *Social Contract,* this social being is portrayed as a phenomenon defying natural instinct; the being speaks through a "general will" and is concretely to be recognized as a personage Rousseau calls the "legislator." The legislator is what everyone in society should be like; his personality is a model, a law. Thus the legislator is not a phantom force to Rousseau, but an image in which power, in his words, "has a human face." And therefore, just as Rousseau reproached Hobbes for using psychology to justify tyranny, Rousseau's critics reproach him for a psychological idea which may lead to a justification of personal dictatorship.

One need not use the idea of a movement from a state of nature to society in order to conceive of uniquely collective forms of personality. In the work of the nineteenth-century psychologist Gustave Le Bon, crowds are analyzed as collective experiences which transform the personalities of individuals; Le Bon deduces a "crowd mentality" unlike the mentality of any of the persons in the crowd when they are alone. Sometimes it is useful to see what one writer cannot understand about the work of another; for this reason Freud's commentary on Le Bon is presented along with the selection from Le Bon's *The Crowd.* Freud believed Le Bon was mainly after the unconscious element in crowd behavior and that this meant Le Bon was working in the same vein as he, Freud, was. In fact, Le Bon's project was quite different; he wanted to show how the anonymity of crowds permits eruptions of unconscious feeling to take place, but as a result, a collective phenomenon is produced; this group experience is not comparable to the unconscious experience of the individual.

Again, if we ask what is the consequence of conceiving of

collective personality as something unique, Tocqueville gives an apt example. Five years elapsed between the writing of the first and second volumes of the *Democracy,* and during this time he moved away from his belief that society is like an individual to a belief that unique traits of character are produced by social experience. In the chapter from Volume II of the *Democracy* presented here, Tocqueville takes a new view of democractic tyranny; now he is concerned with the majority's self-destructive qualities rather than with the suppression of minority dissidents.

3. Thomas Hobbes: *Leviathan*   [1588–1679]

Nature, the art whereby God hath made and governs the world, is by the *art* of man, as in many other things, so in this also imitated, that it can make an artificial animal. For seeing life is but a motion of limbs, the beginning whereof is in some principal part within; why may we not say, that all *automata* (engines that move themselves by springs and wheels as doth a watch) have an artificial life? For what is the *heart,* but a *spring;* and the *nerves,* but so many *strings;* and the *joints,* but so many *wheels,* giving motion to the whole body, such as was intended by the artificer? *Art* goes yet further, imitating that rational and most excellent work of nature, *man.* For by art is created that great LEVIATHAN called a COMMONWEALTH, or STATE, in Latin CIVITAS, which is but an artificial man; though of greater stature and strength than the natural, for whose protection and defence it was intended; and in which the *sovereignty* is an artificial *soul,* as giving life and motion to the whole body; the *magistrates,* and other *officers* of judicature and execution, artificial *joints; reward* and *punishment,* by which fastened to the seat of the sovereignty every joint and member is moved to perform his duty, are the *nerves,* that do the same in the body natural; the *wealth* and *riches* of all the particular members, are the *strength; salus populi,* the *people's safety,* its *business; counsellors,* by whom all things needful for it to know are suggested unto it, are the *memory; equity,* and *laws,* an artificial *reason* and *will; concord, health; sedition, sickness;* and *civil war, war, death.* Lastly, the *pacts* and *covenants,* by which the parts of this body politic were at first made, set together, and united, resemble that *fiat,* or the *let us make man,* prounounced by God in the creation.

To describe the nature of this artificial man, I will consider.

First, the *matter* thereof, and the *artificer;* both which is *man.*

Secondly, *how,* and by what *covenants* it is made; what are the *rights* and just *power* or *authority* of a *sovereign;* and what it is that *preserveth* or *dissolveth* it.

Thirdly, what is a *Christian commonwealth.*

Lastly, what is the *kingdom of darkness.*

Concerning the first, there is a saying much usurped of late, that *wisdom* is acquired, not by reading of *books,* but of *men. . . .*

But there is another saying not of late understood, by which they might learn truly to read one another, if they would take the pains; that is, *nosce teipsum, read thyself:* which was not meant, as it is now used, to countenance, either the barbarous state of men in power, towards their inferiors; or to encourage men of low degree, to a saucy behaviour towards their betters; but to teach us, that for the similitude of the thoughts and passions of one man, to the thoughts and passions of another, whosoever looketh into himself, and considereth what he doth, when he does *think, opine, reason, hope, fear,* &c. and upon what grounds; he shall thereby read and know, what are the thoughts and passions of all other men upon the like occasions. I say the similitude of *passions,* which are the same in all men, *desire, fear, hope,* &c.; not the similitude of the *objects* of the passions, which are the things *desired, feared, hoped,* &c.: for these the constitution individual, and particular education, do so vary, and they are so easy to be kept from our knowledge, that the characters of man's heart, blotted and confounded as they are with dissembling, lying, counterfeiting, and erroneous doctrines, are legible only to him that searcheth hearts. And though by men's actions we do discover their design sometimes; yet to do it without comparing them with our own, and distinguishing all circumstances, by which the case may come to be altered, is to decypher without a key, and be for the most part deceived, by too much trust, or by too much diffidence; as he that reads, is himself a good or evil man. . . .

Much memory, or memory of many things, is called *experience*. Again, imagination being only of those things which have been formerly perceived by sense, either all at once, or by parts at several times; the former, which is the imagining the whole object as it was presented to the sense, *is simple* imagination, as when one imagineth a man, or horse, which he hath seen before. The other is *compounded;* as when, from the sight of a man at one time, and of a horse at another, we conceive in our mind a Centaur. So when a man compoundeth the image of his own person with the image of the actions of another man, as when a man imagines himself a Hercules or an Alexander, which happeneth often to them that are much taken with reading of romances, it is a compound imagination, and properly but a fiction of the mind. . . .

A PERSON, is he, *whose words or actions are considered, either as his own, or as representing the words or actions of another man, or of any other thing, to whom they are attributed, whether truly or by fiction.*

When they are considered as his own, then is he called a *natural person:* and when they are considered as representing the words and actions of another, then is he a *feigned* or *artificial person.*

The word person is Latin: instead whereof the Greeks have πρόσωπον, which signifies the *face,* as *persona* in Latin signifies the *disguise,* or *outward appearance* of a man, counterfeited on the stage; and sometimes more particularly that part of it, which disguiseth the face, as a mask or vizard: and from the stage, hath been translated to any representer of speech and action, as well in tribunals, as theatres. So that a *person,* is the same that an *actor* is, both on the stage and in common conversation; and to *personate,* is to *act,* or *represent* himself, or another; and he that acteth another, is said to bear his person, or act in his name; in which sense Cicero useth it where he says, *Unus sustineo tres personas; mei, adversarii, et judicis*: I bear three persons; my own, my adversary's, and the judge's; and is called in divers occasions, diversly; as a *representer,* or *representative,* a *lieutenant,* a *vicar,* an *attorney,* a *deputy,* a *procurator,* an *actor,* and the like.

Of persons artificial, some have their words and actions *owned* by those whom they represent. And then the person is the *actor;* and he that owneth his words and actions, is the AUTHOR: in which case the actor acteth by authority. For that which in speaking of goods and possessions, is called an *owner,* and in Latin *dominus,* in Greek κύριος speaking of actions, is called author. And as the right of possession, is called dominion; so the right of doing any action, is called AUTHORITY. So that by authority, is always understood a right of doing any act; and *done by authority,* done by commission, or licence from him whose right it is. . . .

There are few things, that are incapable of being represented by fiction. Inanimate things, as a church, an hospital, a bridge, may be personated by a rector, master, or overseer. But things inanimate, cannot be authors, nor therefore give authority to their actors: yet the actors may have authority to procure their maintenance, given them by those that are owners, or governors of those things. And therefore, such things cannot be personated, before there be some state of civil government. Likewise children, fools, and madmen that have no use of reason, may be personated by guardians, or curators; but can be no authors, during that time, of any action done by them, longer than, when they shall recover the use of reason, they shall judge the same reasonable. Yet during the folly, he that hath right of governing them, may give authority to the guardian. But this again has no place but in a state civil, because before such estate, there is no dominion of persons

An idol, or mere figment of the brain, may be personated; as were the gods of the heathen: which by such officers as the state appointed, were personated, and held possessions, and other goods, and rights, which men from time to time dedicated, and consecrated unto them. But idols cannot be authors: for an idol is nothing. The authority proceeded from the state: and therefore before introduction of civil government, the gods of the heathen could not be personated.

A multitude of men, are made *one* person, when they are by one man, or one person, represented; so that it be done with the consent of every one of that multitude in particular. For it is the *unity* of the representer, not the *unity* of the represented, that maketh the person *one*. And it is the representer that beareth the person, and but one person: and *unity*, cannot otherwise be understood in multitude.

And because the multitude naturally is not *one*, but *many;* they cannot be understood for one; but many authors, of every thing their representative saith, or doth in their name; every man giving their common representer, authority from himself in particular; and owning all the actions the representer doth, in case they give him authority without stint: otherwise, when they limit him in what, and how far he shall represent them, none of them owneth more than they gave him commission to act.

And if the representative consist of many men, the voice of the greater number, must be considered as the voice of them all. For if the lesser number pronounce, for example, in the affirmative, and the greater in the negative, there will be negatives more than enough to destroy the affirmatives; and thereby the excess of negatives, standing uncontradicted, are the only voice the representative hath. . . .

The only way to erect such a common power, as may be able to defend them from the invasion of foreigners, and the injuries of one another, and thereby to secure them in such sort, as that by their own industry, and by the fruits of the earth, they may nourish themselves and live contentedly; is, to confer all their power and strength upon one man, or upon one assembly of men, that may reduce all their wills, by plurality of voices, unto one will: which is as much as to say, to appoint one man, or assembly of men, to bear their person; and every one to own, and acknowledge himself to be author of whatsoever he that so beareth their person, shall act, or cause to be acted, in those things which concern the common peace and safety; and therein to submit their wills, every one to his will, and their judgments, to his judgment. This is more than consent, or concord; it is a real unity of them all, in one and the same person, made by covenant of every man with every man, in such manner, as if every man should say to every man, *I authorize and give up my right of governing myself, to this man, or to this assembly of men, on this condition, that thou give up thy right to him, and authorize all his actions in like manner.* This done, the multitude so united in one person, is called a COMMONWEALTH, in Latin CIVITAS. This is the generation of the great LEVIATHAN, or rather, to speak more reverently, of that *mortal god,* to which we owe under the *immortal God,* our peace and defence. For by this authority, given him by every particular man in the commonwealth, he hath the use of so much power and strength conferred on him, that by terror thereof, he is enabled to perform the wills of them all, to peace at home, and mutual aid against their enemies abroad. And in him consisteth the essence of the commonwealth; which, to define it, is *one person, of whose acts a great multitude, by mutual covenants one with another, have made themselves every one the author, to the end he may use the strength and means of them all, as he shall think expedient, for their peace and common defence.*

And he that carrieth this person, is called SOVEREIGN, and said to have *sovereign power;* and every one besides, his SUBJECT.

The attaining to this sovereign power, is by two ways. One, by natural force; as when a man maketh his children, to submit themselves, and their children to his government, as being able to destroy them if they refuse; or by war subdueth his enemies to his will, giving them their lives on that condition. The other, is when men agree amongst themselves, to submit to some man, or assembly of men, voluntarily, on confidence to be protected by him against all others. This latter, may be called a political commonwealth, or commonwealth by *institution;* and the former, a commonwealth by *acquisition.* . . .

Men, for the attaining of peace, and conservation of themselves thereby, have made an artificial man, which we call a commonwealth; so also have they made artificial chains, called *civil laws,* which they themselves, by mutual covenants, have fastened at one end, to the lips of that man, or assembly, to whom they have given the sovereign power; and at the other end to their own ears. These bonds, in their own nature but weak, may nevertheless be made to hold, by the danger, though not by the difficulty of breaking them.

4. Sigmund Freud: *Group Psychology and the Analysis of the Ego*   [1856–1939]

The contrast between individual psychology and social or group psychology, which at a first glance may seem to be full of significance, loses a great deal of its sharpness when it is examined more closely. It is true that individual psychology is concerned with the individual man and explores the paths by which he seeks to find satisfaction for his instinctual impulses; but only rarely and under certain exceptional conditions is individual psychology in a position to disregard the relations of this individual to others. In the individual's mental life someone else is invariably involved, as a model, as an object, as a helper, as an opponent; and so from the very first individual psychology, in this extended but entirely justifiable sense of the words, is at the same time social psychology as well.

The relations of an individual to his parents and to his brothers and sisters, to the object of his love, and to his physician—in fact all the relations which have hitherto been the chief subject of psycho-analytic research—may claim to be considered as social phenomena; and in this respect they may be contrasted with certain other processes, described by us as 'narcissistic', in which the satisfaction of the instincts is partially or totally withdrawn from the influence of other people. The contrast between social and narcissistic—Bleuler would perhaps call them 'autistic'—mental acts therefore falls wholly within the domain of individual psychology, and is not well calculated to differentiate it from a social or group psychology.

The individual in the relations which have already been mentioned—to his parents and to his brothers and sisters, to the person he is in love with, to his friend, and to his physician— comes under the influence of only a single person, or of a very small number of persons, each one of whom has become enormously important to him. Now in speaking of social or group psychology it has become usual to leave these relations on one side and to isolate as the subject of inquiry the influencing of an individual by a large number of people simultaneously, people with whom he is connected by something, though otherwise they may in many respects be strangers to him. Group psychology is therefore concerned with the individual man as a member of a race, of a nation, of a caste, of a profession, of an institution, or as a component part of a crowd of people who have been organized into a group at some particular time for some definite purpose. . . .

If a psychology, concerned with exploring the predispositions, the instinctual impulses, the motives and the aims of an individual man down to his actions and his relations with those who are nearest to him, had completely achieved its task, and had cleared up the whole of these matters with their interconnections, it would then suddenly find itself confronted by a new task which would lie before it unachieved. It would be obliged to explain the surprising fact that under a certain condition this individual, whom it had come to understand, thought, felt and acted in quite a different way from what would have been expected. And this condition is his insertion into a collection of people which has acquired the characteristic of a 'psychological group'. What, then, is a 'group'? How does it acquire the capacity for exercising such a decisive influence over the mental life of the individual? And what is the nature of the mental change which it forces upon the individual?

It is the task of a theoretical group psychology to answer these three questions. The best way of approaching them is evidently to start with the third. Observation of the changes in the individual's reactions is what provides group psychology with its material; for every attempt at an explanation must be preceded by a description of the thing that is to be explained. . . .

I shall make an attempt at using the concept of *libido* for the purpose of throwing light upon group psychology, a concept which has done us such good service in the study of psychoneuroses.

Libido is an expression taken from the theory of the emotions. We call by that name the energy, regarded as a quantitative magnitude (though not at present actually measurable), of those instincts which have to do with all that may be comprised under the word 'love'. The nucleus of what we mean by love naturally consists (and this is what is commonly called love, and what the poets sing of) in sexual love with sexual union as its aim. But we do not separate from this—what in any case has a share in the name 'love'—on the one hand, self-love, and on the other, love for parents and children, friendship and love for humanity in general, and also devotion to concrete objects and to abstract ideas. Our justification lies in the fact that psychoanalytic research has taught us that all these tendencies are an expression of the same instinctual impulses; in relations between the sexes these impulses force their way towards sexual union, but in other circumstances they are diverted from this aim or are prevented from reaching it, though always preserving enough of their original nature to keep their identity recognizable (as in such features as the longing for proximity, and self-sacrifice). . . .

The evidence of psycho-analysis shows that almost every intimate emotional relation between two people which lasts for some time—marriage, friendship, the relations between parents and children—contains a sediment of feelings of aversion and hostility, which only escapes perception as a result of a repression. This is less disguised in the common wrangles between business partners or in the grumbles of a subordinate at his superior. The same thing happens when men come together in larger units. Every time two families become connected by a marriage, each of them thinks itself superior to or of better birth than the other. Of two neighbouring towns each is the other's most jealous rival; every little canton looks down upon the others with contempt. Closely related races keep one another at arm's length; the South German cannot endure the North German, the Englishman casts every kind of aspersion upon the Scot, the Spaniard despises the Portuguese. We are no longer astonished that greater differences should lead to an almost insuperable repugnance, such as the Gallic people feel for the German, the Aryan for the Semite, and the white races for the coloured.

When this hostility is directed against people who are otherwise loved we describe it as ambivalence of feeling; and we explain the fact, in what is probably far too rational a manner, by means of the numerous occasions for conflicts of interest which arise precisely in such intimate relations. In the undisguised antipathies and aversions which people feel towards strangers with whom they have to do we may recognize the expression of self-love—of narcissism. This self-love works for the preservation of the individual, and behaves as though the occurrence of any divergence from his own particular lines of development involved a criticism of them and a demand for their alteration. We do not know why such sensitiveness should have been directed to just these details of differentiation; but it is unmistakable that in this whole connection men give evidence of a readiness for hatred, an aggressiveness, the source of which is unknown, and to which one is tempted to ascribe an elementary character.

But when a group is formed the whole of this intolerance vanishes, temporarily or permanently, within the group. So long as a group formation persists or so far as it extends, individuals in the group behave as though they were uniform, tolerate the peculiarities of its other members, equate themselves with them, and have no feeling of aversion towards them. Such a limitation of narcissism can, according to our theoretical views, only be produced by one factor, a libidinal tie with other people. Love for oneself knows only one barrier—love for others, love for objects. The question will at once be raised whether community of interest in itself, without any addition of libido, must not necessarily lead to the toleration of other people and to considerateness for them. This objection may be met by the reply that nevertheless no lasting limitation of narcissism is effected in this way, since this tolerance does not persist longer than the immediate advantage gained from the other people's collaboration. But the practical importance of this discussion is less than might be supposed, for experience has shown that in cases of collaboration libidinal ties are regularly formed between the fellow-workers which prolong and solidify the relation between them to a point beyond what is merely profitable. The same thing occurs in men's social relations as has become familiar to psycho-analytic research in the course of the development of the individual libido. The libido attaches itself to the satisfaction of the great vital needs, and chooses as its first objects the people who have a share in that process. And in the development of mankind as a whole, just as in individuals, love alone acts as the civilizing factor in the sense that it brings a change from egoism to altruism. And this is true both of sexual love for women, with all the obligations which it involves of not harming the things that are dear to women, and also of desexualized, sublimated homosexual love for other men, which springs from work in common.

If therefore in groups narcissistic self-love is subject to limitations which do not operate outside them, that is cogent evidence that the essence of a group formation consists in new kinds of libidinal ties among the members of the group. . . .

In 1912 I took up a conjecture of Darwin's to the effect that the primitive form of human society was that of a horde ruled over despotically by a powerful male. I attempted to show that the fortunes of this horde have left indestructible traces upon the history of human descent; and, especially, that the development of totemism, which comprises in itself the beginnings of religion, morality, and social organization, is connected with the killing of the chief by violence and the transformation of the paternal horde into a community of brothers. To be sure, this is only a hypothesis . . . but I think it is creditable to such a hypothesis if it proves able to bring coherence and understanding into more and more new regions.

Human groups exhibit once again the familiar picture of an individual of superior strength among a troop of equal companions, a picture which is also contained in our idea of the primal horde. The psychology of such a group, as we know it from the descriptions to which we have so often referred—the dwindling of the conscious individual personality, the focusing of thoughts and feelings into a common direction, the predominance of the affective side of the mind and of unconscious psychical life, the tendency to the immediate carrying out of intentions as they emerge—all this corresponds to a state of regression to a primitive mental activity, of just such a sort as we should be inclined to ascribe to the primal horde.

Thus the group appears to us as a revival of the primal horde. Just as primitive man survives potentially in every individual, so the primal horde may arise once more out of any random collection; in so far as men are habitually under the sway of group formation we recognize in it the survival of the primal horde. . . . from the first there were two kinds of psychologies, that of the individual members of the group and that of the father, chief, or leader. The members of the group were subject to ties just as we see them to-day, but the father of the primal horde was free. His intellectual acts were strong and independent even in isolation, and his will needed no reinforcement from others. Consistency leads us to assume that his ego had few libidinal ties; he loved no one but himself, or other people only in so far as they served his needs. To objects his ego gave away no more than was barely necessary.

He, at the very beginning of the history of mankind, was the 'superman' whom Nietzsche only expected from the future. Even to-day the members of a group stand in need of the illusion that they are equally and justly loved by their leader; but the leader himself need love no one else, he may be of a masterful nature, absolutely narcissistic, self-confident and independent. We know that love puts a check upon narcissism, and it would be possible to show how, by operating in this way, it became a factor of civilization.

The primal father of the horde was not yet immortal, as he later became by deification. If he died, he had to be replaced; his place was probably taken by a youngest son, who had up to then been a member of the group like any other. There must therefore be a possibility of transforming group psychology into individual psychology; a condition must be discovered under which such a transformation is easily accomplished, just as it is possible for bees in case of necessity to turn a larva into a queen instead of into a worker. One can imagine only one possibility: the primal father had prevented his sons from satisfying their directly sexual impulsions; he forced them into abstinence and consequently into the emotional ties with him and with one another which could arise out of those of their impulsions that were inhibited in their sexual aim. He forced them, so to speak, into group psychology. His sexual jealousy and intolerance became in the last resort the causes of group psychology.

Whoever became his successor was also given the possibility of sexual satisfaction, and was by that means offered a way out of the conditions of group psychology. The fixation of the libido to woman and the possibility of satisfaction without any need for delay or accumulation made an end of the importance of those of his sexual impulsions that were inhibited in their aim, and allowed his narcissism always to rise to its full height. We shall return in a postscript to this connection between love and character formation.

We may further emphasize, as being specially instructive, the relation that holds between the contrivance by means of which an artificial group is held together and the constitution of the primal horde. We have seen that with an army and a Church this contrivance is the illusion that the leader loves all of the individuals equally and justly. But this is simply an idealistic remodelling of the state of affairs in the primal horde, where all of the sons knew that they were equally *persecuted* by the primal father, and *feared* him equally. This same recasting upon which all social duties are built up is already presupposed by the next form of human society, the totemic clan. The indestructible strength of the family as a natural group formation rests upon the fact that this necessary presupposition of the father's equal love can have a real application in the family. . . .

The leader of the group is still the dreaded primal father; the group still wishes to be governed by unrestricted force; it has an extreme passion for authority; in Le Bon's phrase, it has a thirst for obedience. The primal father is the group ideal. . . .

We have said that it would be possible to specify the point in the mental development of mankind at which the advance from group psychology to individual psychology was achieved also by the individual members of the group.

For this purpose we must return for a moment to the scientific myth of the father of the primal horde. He was later on exalted into the creator of the world, and with justice, for he had produced all the sons who composed the first group. He was the ideal of each one of them, at once feared and honoured, a fact which led later to the idea of taboo. These many individuals eventually banded themselves together, killed him and cut him in pieces. None of the group of victors could take his place, or, if one of them did, the battles began afresh, until they understood that they must all renounce their father's heritage. They then formed the totemic community of brothers, all with equal rights and united by the totem prohibitions which were to preserve and to expiate the memory of the murder. But the dissatisfaction with what had been achieved still remained, and it became the source of new developments. The persons who were united in this group of brothers gradually came towards a revival of the old state of things at a new level. The male became once more the chief of a family, and broke down the prerogatives of the gynaecocracy which had become established during the fatherless period. As a compensation for this he may at that time have acknowledged the mother deities, whose priests were castrated for the mother's protection, after the example that had been given by the father of the primal horde. And yet the new family was only a shadow of the old one; there were numbers of fathers and each one was limited by the rights of the others.

It was then, perhaps, that some individual, in the exigency of his longing, may have been moved to free himself from the group and take over the father's part. He who did this was the first epic poet; and the advance was achieved in his imagination. This poet disguised the truth with lies in accordance with his longing. He invented the heroic myth. The hero was a man who by himself had slain the father—the father who still appeared in the myth as a totemic monster. Just as the father had been the boy's first ideal, so in the hero who aspires to the father's place the poet now created that first ego ideal. The transition to the hero was probably afforded by the youngest son, the mother's favourite, whom she had protected from paternal jealousy, and who, in the era of the primal horde, had been the father's successor. In the lying poetic fancies of prehistoric times the woman, who had been the prize of battle and the temptation to murder, was probably turned into the active seducer and instigator to the crime.

The hero claims to have acted alone in accomplishing the deed, which certainly only the horde as a whole would have ventured upon. But, as Rank has observed, fairy tales have preserved clear traces of the facts which were disavowed. For we often find in them that the hero who has to carry out some difficult task (usually the youngest son, and not infrequently one who has represented himself to the father-substitute as being stupid, that is to say, harmless)—we often find, then, that this hero can carry out his task only by the help of a crowd of small animals, such as bees or ants. These would be the brothers in the primal horde, just as in the same way in dream symbolism insects or vermin signify brothers and sisters (contemptuously, considered as babies). Moreover every one of the tasks in myths and fairy tales is easily recognizable as a substitute for the heroic deed.

The myth, then, is the step by which the individual emerges from group psychology. The first myth was certainly the psychological, the hero myth; the explanatory nature myth must have followed much later. The poet who had taken this step and had in this way set himself free from the group in his imagination, is nevertheless able (as Rank has further observed) to find his way back to it in reality. For he goes and relates to the group his hero's deeds which he has invented. At bottom this hero is no one but himself. Thus he lowers himself to the level of reality, and raises his hearers to the level of imagination. But his hearers understand the poet, and, in virtue of their having the same relation of longing towards the primal father, they can identify themselves with the hero.

The lie of the heroic myth culminates in the deification of the hero. Perhaps the deified hero may have been earlier than the Father God and may have been a precursor to the return of the primal father as a deity. The series of gods, then, would run chronologically: Mother Goddess—Hero—Father God. But it is only with the elevation of the never-forgotten primal father that the deity acquires the features that we still recognize in him to-day.

Sigmund Freud: *Civilization and Its Discontents*

Of all the slowly developed parts of analytic theory, the theory of the instincts is the one that has felt its way the most painfully forward. And yet that theory was so indispensable to the whole structure that something had to be put in its place. In what was at first my utter perplexity, I took as my starting-point a saying of the poet-philosopher, Schiller, that 'hunger and love are what moves the world'. Hunger could be taken to represent the instincts which aim at preserving the individual; while love strives after objects, and its chief function, favoured in every way by nature, is the preservation of the species. Thus, to begin with, ego-instincts and object-instincts confronted each other. It was to denote the energy of the latter and only the latter instincts that I introduced the term 'libido'. Thus the antithesis was between the ego-instincts and the 'libidinal' instincts of love (in its widest sense) which were directed to an object. . . .

Neurosis was regarded as the outcome of a struggle between the interest of self-preservation and the demands of the libido, a struggle in which the ego had been victorious but at the price of severe sufferings and renunciations. . . .

Every analyst will admit that even to-day this view has not the sound of a long-discarded error. Nevertheless, alterations in it became essential, as our enquiries advanced from the repressed to the repressing force, from the object-instincts to the ego. The decisive step forward was the introduction of the concept of narcissism. . . .

The concept of narcissism made it possible to obtain an analytic understanding of the traumatic neuroses and of many of the affections bordering on the psychoses, as well as of the latter themselves. . . .

Nevertheless, there still remained in me a kind of conviction, for which I was not as yet able to find reasons, that the instincts could not all be of the same kind. My next step was taken in *Beyond the Pleasure Principle,* when the compulsion to repeat and the conservative character of instinctual life first attracted my attention. Starting from speculations on the beginning of life and from biological parallels, I drew the conclusion that, besides the instinct to preserve living substance and to join it into ever larger units, there must exist another, contrary instinct seeking to dissolve those units and to bring them back to their primaeval, inorganic state. That is to say, as well as Eros there was an instinct of death. The phenomena of life could be explained from the concurrent or mutually opposing action of these two instincts. It was not easy, however, to demonstrate the activities of this supposed death instinct. The manifestations of Eros were conspicuous and noisy enough. It might be assumed that the death instinct operated silently within the organism towards its dissolution, but that, of course, was no proof. A more fruitful idea was that a portion of the instinct is diverted towards the external world and comes to light as an instinct of aggressiveness and destructiveness. In this way the instinct itself could be pressed into the service of Eros, in that the organism was destroying some other thing, whether animate or inanimate, instead of destroying its own self. Conversely, any restriction of this aggressiveness directed outwards would be bound to increase the self-destruction, which is in any case proceeding. At the same time one can suspect from this example that the two kinds of instinct seldom—perhaps never—appear in isolation from each other, but are alloyed with each other in varying and very different proportions and so become unrecognizable to our judgment. In sadism, long since known to us as a component instinct of sexuality, we should have before us a particularly strong alloy of this kind between trends of love and the destructive instinct; while its counterpart, masochism, would be a union between destructiveness directed inwards and sexuality—a union which makes what is otherwise an imperceptible trend into a conspicuous and tangible one. . . .

In all that follows I adopt the standpoint, therefore, that the inclination to aggression is an original, self-subsisting instinctual disposition in man, and I return to my view [p. 59] that it constitutes the greatest impediment to civilization. At one point in the course of this enquiry [p. 43] I was led to the idea that civilization was a special process which mankind undergoes, and I am still under the influence of that idea. I may now add that civilization is a process in the service of Eros, whose purpose is to combine single human individuals, and after that families, then races, peoples and nations, into one great unity, the unity of mankind. Why this has to happen, we do not know; the work of Eros is precisely this. These collections of men are to be libidinally bound to one another. Necessity alone, the advantages of work in common, will not hold them together. But man's natural aggressive instinct, the hostility of each against all and of all against each, opposes this programme of civilization. This aggressive instinct is the derivative and the main representative of the death instinct which we have found alongside of Eros and which shares world-dominion with it. And now, I think, the meaning of the evolution of civilization is no longer obscure to us. It must present the struggle between Eros and Death, between the instinct of life and the instinct of destruction, as it works itself out in the human species. This struggle is what all life essentially consists of, and the evolution of civilization may therefore be simply described as the struggle for life of the human species. And it is this battle of the giants that our nurse-maids try to appease with their lullaby about Heaven. . . .

What means does civilization employ in order to inhibit the aggressiveness which opposes it, to make it harmless, to get rid of it, perhaps? We have already become acquainted with a few of these methods, but not yet with the one that appears to be the most important. This we can study in the history of the development of the individual. What happens in him to render his desire for aggression innocuous? Something very remarkable, which we should never have guessed and which is nevertheless quite obvious. His aggressiveness is introjected, internalized; it is, in point of fact, sent back to where it came from—that is, it is directed towards his own ego. There it is taken over by a portion of the ego, which sets itself over against the rest of the ego as super-ego, and which now, in the form of 'conscience', is ready to put into action against the ego the same harsh aggressiveness that the ego would have liked to satisfy upon other, extraneous individuals. The tension between the harsh super-ego and the ego that is subjected to it, is called by us the sense of guilt; it expresses itself as a need for punishment. Civilization, therefore, obtains mastery over the individual's dangerous desire for aggression by weakening and disarming it and by setting up an agency within him to watch over it, like a garrison in a conquered city. . . .

Thus we know of two origins of the sense of guilt: one arising from fear of an authority, and the other, later on, arising from fear of the super-ego. The first insists upon a renunciation of instinctual satisfactions; the second, as well as doing this, presses for punishment, since the continuance of the forbidden wishes cannot be concealed from the super-ego. We have also learned how the severity of the super-ego—the demands of conscience—is to be understood. It is simply a continuation of the severity of the external authority, to which it has succeeded and which it has in part replaced. We now see in what relationship the renunciation of instinct stands to the sense of guilt. Originally, renunciation of instinct was the result of fear of an external authority: one renounced one's satisfactions in order not to lose its love. If one has carried out this renunciation, one is, as it were, quits with the authority and no sense of guilt should remain. But with fear of the super-ego the case is different. Here, instinctual renunciation is not enough, for the wish persists and cannot be concealed from the super-ego. Thus, in spite of the renunciation that has been made, a sense of guilt comes about. This constitutes a great economic disadvantage in the erection of a super-ego, or, as we may put it, in the formation of a conscience. Instinctual renunciation now no longer has a completely liberating effect; virtuous continence is no longer rewarded with the assurance of love. A threatened external unhappiness—loss of love and punishment on the part of the external authority—has been exchanged for a permanent internal unhappiness, for the tension of the sense of guilt. . . .

Now, I think, we can at last grasp two things perfectly clearly: the part played by love in the origin of conscience and the fatal inevitability of the sense of guilt. Whether one has killed one's father or has abstained from doing so is not really the decisive thing. One is bound to feel guilty in either case, for the sense of guilt is an expression of the conflict due to ambivalence, of the eternal struggle between Eros and the instinct of destruction or death. This conflict is set going as soon as men are faced with the task of living together. So long as the community assumes no other form than that of the family, the conflict is bound to express itself in the Oedipus complex, to establish the conscience and to create the first sense of guilt. When an attempt is made to widen the community, the same conflict is continued in forms which are dependent on the past; and it is strengthened and results in a further intensification of the sense of guilt. Since civilization obeys an internal erotic impulsion which causes human beings to unite in a closely-knit group, it can only achieve this aim through an ever-increasing reinforcement of the sense of guilt. What began in relation to the father is completed in relation to the group. If civilization is a necessary course of development from the family to humanity as a whole, then—as a result of the inborn conflict arising from ambivalence, of the eternal struggle between the trends of love and death—there is inextricably bound up with it an increase of the sense of guilt, which will perhaps reach heights that the individual finds hard to tolerate.

5. Alexis de Tocqueville:
Democracy in America, Vol. I   [1805–1859]

TYRANNY OF THE MAJORITY.

I hold it to be an impious and detestable maxim that, politically speaking, the people have a right to do anything; and yet I have asserted that all authority originates in the will of the majority. Am I, then, in contradiction with myself?

A general law, which bears the name of justice, has been made and sanctioned, not only by a majority of this or that people, but by a majority of mankind. The rights of every people are therefore confined within the limits of what is just. A nation may be considered as a jury which is empowered to represent society at large and to apply justice, which is its law. Ought such a jury, which represents society, to have more power than the society itself whose laws it executes?

When I refuse to obey an unjust law, I do not contest the right of the majority to command, but I simply appeal from the sovereignty of the people to the sovereignty of mankind. Some have not feared to assert that a people can never outstep the boundaries of justice and reason in those affairs which are peculiarly its own; and that consequently full power may be given to the majority by which it is represented. But this is the language of a slave.

A majority taken collectively is only an individual, whose opinions, and frequently whose interests, are opposed to those of another individual, who is styled a minority. If it be admitted that a man possessing absolute power may misuse that power by wronging his adversaries, why should not a majority be liable to the same reproach? Men do not change their characters by uniting with one another; nor does their patience in the presence of obstacles increase with their strength. For my own part, I cannot believe it; the power to do everything, which I should refuse to one of my equals, I will never grant to any number of them.

I do not think that, for the sake of preserving liberty, it is possible to combine several principles in the same government so as really to oppose them to one another. The form of government that is usually termed *mixed* has always appeared to me a mere chimera. Accurately speaking, there is no such thing as a *mixed government,* in the sense usually given to that word, because in all communities some one principle of action may be discovered which preponderates over the others. England in the last century, which has been especially cited as an example of this sort of government, was essentially an aristocratic state, although it comprised some great elements of democracy; for the laws and customs of the country were such that the aristocracy could not but preponderate in the long run and direct public affairs according to its own will. The error arose from seeing the interests of the nobles perpetually contending with those of the people, without considering the issue of the contest, which was really the important point. When a community actually has a mixed government—that is to say, when it is equally divided between adverse principles—it must either experience a revolution or fall into anarchy.

I am therefore of the opinion that social power superior to all others must always be placed somewhere; but I think that liberty is endangered when this power finds no obstacle which can retard its course and give it time to moderate its own vehemence.

Unlimited power is in itself a bad and dangerous thing. Human beings are not competent to exercise it with discretion. God alone can be omnipotent, because his wisdom and his justice are always equal to his power. There is no power on earth so worthy of honor in itself or clothed with rights so sacred that I would admit its uncontrolled and all-predominant authority. When I see that the right and the means of absolute command are conferred on any power whatever, be it called a people or a king, an aristocracy or a democracy, a monarchy or a republic, I say there is the germ of tyranny, and I seek to live elsewhere, under other laws.

In my opinion, the main evil of the present democratic institutions of the United States does not arise, as is often asserted in Europe, from their weakness, but from their irresistible strength. I am not so much alarmed at the excessive liberty which reigns in that country as at the inadequate securities which one finds there against tyranny.

When an individual or a party is wronged in the United States, to whom can he apply for redress? If to public opinion, public opinion constitutes the majority; if to the legislature, it represents the majority and implicitly obeys it; if to the executive power, it is appointed by the majority and serves as a passive tool in its hands. The public force consists of the majority under arms; the jury is the majority invested with the right of hearing judicial cases; and in certain states even the judges are elected by the majority. However iniquitious or absurd the measure of which you complain, you must submit to it as well as you can. . . .

If, on the other hand, a legislative power could be so constituted as to represent the majority without necessarily being the slave of its passions, an executive so as to retain a proper share of authority, and a judiciary so as to remain independent of the other two powers, a government would be formed which would still be democratic while incurring scarcely any risk of tyranny.

I do not say that there is a frequent use of tyranny in America at the present day; but I maintain that there is no sure barrier against it, and that the causes which mitigate the government there are to be found in the circumstances and the manners of the country more than in its laws.

6. Jean-Jacques Rousseau: *The Social Contract* [1712–1778]

Man was born free, and he is everywhere in chains. Those who think themselves the masters of others are indeed greater slaves than they. How did this transformation come about? I do not know. How can it be made legitimate? That question I believe I can answer.

If I were to consider only force and the effects of force, I should say: 'So long as a people is constrained to obey, and obeys, it does well; but as soon as it can shake off the yoke, and shakes it off, it does better; for since it regains its freedom by the same right as that which removed it, a people is either justified in taking back its freedom, or there is no justifying those who took it away.' But the social order is a sacred right which serves as a basis for all other rights. And as it is not a natural right, it must be one founded on covenants. The problem is to determine what those covenants are. . . .

I assume that men reach a point where the obstacles to their preservation in a state of nature prove greater than the strength that each man has to preserve himself in that state. Beyond this point, the primitive condition cannot endure, for then the human race will perish if it does not change its mode of existence.

Since men cannot create new forces, but merely combine and control those which already exist, the only way in which they can preserve themselves is by uniting their separate powers in a combination strong enough to overcome any resistance, uniting them so that their powers are directed by a single motive and act in concert.

Such a sum of forces can be produced only by the union of

separate men, but as each man's own strength and liberty are the chief instruments of his preservation, how can he merge his with others' without putting himself in peril and neglecting the care he owes to himself? This difficulty, which brings me back to my present subject, may be expressed in these words:

'How to find a form of association which will defend the person and goods of each member with the collective force of all, and under which each individual, while uniting himself with the others, obeys no one but himself, and remains as free as before.' This is the fundamental problem to which the social contract holds the solution.

The articles of this contract are so precisely determined by the nature of the act, that the slightest modification must render them null and void; they are such that, though perhaps never formally stated, they are everywhere the same, everywhere tacitly admitted and recognized; and if ever the social pact is violated, every man regains his original rights and, recovering his natural freedom, loses that social freedom for which he exchanged it.

These articles of association, rightly understood, are reducible to a single one, namely the total alienation by each associate of himself and all his rights to the whole community. Thus, in the first place, as every individual gives himself absolutely, the conditions are the same for all, and precisely because they are the same for all, it is in no one's interest to make the conditions onerous for others.

Secondly, since the alienation is unconditional, the union is as perfect as it could be, and no individual associate has any longer any rights to claim; for if rights were left to individuals, in the absence of any higher authority to judge between them and the public, each individual, being his own judge in some causes, would soon demand to be his own judge in all; and in this way the state of nature would be kept in being, and the association inevitably become either tyrannical or void.

Finally, since each man gives himself to all, he gives himself to no one; and since there is no associate over whom he does not gain the same rights as others gain over him, each man recovers the equivalent of everything he loses, and in the bargain he acquires more power to preserve what he has.

If, then, we eliminate from the social pact everything that is not essential to it, we find it comes down to this: 'Each one of us puts into the community his person and all his powers under the supreme direction of the general will; and as a body, we incorporate every member as an indivisible part of the whole.'

Immediately, in place of the individual person of each contracting party, this act of association creates an artificial and collective body composed of as many members as there are voters in the assembly, and by this same act that body acquires its unity, its common *ego,* its life and its will. The public person thus formed by the union of all other persons was once called the *city,** and is now known as the *republic* or the *body politic.* In its passive role it is called the *state,* when it plays an active role it is the *sovereign;* and when it is compared to others of its own kind, it is a *power.* Those who are associated in it take collectively the name of a *people,* and call themselves individually *citizens,* in so far as they share in the sovereign power, and *subjects,* in so far as they put themselves under the laws of the state. However, these words are often confused, each being mistaken for another; but the essential thing is to know how to recognize them when they are used in their precise sense. . . .

It follows from what I have argued that the general will is always rightful and always tends to the public good; but it does not follow that the decisions of the people are always equally

---

* The real meaning of this word has been almost entirely lost in the modern world, when a town and a city are thought to be identical, and a citizen the same as a burgess. People forget that houses may make a town, while only citizens can make a city. The Carthaginians once paid dearly for this mistake. I have never read of the title *cives* being given to the subject of any prince, not even to the Macedonians in ancient times or the English today, in spite of their being closer to liberty than any other people. The French alone apply the name 'Citizen' freely to everyone, and that is because they do not know what it means, as their Dictionaries prove; if they did know, they would be guilty, in usurping it, of *lèse-majesté;* as it is, they use the word to designate social status and not legal right. When Bodin wanted to speak of citizens and burgesses, he made the gross error of mistaking the one for the other. Monsieur d'Alembert avoids this mistake; and in his article on 'Geneva' he correctly distinguishes between the four orders of men (five, if aliens are included) which are found in our town, and of which only two compose the republic. No other French author to my knowledge has understood the real meaning of the word 'citizen'.

right. We always want what is advantageous but we do not always discern it. The people is never corrupted, but it is often misled; and only then does it seem to will what is bad.

There is often a great difference between the will of all [what all individuals want] and the general will; the general will studies only the common interest while the will of all studies private interest, and is indeed no more than the sum of individual desires. But if we take away from these same wills, the pluses and minuses which cancel each other out, the sum of the difference is the general will.

From the deliberations of a people properly informed, and provided its members do not have any communication among themselves, the great number of small differences will always produce a general will and the decision will always be good. But if groups, sectional associations are formed at the expense of the larger association, the will of each of these groups will become general in relation to its own members and private in relation to the state; we might then say that there are no longer as many votes as there are men but only as many votes as there are groups. The differences become less numerous and yield a result less general. Finally, when one of these groups becomes so large that it can dominate the rest, the result is no longer the sum of many small differences, but one great divisive difference; then there ceases to be a general will, and the opinion which prevails is no more than a private opinion.

Thus if the general will is to be clearly expressed, it is imperative that there should be no sectional associations in the state, and that every citizen should make up his own mind for himself—such was the unique and sublime invention of the great Lycurgus. But if there are sectional associations, it is wise to multiply their number and to prevent inequality among them, as Solon, Numa and Servius did. These are the only precautions which can ensure that the general will is always enlightened and the people protected from error. . . .

Just as an architect who puts up a large building first surveys and tests the ground to see if it can bear the weight, so the wise lawgiver begins not by laying down laws good in themselves, but by finding out whether the people for whom the laws are intended is able to support them. Such reasoning led Plato to refuse to provide laws for the Arcadians or the Cyreneans, because he well knew that those peoples, being rich, would not tolerate equality. Crete, too, provides an example of good laws and bad men, for the people Milos tried to discipline were dominated by their vices.

The world has seen a thousand splendid nations that could not have accepted good laws, and even those that might have accepted them could have done so only for short periods of their long history. Nations, like men, are teachable only in their youth; with age they become incorrigible. Once customs are established and prejudices rooted, reform is a dangerous and fruitless enterprise; a people cannot bear to see its evils touched, even if only to be eradicated; it is like a stupid, pusillanimous invalid who trembles at the sight of a physician.

I am not denying that just as certain afflictions unhinge men's minds and banish their memory of the past, so there are certain violent epochs and revolutions in states which have the same effect on peoples that psychological shocks may have on individuals; only instead of forgetting the past, they look back on it in horror, and then the state, after being consumed by civil war, is born again, so to speak, from its own ashes, and leaps from the arms of death to regain the vigour of youth. Such was the experience of Sparta at the time of Lycurgus, of Rome after the Tarquins, and, in the modern world, of Holland and Switzerland after the expulsion of the tyrants.

But such events are unusual; they are exceptional cases to be explained by the special constitution of the states concerned. It could not even happen twice to the same people; because although a people can make itself free while it is still uncivilized, it cannot do so when its civil energies are worn out. Disturbances may well destroy a civil society without a revolution being able to restore it, so that as soon as the chains are broken, the state falls apart and exists no longer; then what is needed is a master, not a liberator. Free peoples, remember this maxim: liberty can be gained, but never *regained*.

For nations, as for men, there is a time of maturity which

they must reach before they are made subject to law; but the maturity of a people is not always easily recognized; and something done too soon will prove abortive. Peoples differ; one is amenable to discipline from the beginning; another is not, even after ten centuries. The Russians have never been effectively governed because the attempt to govern them was made too early. Peter the Great had the talent of a copyist; he had no true genius, which is creative and makes everything from nothing. Some of the things he did were sound; most were misguided. He saw that his people was uncivilized, but he did not see that it was unready for government; he sought to civilize his subjects when he ought rather to have drilled them. He tried to turn them into Germans or Englishmen instead of making them Russians. He urged his subjects to be what they were not and so prevented them from becoming what they might have been. This is just how a French tutor trains his pupil to shine for a brief moment in his childhood and then grow up into a nonentity. The Russian Empire would like to subjugate Europe and will find itself subjugated. The Tartars, its subjects or neighbours, will become its masters—and ours. Such a revolution seems to me inevitable. All the kings of Europe are labouring in concert to hasten its coming.

Just as nature has set bounds to the stature of a well-formed man, outside which he is either a giant or a dwarf, so, in what concerns the best constitution for a state, there are limits to the size it can have if it is to be neither too large to be well-governed nor too small to maintain itself. In the body politic there is a maximum of strength which must not be exceeded, and which is often fallen short of as a result of expansion. The more the social bond is stretched, the slacker it becomes; and in general a small state is relatively stronger for its size than a large one.

7. Gustave Le Bon: *The Crowd*   [1841–1931]

The whole of the common characteristics with which heredity endows the individuals of a race constitute the genius of the race. When, however, a certain number of these individuals are gathered together in a crowd for purposes of action, observation proves that, from the mere fact of their being assembled, there result certain new psychological characteristics, which are added to the racial characteristics and differ from them at times to a very considerable degree.

Organised crowds have always played an important part in the life of peoples, but this part has never been of such moment as at present. The substitution of the unconscious action of crowds for the conscious activity of individuals is one of the principal characteristics of the present age. . . .

Men are ruled by ideas, sentiments, and customs—matters which are of the essence of ourselves. Institutions and laws are the outward manifestation of our character, the expression of its needs. Being its outcome, institutions and laws cannot change this character. . . . It is necessary, in consequence, when studying a social phenomenon, to consider it successively under two very different aspects. It will then be seen that the teachings of pure reason are very often contrary to those of practical reason. . . .

Crowds, doubtless, are always unconscious, but this very unconsciousness is perhaps one of the secrets of their strength. In the natural world beings exclusively governed by instinct accomplish acts whose marvellous complexity astounds us. Reason is an attribute of humanity of too recent date and still too imperfect to reveal to us the laws of the unconscious, and still more to take its place. The part played by the unconscious in all our acts is immense, and that played by reason very small. The unconscious acts like a force still unknown. . . .

In its ordinary sense the word "crowd" means a gathering of individuals of whatever nationality, profession, or sex, and whatever be the chances that have brought them together. From the psychological point of view the expression "crowd" assumes quite a different signification. Under certain given circumstances, and only under those circumstances, an agglomeration of men presents new characteristics very different from those of the individuals composing it. The sentiments and ideas of all the persons in the gathering take one and the same direction, and their conscious personality vanishes. . . .

The most striking peculiarity presented by a psychological crowd is the following: Whoever be the individuals that compose it, however like or unlike be their mode of life, their occupations, their character, or their intelligence, the fact that they have been transformed into a crowd puts them in possession of a sort of collective mind which makes them feel, think, and act in a manner quite different from that in which each individual of them would feel, think, and act were he in a state of isolation. There are certain ideas and feelings which do not come into being, or do not transform themselves into acts except in the case of individuals forming a crowd. . . .

In the aggregate which constitutes a crowd there is in no sort a summing-up of or an average struck between its elements. What really takes place is a combination followed by the creation of new characteristics, just as in chemistry certain elements, when brought into contact—bases and acids, for example—combine to form a new body possessing properties quite different from those of the bodies that have served to form it.

It is easy to prove how much the individual forming part of a crowd differs from the isolated individual, but it is less easy to discover the causes of this difference.

To obtain at any rate a glimpse of them it is necessary in the first place to call to mind the truth established by modern psychology, that unconscious phenomena play an altogether preponderating part not only in organic life, but also in the operations of the intelligence. The conscious life of the mind is of small importance in comparison with its unconscious life. . . .

It is more especially with respect to those unconscious elements which constitute the genius of a race that all the individuals belonging to it resemble each other, while it is principally in respect to the conscious elements of their character—the fruit of education, and yet more of exceptional hereditary conditions—that they differ from each other. Men the most unlike in the matter of their intelligence possess instincts, passions, and feelings that are very similar. In the case of everything that belongs to the realm of sentiment—religion, politics, morality, the affections and antipathies, etc.—the most eminent men seldom surpass the standard of the most ordinary individuals. From the intellectual point of view an abyss may exist between a great mathematician and his bootmaker, but from the point of view of character the difference is most often slight or non-existent.

It is precisely these general qualities of character, governed by forces of which we are unconscious, and possessed by the majority of the normal individuals of a race in much the same degree—it is precisely these qualities, I say, that in crowds become common property. In the collective mind the intellectual aptitudes of the individuals, and in consequence their individuality, are weakened. The heterogeneous is swamped by the homogeneous, and the unconscious qualities obtain the upper hand. . . .

This very fact that crowds possess in common ordinary qualities explains why they can never accomplish acts demanding a high degree of intelligence. In crowds it is stupidity and not mother-wit that is accumulated. . . .

If the individuals of a crowd confined themselves to putting in common the ordinary qualities of which each of them has his share, there would merely result the striking of an average, and not, as we have said is actually the case, the creation of new characteristics. How is it that these new characteristics are created? This is what we are now to investigate.

Different causes determine the appearance of these characteristics peculiar to crowds, and not possessed by isolated individuals. The first is that the individual forming part of a crowd acquires, solely from numerical considerations, a sentiment of invincible power which allows him to yield to instincts which, had he been alone, he would perforce have kept under restraint. He will be the less disposed to check himself from the consideration that, a crowd being anonymous, and in consequence irresponsible, the sentiment of responsibility which always controls individuals disappears entirely.

The second cause, which is contagion, also intervenes to determine the manifestation in crowds of their special characteristics, and at the same time the trend they are to take. Contagion is a phenomenon of which it is easy to establish the presence, but that it is not easy to explain. It must be classed among those phenomena of a hypnotic order, which we shall shortly study. In a crowd every sentiment and act is contagious, and contagious to such a degree that an individual readily sacrifices his personal interest to the collective interest. This is an aptitude very contrary to his nature, and of which a man is scarcely capable, except when he makes part of a crowd.

A third cause, and by far the most important, determines in the individuals of a crowd special characteristics which are quite contrary at times to those presented by the isolated individual. I allude to that suggestibility of which, moreover, the contagion mentioned above is neither more nor less than an effect.

To understand this phenomenon it is necessary to bear in mind certain recent physiological discoveries. We know to-day that by various processes an individual may be brought into such a condition that, having entirely lost his conscious personality, he obeys all the suggestions of the operator who has deprived him of it, and commits acts in utter contradiction with his character and habits.

Such also is approximately the state of the individual forming part of a psychological crowd. He is no longer conscious of his acts. In his case, as in the case of the hypnotised subject, at the same time that certain faculties are destroyed, others may be brought to a high degree of exaltation. Under the influence of a suggestion, he will undertake the accomplishment of certain acts

with irresistible impetuosity. This impetuosity is the more irresistible in the case of crowds than in that of the hypnotised
subject, from the fact that, the suggestion being the same for all
the individuals of the crowd, it gains in strength by reciprocity.
The individualities in the crowd who might possess a personality sufficiently strong to resist the suggestion are too few in
number to struggle against the current. At the utmost, they may
be able to attempt a diversion by means of different suggestions.
It is in this way, for intance, that a happy expression, an image
opportunely evoked, have occasionally deterred crowds from
the most bloodthirsty acts.

We see, then, that the disappearance of the conscious
personality, the predominance of the unconscious personality,
the turning by means of suggestion and contagion of feelings
and ideas in an identical direction, the tendency immediately to
transform the suggested ideas into acts; these we see, are the
principal characteristics of the individual forming part of a
crowd. He is no longer himself, but has become an automaton
who has ceased to be guided by his will.

Moreover, by the mere fact that he forms part of an
organised crowd, a man descends several rungs in the ladder of
civilisation. Isolated, he may be a cultivated individual; in a
crowd, he is a barbarian—that is, a creature acting by instinct.
He possesses the spontaneity, the violence, the ferocity, and
also the enthusiasm and heroism of primitive beings, whom he
further tends to resemble by the facility with which he allows
himself to be impressed by words and images—which would be
entirely without action on each of the isolated individuals composing the crowd—and to be induced to commit acts contrary
to his most obvious interests and his best-known habits. An
individual in a crowd is a grain of sand amid other grains of
sand, which the wind stirs up at will.

It is for these reasons that juries are seen to deliver ver-
dicts of which each individual juror would disapprove, that
parliamentary assemblies adopt laws and measures of which
each of their members would disapprove in his own person.
Taken separately, the men of the French Revolutionary Convention were enlightened citizens of peaceful habits. United in a

crowd, they did not hesitate to give their adhesion to the most savage proposals, to guillotine individuals most clearly innocent, and, contrary to their interests, to renounce their inviolability and to decimate themselves.

It is not only by his acts that the individual in a crowd differs essentially from himself. Even before he has entirely lost his independence, his ideas and feelings have undergone a transformation, and the transformation is so profound as to change the miser into a spendthrift, the sceptic into a believer, the honest man into a criminal, and the coward into a hero. The renunciation of all its privileges which the French nobility voted in a moment of enthusiasm during the celebrated night of August 4, 1789, would certainly never have been consented to by any of its members taken singly.

The conclusion to be drawn from what precedes is, that the crowd is always intellectually inferior to the isolated individual, but that, from the point of view of feelings and of the acts these feelings provoke, the crowd may, according to circumstances, be better or worse than the individual. All depends on the nature of the suggestion to which the crowd is exposed. This is the point that has been completely misunderstood by writers, who have only studied crowds from the criminal point of view. Doubtless a crowd is often criminal, but also it is often heroic. It is crowds rather than isolated individuals that may be induced to run the risk of death to secure the triumph of a creed or an idea, that may be fired with enthusiasm for glory and honour, that are led on—almost without bread and without arms, as in the age of the Crusades—to deliver the tomb of Christ from the infidel, or, as in '93, to defend the fatherland. Such heroism is without doubt somewhat unconscious, but it is of such heroism that history is made. Were peoples only to be credited with the great actions performed in cold blood, the annals of the world would register but few of them. . . .

When studying the fundamental characteristics of a crowd we stated that it is guided almost exclusively by unconscious motives. Its acts are far more under the influence of the spinal cord than of the brain. In this respect a crowd is closely akin to quite primitive beings. The acts performed may be perfect so far as their execution is concerned, but as they are not directed by the brain, the individual conducts himself according as the exciting causes to which he is submitted may happen to decide. A crowd is at the mercy of all external exciting causes, and reflects their incessant variations. It is the slave of the impulses which it receives. The isolated individual may be submitted to the same exciting causes as the man in a crowd, but as his brain shows him the inadvisability of yielding to them, he refrains from yielding. This truth may be physiologically expressed by saying that the isolated individual possesses the capacity of dominating his reflex actions, while a crowd is devoid of this capacity. . . .

The exciting causes that may act on crowds being so varied, and crowds always obeying them, crowds are in consequence extremely mobile. This explains how it is that we see them pass in a moment from the most bloodthirsty ferocity to the most extreme generosity and heroism. . . . Any display of premeditation by crowds is in consequence out of the question. . . . A crowd is not merely impulsive and mobile. Like a savage, it is not prepared to admit that anything can come between its desire and the realisation of its desire. It is the less capable of understanding such an intervention, in consequence of the feeling of irresistible power given it by its numerical strength. The notion of impossibility disappears for the individual in a crowd. An isolated individual knows well enough that alone he cannot set fire to a palace or loot a shop, and should he be tempted to do so, he will easily resist the temptation. Making part of a crowd, he is conscious of the power given him by number, and it is sufficient to suggest to him ideas of murder or pillage for him to yield immediately to temptation. An unexpected obstacle will be destroyed with frenzied rage. Did the human organism allow of the perpetuity of furious passion, it might be said that the normal condition of a crowd baulked in its wishes is just such a state of furious passion. . . .

The simplest event that comes under the observation of a crowd is soon totally transformed. A crowd thinks in images, and the image itself immediately calls up a series of other images, having no logical connection with the first. We can easily conceive this state by thinking of the fantastic succession of ideas to which we are sometimes led by calling up in our minds any fact. Our reason shows us the incoherence there is in these images, but a crowd is almost blind to this truth, and confuses with the real event what the deforming action of its imagination has superimposed thereon. A crowd scarcely distinguishes between the subjective and the objective. It accepts as real the images evoked in its mind, though they most often have only a very distant relation with the observed fact.

The ways in which a crowd perverts any event of which it is a witness ought, it would seem, to be innumerable and unlike each other, since the individuals composing the gathering are of very different temperaments. But this is not the case. As the result of contagion the perversions are of the same kind, and take the same shape in the case of all the assembled individuals.

The first perversion of the truth effected by one of the individuals of the gathering is the starting-point of the contagious suggestion. Before St. George appeared on the walls of Jerusalem to all the Crusaders he was certainly perceived in the first instance by one of those present. By dint of suggestion and contagion the miracle signalised by a single person was immediately accepted by all.

Such is always the mechanism of the collective hallucinations so frequent in history—hallucinations which seem to have all the recognised characteristics of authenticity, since they are phenomena observed by thousands of persons. . . .

The following fact is one of the most typical. . . . The frigate, the *Belle Poule,* was cruising in the open sea for the purpose of finding the cruiser *Le Berceau,* from which she had been separated by a violent storm. It was broad daylight and in full sunshine. Suddenly the watch signalled a disabled vessel; the crew looked in the direction signalled, and every one, officers and sailors, clearly perceived a raft covered with men towed by boats which were displaying signals of distress. Yet this was nothing more than a collective hallucination. Admiral Desfossés lowered a boat to go to the rescue of the wrecked sailors. On nearing the object sighted, the sailors and officers on board the boat saw "masses of men in motion, stretching out their hands, and heard the dull and confused noise of a great number of voices." When the object was reached those in the boat found themselves simply and solely in the presence of a few branches of trees covered with leaves that had been swept out from the neighbouring coast. Before evidence so palpable the hallucination vanished.

The mechanism of a collective hallucination of the kind we have explained is clearly seen at work in this example. On the one hand we have a crowd in a state of expectant attention, on the other a suggestion made by the watch signalling a disabled vessel at sea, a suggestion which, by a process of contagion, was accepted by all those present, both officers and sailors. . . .

Crowds are only cognisant of simple and extreme sentiments; the opinions, ideas, and beliefs suggested to them are accepted or rejected as a whole, and considered as absolute truths or as not less absolute errors. This is always the case with beliefs induced by a process of suggestion instead of engendered by reasoning. Everyone is aware of the intolerance that accompanies religious beliefs, and of the despotic empire they exercise on men's minds.

Being in doubt as to what constitutes truth or error, and having, on the other hand, a clear notion of its strength, a crowd is as disposed to give authoritative effect to its inspirations as it is intolerant. An individual may accept contradiction and discussion; a crowd will never do so. At public meetings the slightest contradiction on the part of an orator is immediately received with howls of fury and violent invective, soon followed by blows and expulsion should the orator stick to the point. Without the restraining presence of the representatives of authority the contradictor, indeed, would often be done to death. . . .

Authoritativeness and intolerance are sentiments of which crowds have a very clear notion, which they easily conceive and which they entertain as readily as they put them in practice when once they are imposed upon them. Crowds exhibit a docile respect for force, and are but slightly impressed by kindness, which for them is scarcely other than a form of weakness. Their sympathies have never been bestowed on easy-going masters, but on tyrants who vigorously oppressed them. It is to these latter that they always erect the loftiest statues. It is true that they willingly trample on the despot whom they have stripped of his power, but it is because, having lost his strength, he has resumed his place among the people, who are to be despised because they are not to be feared. The type of hero dear to crowds will always have the semblance of a Cæsar. His insignia attracts them, his authority overawes them, and his sword instils them with fear.

A crowd is always ready to revolt against a feeble and to bow down servilely before a strong authority. Should the strength of an authority be intermittent, the crowd, always obedient to its extreme sentiments, passes alternately from anarchy to servitude, and from servitude to anarchy.

However, to believe in the predominance among crowds of revolutionary instincts would be to misconstrue entirely their psychology. It is merely their tendency to violence that deceives us on this point. Their rebellious and destructive outbursts are always very transitory. Crowds are too much governed by unconscious considerations, and too much subject in consequence to secular hereditary influences not to be extremely conservative. Abandoned to themselves, they soon weary of disorder, and instinctively turn to servitude. It was the proudest and most intractable of the Jacobins who acclaimed Bonaparte with greatest energy when he suppressed all liberty and made his hand of iron severely felt.

It is difficult to understand history, and popular revolutions in particular, if one does not take sufficiently into account the profoundly conservative instincts of crowds. . . . Their incessant mobility only exerts its influence on quite superficial matters. In fact, they possess conservative instincts as indestructible as those of all primitive beings. Their fetish-like respect for all traditions is absolute; their unconscious horror of all novelty capable of changing the essential conditions of their existence is very deeply rooted.

Sigmund Freud: *Group Psychology and the Analysis of the Ego*

We shall take the liberty of interrupting Le Bon's exposition with glosses of our own, and shall accordingly insert an observation at this point. If the individuals in the group are combined into a unity, there must surely be something to unite them, and this bond might be precisely the thing that is characteristic of a group. But Le Bon does not answer this question; he goes on to consider the alteration which the individual undergoes when in a group and describes it in terms which harmonize well with the fundamental postulates of our own depth-psychology. . . .

Le Bon thinks that the particular acquirements of individuals become obliterated in a group, and that in this way their distinctiveness vanishes. The racial unconscious emerges; what is heterogeneous is submerged in what is homogeneous. As we should say, the mental superstructure, the development of which in individuals shows such dissimilarities, is removed, and the unconscious foundations, which are similar in everyone, stand exposed to view. In this way individuals in a group would come to show an average character. But Le Bon believes that they also display new characteristics which they have not previously possessed. . . .

From our point of view we need not attribute so much importance to the appearance of new characteristics. For us it would be enough to say that in a group the individual is brought under conditions which allow him to throw off the repressions of his unconscious instinctual impulses. The apparently new characteristics which he then displays are in fact the manifestations of this unconscious, in which all that is evil in the human · mind is contained as a predisposition. We can find no difficulty in understanding the disappearance of conscience or of a sense of responsibility in these circumstances. It has long been our contention that 'social anxiety' is the essence of what is called conscience. . . .

What Le Bon says on the subject of leaders of groups is less exhaustive, and does not enable us to make out an underlying principle so clearly. He thinks that as soon as living beings are gathered together in certain numbers, no matter whether they are a herd of animals or a collection of human beings, they place themselves instinctively under the authority of a chief.

A group is an obedient herd, which could never live without a master. It has such a thirst for obedience that it submits instinctively to anyone who appoints himself its master.

Although in this way the needs of a group carry it half-way to meet the leader, yet he too must fit in with it in his personal qualities. He must himself be held in fascination by a strong faith (in an idea) in order to awaken the group's faith; he must possess a strong and imposing will, which the group, which has no will of its own, can accept from him. Le Bon then discusses the different kinds of leaders, and the means by which they work upon the group. On the whole he believes that the leaders make themselves felt by means of the ideas in which they themselves are fanatical believers.

Moreover, he ascribes both to the ideas and to the leaders a mysterious and irresistible power, which he calls 'prestige'. Prestige is a sort of domination exercised over us by an individual, a work or an idea. It entirely paralyses our critical faculty, and fills us with wonderment and respect. It would seem to arouse a feeling like that of 'fascination' in hypnosis. He distinguishes between acquired or artificial and personal prestige. The former is attached to persons in virtue of their name, fortune and reputation, and to opinions, works of art, etc., in virtue of tradition. Since in every case it harks back to the past, it cannot be of much help to us in understanding this puzzling influence. Personal prestige is attached to a few people, who become leaders by means of it, and it has the effect of making everyone obey them as though by the operation of some magnetic magic. All prestige, however, is also dependent upon success, and is lost in the event of failure.

Le Bon does not give the impression of having succeeded in bringing the function of the leader and the importance of prestige completely into harmony with his brilliantly executed picture of the group mind.

We have made use of Le Bon's description by way of introduction, because it fits in so well with our own psychology in the emphasis which it lays upon unconscious mental life. But we must now add that as a matter of fact none of that author's statements bring forward anything new. Everything that he says to the detriment and depreciation of the manifestations of the group mind had already been said by others before him with equal distinctness and equal hostility, and has been repeated in unison by thinkers, statesmen and writers since the earliest periods of literature. The two theses which comprise the most important of Le Bon's opinions, those touching upon the collective inhibition of intellectual functioning and the heightening of affectivity in groups, had been formulated shortly before by Sighele. At bottom, all that is left over as being peculiar to Le Bon are the two notions of the unconscious and of the comparison with the mental life of primitive people, and even these had naturally often been alluded to before him.

8. Alexis de Tocqueville: *Democracy in America*, Vol. II

WHAT SORT OF DESPOTISM DEMOCRATIC NATIONS HAVE TO FEAR

I had remarked during my stay in the United States that a democratic state of society, similar to that of the Americans, might offer singular facilties for the establishment of despotism; and I perceived, upon my return to Europe, how much use had already been made, by most of our rulers, of the notions, the sentiments, and the wants created by this same social condition, for the purpose of extending the circle of their power. This led me to think that the nations of Christendom would perhaps eventually undergo some oppression like that which hung over several of the nations of the ancient world.

A more accurate examination of the subject, and five years of further meditation, have not diminished my fears, but have changed their object.

No sovereign ever lived in former ages so absolute or so powerful as to undertake to administer by his own agency, and without the assistance of intermediate powers, all the parts of a great empire; none ever attempted to subject all his subjects indiscriminately to strict uniformity of regulation and personally to tutor and direct every member of the community. The notion of such an undertaking never occurred to the human mind; and if any man had conceived it, the want of information, the imperfection of the administrative system, and, above all, the natural obstacles caused by the inequality of conditions would speedily have checked the execution of so vast a design.

When the Roman emperors were at the height of their power, the different nations of the empire still preserved usages and customs of great diversity; although they were subject to the same monarch, most of the provinces were separately administered; they abounded in powerful and active municipalities; and although the whole government of the empire was centered in the hands of the Emperor always and he always remained, in case of need, the supreme arbiter in all matters, yet the details of social life and private occupations lay for the most part beyond his control. The emperors possessed, it is true, an immense and unchecked power, which allowed them to gratify all their whimsical tastes and to employ for that purpose the whole strength of the state. They frequently abused that power arbitrarily to deprive their subjects of property or of life; their tyranny was extremely onerous to the few, but it did not reach the many; it was confined to some few main objects and neglected the rest; it was violent, but its range was limited.

It would seem that if despotism were to be established among the democratic nations of our days, it might assume a different character; it would be more extensive and more mild; it would degrade men without tormenting them. I do not question that, in an age of instruction and equality like our own, sovereigns might more easily succeed in collecting all political power into their own hands and might interfere more habitually and decidedly with the circle of private interests than any sovereign of antiquity could ever do. But this same principle of equality which facilitates despotism tempers its rigor. We have seen how the customs of society become more humane and gentle in proportion as men become more equal and alike. When no member of the community has much power or much wealth, tyranny is, as it were, without opportunities and a field of action. As all fortunes are scanty, the passions of men are naturally circumscribed, their imagination limited, their pleasures simple. This universal moderation moderates the sovereign himself and checks within certain limits the inordinate stretch of his desires.

Independently of these reasons, drawn from the nature of the state of society itself, I might add many others arising from causes beyond my subject; but I shall keep within the limits I have laid down.

Democratic governments may become violent and even cruel at certain periods of extreme effervescence or of great danger, but these crises will be rare and brief. When I consider the petty passions of our contemporaries, the mildness of their manners, the extent of their education, the purity of their religion, the gentleness of their morality, their regular and industrious habits, and the restraint which they almost all observe in their vices no less than in their virtues, I have no fear that they will meet with tyranny in their rules, but rather with guardians.

I think, then, that the species of oppression by which democratic nations are menaced is unlike anything that ever before existed in the world; our contemporaries will find no prototype of it in their memories. I seek in vain for an expression that will accurately convey the whole of the idea I have formed of it; the old words *despotism* and *tyranny* are inappropriate: the thing itself is new, and since I cannot name, I must attempt to define it.

I seek to trace the novel features under which despotism

may appear in the world. The first thing that strikes the observation is an innumerable multitude of men, all equal and alike, incessantly endeavoring to procure the petty and paltry pleasures with which they glut their lives. Each of them, living apart, is as a stranger to the fate of all the rest; his children and his private friends constitute to him the whole of mankind. As for the rest of his fellow citizens, he is close to them, but does not see them; he touches them, but he does not feel them; he exists only in himself and for himself alone; and if his kindred still remain to him, he may be said at any rate to have lost his country.

Above this race of men stands an immense and tutelary power, which takes upon itself alone to secure their gratifications and to watch over their fate. That power is absolute, minute, regular, provident, and mild. It would be like the authority of a parent if, like that authority, its object was to prepare men for manhood; but it seeks, on the contrary, to keep them in perpetual childhood: it is well content that the people should rejoice, provided they think of nothing but rejoicing. For their happiness such a government willingly labors, but it chooses to be the sole agent and the only arbiter of that happiness; it provides for their security, foresees and supplies their necessities, facilitates their pleasures, manages their principal concerns, directs their industry, regulates the descent of property, and subdivides their inheritances; what remains, but to spare them all the care of thinking and all the trouble of living?

Thus it every day renders the exercise of the free agency of man less useful and less frequent; it circumscribes the will within a narrower range and gradually robs a man of all the uses of himself. The principle of equality has prepared men for these things; it has predisposed men to endure them and often to look on them as benefits.

After having thus successively taken each member of the community in its powerful grasp and fashioned him at will, the supreme power then extends its arm over the whole community. It covers the surface of society with a network of small complicated rules, minute and uniform, through which the most original minds and the most energetic characters cannot penetrate, to rise above the crowd. The will of man is not shattered, but softened, bent, and guided; men are seldom forced by it to act, but they are constantly restrained from acting. Such a power does not destroy, but it prevents existence; it does not tyrannize, but it compresses, enervates, extinguishes, and stupefies a people, till each nation is reduced to nothing better than a flock of timid and industrious animals, of which the government is the shepherd.

I have always thought that servitude of the regular, quiet, and gentle kind which I have just described might be combined more easily than is commonly believed with some of the outward forms of freedom, and that it might even establish itself under the wing of the sovereignty of the people.

Our contemporaries are constantly excited by two conflicting passions: they want to be led, and they wish to remain free. As they cannot destroy either the one or the other of these contrary propensities, they strive to satisfy them both at once. They devise a sole, tutelary, and all-powerful form of government, but elected by the people. They combine the principle of centralization and that of popular sovereignty; this gives them a respite: they console themselves for being in tutelage by the reflection that they have chosen their own guardians. Every man allows himself to be put in leading-strings, because he sees that it is not a person or a class of persons, but the people at large who hold the end of his chain.

By this system the people shake off their state of dependence just long enough to select their master and then relapse into it again. A great many persons at the present day are quite contented with this sort of compromise between administrative despotism and the sovereignty of the people; and they think they have done enough for the protection of individual freedom when they have surrendered it to the power of the nation at large. This does not satisfy me: the nature of him I am to obey signifies less to me than the fact of extorted obedience.

I do not deny, however, that a constitution of this kind appears to me to be infinitely preferable to one which, after having concentrated all the powers of government, should vest them in the hands of an irresponsible person or body of persons. Of all the forms that democratic despotism could assume, the latter would assuredly be the worst.

When the sovereign is elective, or narrowly watched by a legislature which is really elective and independent, the oppression that he exercises over individuals is sometimes greater, but it is always less degrading; because every man, when he is oppressed and disarmed, may still imagine that, while he yields obedience, it is to himself he yields it, and that it is to one of his own inclinations that all the rest give way. In like manner, I can understand that when the sovereign represents the nation and is dependent upon the people, the rights and the power of which every citizen is deprived serve not only the head of the state, but the state itself; and that private persons derive some return from the sacrifice of their independence which they have made to the public. To create a representation of the people in every centralized country is, therefore, to diminish the evil that extreme centralization may produce, but not to get rid of it.

I admit that, by this means, room is left for the intervention of individuals in the more important affairs; but it is not the less suppressed in the smaller and more private ones. It must not be forgotten that it is especially dangerous to enslave men in the minor details of life. For my own part, I should be inclined to think freedom less necessary in great things than in little ones, if it were possible to be secure of the one without possessing the other.

Subjection in minor affairs breaks out every day and is felt by the whole community indiscriminately. It does not drive men to resistance, but it crosses them at every turn, till they are led to surrender the exercise of their own will. Thus their spirit is gradually broken and their character enervated; whereas that obedience which is exacted on a few important but rare occasions only exhibits servitude at certain intervals and throws the burden of it upon a small number of men. It is in vain to summon a people who have been rendered so dependent on the central power to choose from time to time the representatives of that power; this rare and brief exercise of their free choice, however important it may be, will not prevent them from gradually losing the faculties of thinking, feeling, and acting for themselves, and thus gradually falling below the level of humanity.

I add that they will soon become incapable of exercising the great and only privilege which remains to them. The democratic nations that have introduced freedom into their political constitution at the very time when they were augmenting the despotism of their administrative constitution have been led into strange paradoxes. To manage those minor affairs in which good sense is all that is wanted, the people are held to be unequal to the task; but when the government of the country is at stake, the people are invested with immense powers; they are alternately made the playthings of their ruler, and his masters, more than kings and less than men. After having exhausted all the different modes of election without finding one to suit their purpose, they are still amazed and still bent on seeking further; as if the evil they notice did not originate in the constitution of the country far more than in that of the electoral body.

It is indeed difficult to conceive how men who have entirely given up the habit of self-government should succeed in making a proper choice of those by whom they are to be governed; and no one will ever believe that a liberal, wise, and energetic government can spring from the suffrages of a subservient people.

A constitution republican in its head and ultra-monarchical in all its other parts has always appeared to me to be a shortlived monster. The vices of rulers and the ineptitude of the people would speedily bring about its ruin; and the nation, weary of its representatives and of itself, would create freer institutions or soon return to stretch itself at the feet of a single master.

III.

Collective Consciousness

The two most influential modern writers on collective consciousness are also probably the two most misunderstood. Each has been subject to a vulgar formula which reduces his ideas to a mechanical system. For Marx, the formula is that economics determines consciousness, as though economic organization were a stimulus which produced an instant and blind psychological response. For Durkheim, the formula is that the more solidarity people feel, the greater is their collective consciousness, again as though consciousness were a simple mirror of a social fact.

The readings in this section are arranged to dispel these clichés. For each writer, a case study of his method of analysis is offered; for Marx, it is his description of the phenomenon of false consciousness in the Revolution of 1848; for Durkheim, it is his description of suicide patterns in late-nineteenth-century Europe. The case study is then followed by a selection from the theory which prompted each writer to make this specific analysis. What this procedure should make clear is how flexible and nuanced the work of both Marx and Durkheim is.

Both writers, it was earlier remarked, are concerned not so much with the group self-images as with the process by which beliefs and ideas as well as self-images are shared among people. Both writers also separate the forms of collective consciousness from knowledge *per se;* when Marx speaks of false consciousness, for example, he means the objects of knowledge of a group or class are unreal, but the processes of collective awareness which produced these illusions are certainly real and strong enough. Marx and Durkheim diverge sharply in their views of how the process of consciousness works.

One reader of Marx and Durkheim, the philosopher Ernst Cassirer, portrays the difference as follows: the animating energy of consciousness for Marx is external to the act of being conscious, while for Durkheim "internal" and "external" are meaningless measures of consciousness. If we think back to our first reading, Aristotle, we can quickly understand what Cassirer means. For Marx, the energies for conscious belief come from experiences in the productive sphere of society; Aristotle's sense of psyche or soul and Marx's sense of production are analogous; consciousness is like "nous," like the wax upon which the forces of society leave their imprint. An historical consciousness is like a piece of wax upon which several different, conflicting impressions have been made at different points in time; the consciousness of a group thus never mechanically and simply expresses the interests of a class at a given moment—the vulgar formula—but rather exhibits the contradictions and confusions of the multiple impressions of history. Durkheim sees consciousness to contain its own principle of energy—it is the principle of language; because men have available the tools of language there is a continual interchange between the brute material conditions of life and the processes of consciousness. Language organizes these material conditions, leaves an impress upon them, just as the material conditions leave an impress upon language. This interaction is so organically integrated that to speak of "internal" and "external" conditions of consciousness seems, to Durkheim, a false abstraction. What he wants to find is another set of concepts to explain the process.

Because Marx's ideas have had such immense political and practical consequences in the modern world, it is important to understand their "connective tissues" to everyday beliefs, as well as the economic assumptions which form their basis. For this reason, the Marxian theory presented in this section is drawn from Part I of Marx and Engels' *The German Ideology*, the work in which Marx addresses himself to the connections between collective consciousness and social reality. The reader who would like to understand something more of another aspect of Marx's theory of consciousness, the idea of "reification of consciousness" (by which Marx means the techniques of imagining one experience or idea as, falsely, a world of its own with a tantalizing but unfathomable secret), should look at Marx's *Capital,* Chapter 1, especially Part 4. Similarly, in focusing on those aspects of Durkheim's writing which contrast him to Marx, we have had to exclude an element of his theory of consciousness which is important in and of itself. This is the idea of "organic solidarity," and the reader who wishes to understand it should consult the whole of Durkheim's *The Division of Labor in Society.*

9. Karl Marx: "The Eighteenth Brumaire of Louis Bonaparte," in *Surveys from Exile* [1818–1883]

Men make their own history, but not of their own free will; not under circumstances they themselves have chosen but under the given and inherited circumstances with which they are directly confronted. The tradition of the dead generations weighs like a nightmare on the minds of the living. And, just when they appear to be engaged in the revolutionary transformation of themselves and their material surroundings, in the creation of something which does not yet exist, precisely in such epochs of revolutionary crisis they timidly conjure up the spirits of the past to help them; they borrow their names, slogans and costumes so as to stage the new world-historical scene in this venerable disguise and borrowed language. Luther put on the mask of the apostle Paul; the Revolution of 1789–1814 draped itself alternately as the Roman republic and the Roman empire; and the revolution of 1848 knew no better than to parody at some points 1789 and at others the revolutionary traditions of 1793–5. In the same way, the beginner who has learned a new language always retranslates it into his mother tongue: he can only be said to have appropriated the spirit of the new language and to be able to express himself in it freely when he can manipulate it without reference to the old, and when he forgets his original language while using the new one. . . .

As we have said, Legitimists and Orleanists formed the two great fractions of the party of Order. [in 1848] . . . It was therefore not so-called principles which kept these fractions divided, but rather their material conditions of existence, two distinct sorts of property; it was the old opposition between town and country, the old rivalry between capital and landed property. Who would deny that at the same time old memories, personal enmities, fears and hopes, prejudices and illusions, sympathies and antipathies, convictions, articles of faith and principles bound them to one or the other royal house? A whole superstructure of different and specifically formed feelings, illusions, modes of thought and views of life arises on the basis of the different forms of property, of the social conditions of existence. The whole class creates and forms these out of its material foundations and the corresponding social relations. The single individual, who derives these feelings, etc. through tradition and upbringing, may well imagine that they form the real determinants and the starting-point of his activity. The Orleanist and Legitimist fractions each tried to make out to their opponents and themselves that they were divided by their adherence to the two royal houses; facts later proved that it was rather the division between their interests which forbade the unification of the royal houses. A distinction is made in private life between what a man thinks and says of himself and what he really is and does. In historical struggles one must make a still sharper distinction between the phrases and fantasies of the parties and their real organization and real interests, between their conception of themselves and what they really are. Orleanists and Legitimists found themselves side by side in the republic, making equal claims. Each side wanted to secure the *restoration* of its *own* royal house against the other; this had no other meaning than that each of the *two great interests* into which the bourgeoisie is divided—landed property and capital—was endeavouring to restore its own supremacy and the subordination of the other interest. We refer to the two interests of the bourgeoisie because big landed property in fact has been completely bourgeoisified by the development of modern society, despite its feudal coquetry and racial pride. The Tories in England long imagined they were enthusiastic about the monarchy, the church, and the beauties of the old English constitution, until the day of danger wrung from them the confession that they were only enthusiastic about *ground rent*.

The petty bourgeoisie and the workers had formed their own coalition, the so-called *social-democratic* party, in opposition to the coalition of the bourgeoisie. The petty bourgeoisie saw that they had done badly out of the June days. Their material interests were in danger, and the counter-revolution called into question the democratic guarantees which were supposed to secure the assertion of those interests. They therefore drew closer to the workers. . . .

Only one must not take the narrow view that the petty bourgeoisie explicitly sets out to assert its egoistic class interests. It rather believes that the *particular* conditions of its liberation are the only *general* conditions within which modern society can be saved and the class struggle avoided. Nor indeed must one imagine that the democratic representatives are all *shopkeepers* or their enthusiastic supporters. They may well be poles apart from them in their education and their individual situation. What makes them representatives of the petty bourgeoisie is the fact that their minds are restricted by the same barriers which the petty bourgeoisie fails to overcome in real life, and that they are therefore driven in theory to the same problems and solutions to which material interest and social situation drive the latter in practice.

Karl Marx and Friedrich Engels:
The German Ideology

The production of ideas, of conceptions, of consciousness, is at first directly interwoven with the material activity and the material intercourse of men, the language of real life. Concelving, thinking, the mental intercourse of men, appear at this stage as the direct efflux of their material behaviour. The same applies to mental production as expressed in the language of politics, laws, morality, religion, metaphysics, etc. of a people. Men are the producers of their conceptions, ideas, etc.—real, active men, as they are conditioned by a definite development of their productive forces and of the intercourse corresponding to these, up to its furthest forms. Consciousness can never be anything else than conscious existence, and the existence of men is their actual life-process. If in all ideology men and their circumstances appear upside-down as in a *camera obscura,* this phenomenon arises just as much from their historical life-process as the inversion of objects on the retina does from their physical life-process.

In direct contrast to German philosophy which descends from heaven to earth, here we ascend from earth to heaven. That is to say, we do not set out from what men say, imagine, conceive, nor from men as narrated, thought of, imagined, conceived, in order to arrive at men in the flesh. We set out from real, active men, and on the basis of their real life-process we demonstrate the development of the ideological reflexes and echoes of this life-process. The phantoms formed in the human brain are also, necessarily, sublimates of their material life-process, which is empirically verifiable and bound to material premises. Morality, religion, metaphysics, all the rest of ideology and their corresponding forms of consciousness, thus no longer retain the semblance of independence. They have no history, no development; but men, developing their material production and their material intercourse, alter, along with this their real existence, their thinking and the products of their thinking. Life is not determined by consciousness, but consciousness by life. . . .

Only now, after having considered four moments, four aspects of the primary historical relationships, do we find that man also possesses "consciousness", but, even so, not inherent, not "pure" consciousness. From the start the "spirit" is afflicted with the curse of being "burdened" with matter, which here makes its appearance in the form of agitated layers of air, sounds, in short, of language. Language is as old as consciousness, language *is* practical consciousness that exists also for other men, and for that reason alone it really exists for me personally as well; language, like consciousness, only arises from the need, the necessity, of intercourse with other men. . . . Consciousness is at first, of course, merely consciousness concerning the *immediate* sensuous environment and consciousness of the limited connection with other persons and things outside the individual who is growing self-conscious. At the same time it is consciousness of nature, which first appears to men as a completely alien, all-powerful and unassailable force, with which men's relations are purely animal and by which they are overawed like beasts; . . . On the other hand, man's consciousness of the necessity of associating with the individuals around him is the beginning of the consciousness that he is living in society at all. This beginning is as animal as social life itself at this stage. It is mere herd-consciousness, and at this point man is only distinguished from sheep by the fact that with him consciousness takes the place of instinct or that his instinct is a conscious one. This sheep-like or tribal consciousness receives its further development and extension through increased productivity, the increase of needs, and, what is fundamental to both of these, the increase of population. With these there develops the division of labour, which was originally nothing but the division of labour in the sexual act, then that division of labour which develops spontaneously or "naturally" by virtue of natural predisposition (e.g. physical strength), needs, accidents, etc. Division of labour only becomes truly such from the moment when a division of material and mental labour appears. (The first form of ideologists, *priests,* is concurrent.) From this moment onwards consciousness *can* really flatter itself that it is something other than consciousness of existing practice, that it *really* represents something without representing something real; from now on consciousness is in a position to emancipate itself from the world and to proceed to the formation of "pure" theory, theology, philosophy, ethics, etc. But even if this theory, theology, philosophy, ethics, etc. comes into contradiction with the existing relations, this can only occur because existing social relations have come into contradiction with existing forces of production. . . .

The class which has the means of material production at its disposal, has control at the same time over the means of mental production, so that thereby, generally speaking, the ideas of those who lack the means of mental production are subject to it. The ruling ideas are nothing more than the ideal expression of the dominant material relationships, the dominant material relationships grasped as ideas; hence of the relationships which make the one class the ruling one, therefore, the ideas of its dominance. The individuals composing the ruling class possess among other things consciousness, and therefore think. Insofar, therefore, as they rule as a class and determine the extent and compass of an epoch, it is self-evident that they do this in its whole range, hence among other things rule also as thinkers, as producers of ideas, and regulate the production and distribution of the ideas of their age: thus their ideas are the ruling ideas of the epoch. For instance, in an age and in a country where royal power, aristocracy, and bourgeoisie are contending for mastery and where, therefore, mastery is shared, the doctrine of the separation of powers proves to be the dominant idea and is expressed as an "eternal law". . . .

For each new class which puts itself in the place of one ruling before it, is compelled, merely in order to carry through its aim, to represent its interest as the common interest of all the members of society, that is, expressed in ideal form: it has to give its ideas the form of universality, and represent them as the only rational, universally valid ones.

10. Emile Durkheim:
Suicide: A Study in Sociology   [1858–1917]

The population of Paris renews itself very rapidly; yet the share of Paris in the total of French suicides remains practically the same. Although only a few years suffice to change completely the personnel of the army, the rate of military suicides varies only very slowly in a given nation. In all countries the evolution of collective life follows a given rhythm throughout the year; it grows from January to about July and then diminishes. Thus, though the members of the several European societies spring from widely different average types, the seasonal and even monthly variations of suicide take place in accordance with the same law. Likewise, regardless of the diversity of individual temperaments, the relation between the aptitude for suicide of married persons and that of widowers and widows is identically the same in widely differing social groups, from the simple fact that the moral condition of widowhood everywhere bears the same relation to the moral constitution characteristic of marriage. The causes which thus fix the contingent of voluntary deaths for a given society or one part of it must then be independent of individuals, since they retain the same intensity no matter what particular persons they operate on. One would think that an unchanging manner of life would produce unchanging effects. This is true; but a way of life is something, and its unchanging character requires explanation. If a way of life is unchanged while changes occur constantly among those who practice it, it cannot derive its entire reality from them.

It has been thought that this conclusion might be avoided through the observation that this very continuity was the work of individuals and that, consequently, to account for it there was no need to ascribe to social phenomena a sort of transcendency in relation to individual life. Actually, it has been said, "anything social, whether a word of a language, a religious rite, an artisan's skill, an artistic method, a legal statute or a moral maxim is transmitted and passes from an individual parent, teacher, friend, neighbor, or comrade to another individual."

Doubtless if we had only to explain the general way in which an idea or sentiment passes from one generation to another, how it is that the memory of it is not lost, this explanation might as a last resort be considered satisfactory. But the transmission of facts such as suicide and, more broadly speaking, such as the various acts reported by moral statistics, has a very special nature not to be so readily accounted for. It relates, in fact, not merely in general to a certain way of acting, *but to the number of cases in which this way of acting is employed.* Not merely are there suicides every year, but there are as a general rule as many each year as in the year preceding. The state of mind which causes men to kill themselves is not purely and simply transmitted, but—something much more remarkable—transmitted to an equal number of persons, all in such situations as to make the state of mind become an act. How can this be if only individuals are concerned? The number as such cannot be directly transmitted. Today's population has not learned from yesterday's the size of the contribution it must make to suicide; nevertheless, it will make one of identical size with that of the past, unless circumstances change.

Are we then to imagine that, in some way, each suicide had as his initiator and teacher one of the victims of the year before and that he is something like his moral heir? Only thus can one conceive the possibility that the social suicide-rate is perpetuated by way of interindividual traditions. For if the total figure cannot be transmitted as a whole, the units composing it must be transmitted singly. According to this idea, each suicide would have received his tendency from some one of his predecessors and each act of suicide would be something like the echo of a preceding one. But not a fact exists to permit the assumption of such a personal filiation between each of these moral occurrences statistically registered this year, for example, and a similar event of the year before. As has been shown above, it is quite exceptional for an act to be inspired in this way by another of like nature. Besides, why should these ricochets occur regularly from year to year? Why should the generating act require a year to produce its counterpart? Finally, why should it inspire a single copy only? For surely each model must be reproduced only once on the average, or the total would not be constant. Such an hypothesis, as arbitrary as it is difficult to conceive, we need discuss no longer. But if it is dropped, if the numerical equality of annual contingents does not result from each particular case producing its counterpart in the ensuing period, it can only be due to the permanent action of some impersonal cause which transcends all individual cases.

The terms therefore must be strictly understood. Collective tendencies have an existence of their own; they are forces as real as cosmic forces, though of another sort; they, likewise, affect the individual from without, though through other channels. The proof that the reality of collective tendencies is no less than that of cosmic forces is that this reality is demonstrated in the same way, by the uniformity of effects. When we find that the number of deaths varies little from year to year, we explain this regularity by saying that mortality depends on the climate, the temperature, the nature of the soil, in brief on a certain number of material forces which remain constant through changing generations because independent of individuals. Since, therefore, moral acts such as suicide are reproduced not merely with an equal but with a greater uniformity, we must likewise admit that they depend on forces external to individuals. Only, since these forces must be of a moral order and since, except for individual men, there is no other moral order of existence in the world but society, they must be social. But whatever they are called, the important thing is to recognize their reality and conceive of them as a totality of forces which cause us to act from without, like the physico-chemical forces to which we react. So truly are they things *sui generis* and not mere verbal entities that they may be measured, their relative sizes compared, as is done with the intensity of electric currents or luminous foci. Thus, the basic proposition that social facts are objective, a proposition we have had the opportunity to prove in another work and which we consider the fundamental principle of the sociological method, finds a new and especially conclusive proof in moral statistics and above all in the statistics of suicide. Of course, it offends common sense. But science has encountered incredulity whenever it has revealed to men the existence of a force that has been overlooked. Since the system of accepted ideas must be modified to make room for the new order of things and to establish new concepts, men's minds resist through mere inertia. Yet this understanding must be reached. If there is such a science as sociology, it can only be the study of a world hitherto unknown, different from those explored by the other sciences. This world is nothing if not a system of realities.

But just because it encounters traditional prejudices this conception has aroused objections to which we must reply.

First, it implies that collective tendencies and thoughts are of a different nature from individual tendencies and thoughts, that the former have characteristics which the latter lack. How can this be, it is objected, since there are only individuals in society? But, reasoning thus, we should have to say that there is nothing more in animate nature than inorganic matter, since the cell is made exclusively of inanimate atoms. To be sure, it is likewise true that society has no other active forces than individuals; but individuals by combining form a psychical existence of a new species, which consequently has its own manner of thinking and feeling. Of course the elementary qualities of which the social fact consists are present in germ in individual minds. But the social fact emerges from them only when they have been transformed by association since it is only then that it appears. Association itself is also an active factor productive of special effects. In itself it is therefore something new. When the consciousness of individuals, instead of remaining isolated, becomes grouped and combined, something in the world has been altered. Naturally this change produces others, this novelty

engenders other novelties, phenomena appear whose characteristic qualities are not found in the elements composing them.

This proposition could only be opposed by agreeing that a
whole is qualitatively identical with the sum of its parts, that an
effect is qualitatively reducible to the sum of its productive
causes; which amounts to denying all change or to making it
inexplicable. Someone has, however, gone so far as to sustain
this extreme thesis, but only two truly extraordinary reasons
have been found for its defense. First, it has been said that "in
sociology we have through a rare privilege intimate knowledge
both of that element which is our individual consciousness and
of the compound which is the sum of consciousness in individuals"; secondly, that through this two fold introspection
"we clearly ascertain that if the individual is subtracted nothing
remains of the social."

The first assertion is a bold denial of all contemporary
psychology. Today it is generally recognized that psychical life,
far from being directly cognizable, has on the contrary profound
depths inaccessible to ordinary perception, to which we attain
only gradually by devious and complicated paths like those
employed by the sciences of the external world. The nature of
consciousness is therefore far from lacking in mystery for the
future. The second proposition is purely arbitrary. The author
may of course state that in his personal opinion nothing real
exists in society but what is individual, but proofs supporting
this statement are lacking and discussion is therefore impossible. It would be only too easy to oppose to this the contrary
feeling of a great many persons, who conceive of society not as
the form spontaneously assumed by individual nature on expanding outwardly, but as an antagonistic force restricting individual natures and resisted by them! What a remarkable
intuition it is, by the way, that lets us know directly and without
intermediary both the element—the individual—and the compound, society? If we had really only to open our eyes and take
a good look to perceive at once the laws of the social world,
sociology would be useless or, at least very simple. Unfortunately, facts show only too clearly the incompetence of consciousness in this matter. Never would consciousness have

dreamt, of its own accord, of the necessity which annually reproduces demographic phenomena in equal numbers, had it not received a suggestion from without. Still less can it discover their causes, if left to its own devices.

But by separating social from individual life in this manner, we do not mean that there is nothing psychical about the former. On the contrary, it is clear that essentially social life is made up of representations. Only these collective representations are of quite another character from those of the individual. We see no objection to calling sociology a variety of psychology, if we carefully add that social psychology has its own laws which are not those of individual psychology.

Emile Durkheim: *The Elementary Forms of the Religious Life*

We speak a language that we did not make; we use instruments that we did not invent; we invoke rights that we did not found; a treasury of knowledge is transmitted to each generation that it did not gather itself, etc. It is to society that we owe these varied benefits of civilization, and if we do not ordinarily see the source from which we get them, we at least know that they are not our own work. Now it is these things that give man his own place among things; a man is a man only because he is civilized. So he could not escape the feeling that outside of him there are active causes from which he gets the characteristic attributes of his nature and which, as benevolent powers, assist him, protect him and assure him of a privileged fate. And of course he must attribute to these powers a dignity corresponding to the great value of the good things he attributes to them.

Thus the environment in which we live seems to us to be peopled with forces that are at once imperious and helpful, august and gracious, and with which we have relations. Since they exercise over us a pressure of which we are conscious, we are forced to localize them outside ourselves, just as we do for the objective causes of our sensations. But the sentiments which they inspire in us differ in nature from those which we have for simple visible objects. As long as these latter are reduced to their empirical characteristics as shown in ordinary experience, and as long as the religious imagination has not metamorphosed them, we entertain for them no feeling which resembles respect, and they contain within them nothing that is able to raise us outside ourselves. Therefore, the representations which express them appear to us to be very different from those aroused in us by collective influences. The two form two distinct and separate mental states in our consciousness, just as do the two forms of life to which they correspond. Consequently, we get the impression that we are in relations with two distinct sorts of reality and that a sharply drawn line of demarcation separates them from each other: on the one hand is the world of profane things, on the other, that of sacred things. . . .

In fact, if left to themselves, individual consciousnesses are closed to each other; they can communicate only by means of signs which express their internal states. If the communication established between them is to become a real communion, that is to say, a fusion of all particular sentiments into one common sentiment, the signs expressing them must themselves be fused into one single and unique resultant. It is the appearance of this that informs individuals that they are in harmony and makes them conscious of their moral unity. It is by uttering the same cry, pronouncing the same word, or performing the same gesture in regard to some object that they become and feel themselves to be in unison. It is true that individual representations also cause reactions in the organism that are not without importance; however, they can be thought of apart from these physical reactions which accompany them or follow them, but which do not constitute them. But it is quite another matter with collective representations. They presuppose that minds act and react upon one another; they are the product of these actions and reactions which are themselves possible only through material intermediaries. These latter do not confine themselves to revealing the mental state with which they are associated; they aid in creating it. Individual minds cannot come in contact and communicate with each other except by coming out of themselves; but they cannot do this except by movements. So it is the homogeneity of these movements that gives the group consciousness of itself and consequently makes it exist. When this homogeneity is once established and these movements have once taken a stereotyped form, they serve to symbolize the corresponding representations. But they symbolize them only because they have aided in forming them.

Moreover, without symbols, social sentiments could have only a precarious existence. Though very strong as long as men are together and influence each other reciprocally, they exist only in the form of recollections after the assembly has ended, and when left to themselves, these become feebler and feebler; for since the group is now no longer present and active, individual temperaments easily regain the upper hand. The violent passions which may have been released in the heart of a crowd fall away and are extinguished when this is dissolved, and men ask themselves with astonishment how they could ever have been so carried away from their normal character. But if the movements by which these sentiments are expressed are connected with something that endures, the sentiments themselves become more durable. These other things are constantly bringing them to mind and arousing them; it is as though the cause which excited them in the first place continued to act. Thus these systems of emblems, which are necessary if society is to become conscious of itself, are no less indispensable for assuring the continuation of this consciousness. . . .

A concept is not my concept; I hold it in common with other men, or, in any case, can communicate it to them. It is impossible for me to make a sensation pass from my consciousness into that of another; it holds closely to my organism and personality and cannot be detached from them. All that I can do is to invite others to place themselves before the same object as myself and to leave themselves to its action. On the other hand, conversation and all intellectual communication between men is an exchange of concepts. The concept is an essentially impersonal representation; it is through it that human intelligences communicate.*

The nature of the concept, thus defined, bespeaks its origin. If it is common to all it is the work of the community. Since it bears the mark of no particular mind, it is clear that it was elaborated by a unique intelligence, where all others meet each other, and after a fashion, come to nourish themselves. If it has more stability than sensations or images, it is because the collective representations are more stable than the individual ones; for while an individual is conscious even of the slight changes which take place in his environment, only events of a greater gravity can succeed in affecting the mental status of a society. Every time that we are in the presence of a *type*† of thought or action which is imposed uniformly upon particular wills or intelligences, this pressure exercised over the individual betrays the intervention of the group. Also, as we have already said, the concepts with which we ordinarily think are those of our vocabulary. Now it is unquestionable that language, and consequently the system of concepts which it translates, is the product of a collective elaboration. What it expresses is the manner in which society as a whole represents the facts of experience. The ideas which correspond to the diverse elements of language are thus collective representations.

Even their contents bear witness to the same fact. In fact, there are scarcely any words among those which we usually

* This universality of the concept should not be confused with its generality: they are very different things. What we mean by universality is the property which the concept has of being communicable to a number of minds, and in principle, to all minds; but this communicability is wholly independent of the degree of its extension. A concept which is applied to only one object, and whose extension is consequently at the minimum, can be the same for everybody: such is the case with the concept of a deity.

† It may be objected that frequently, as the mere effect of repetition, ways of thinking and acting become fixed and crystallized in the individual, in the form of habits which resist change. But a habit is only a tendency to repeat an act or idea automatically every time that the same circumstances appear; it does not at all imply that the idea or act is in the form of an exemplary type, proposed to or imposed upon the mind or will. It is only when a type of this sort is set up, that is to say, when a rule or standard is established, that social action can and should be presumed.

employ whose meaning does not pass, to a greater or less extent, the limits of our personal experience. Very frequently a term expresses things which we have never perceived or experiences which we have never had or of which we have never been the witnesses. Even when we know some of the objects which it concerns, it is only as particular examples that they serve to illustrate the idea which they would never have been able to form by themselves. Thus there is a great deal of knowledge condensed in the word which I never collected, and which is not individual; it even surpasses me to such an extent that I cannot even completely appropriate all its results. Which of us knows all the words of the language he speaks and the entire signification of each?

This remark enables us to determine the sense in which we mean to say that concepts are collective representations. If they belong to a whole social group, it is not because they represent the average of the corresponding individual representations; for in that case they would be poorer than the latter in intellectual content, while, as a matter of fact, they contain much that surpasses the knowledge of the average individual. They are not abstractions which have a reality only in particular consciousnesses, but they are as concrete representations as an individual could form of his own personal environment: they correspond to the way in which this very special being, society, considers the things of its own proper experience. If, as a matter of fact, the concepts are nearly always general ideas, and if they express categories and classes rather than particular objects, it is because the unique and variable characteristics of things interest society but rarely; because of its very extent, it can scarcely be affected by more than their general and permanent qualities. Therefore it is to this aspect of affairs that it gives its attention: it is a part of its nature to see things in large and under the aspect which they ordinarily have. . . .

Saying that concepts express the manner in which society represents things is also saying that conceptual thought is coeval with humanity itself. We refuse to see in it the product of a more or less retarded culture. A man who did not think with concepts would not be a man, for he would not be a social being. If reduced to having only individual perceptions, he would be indistinguishable from the beasts. If it has been possible to sustain the contrary thesis, it is because concepts have been defined by characteristics which are not essential to them. They have been identified with general ideas and with clearly limited and circumscribed general ideas. In these conditions it has possibly seemed as though the inferior societies had no concepts properly so called; for they have only rudimentary processes of generalization and the ideas which they use are not generally very well defined. But the greater part of our concepts are equally indetermined; we force ourselves to define them only in discussions or when doing careful work. We have also seen that conceiving is not generalizing. Thinking conceptually is not simply isolating and grouping together the common characteristics of a certain number of objects; it is relating the variable to the permanent, the individual to the social.

PART TWO

COLLECTIVE
BEHAVIOR:
ROLES AND CROWDS

I.

Roles

Two forms of collective behavior have appeared in the essays on collective personality. Hobbes introduced the idea of playing a social "role," and Le Bon studied the behavior of crowds. In the present group of essays, we take up each of these activities in greater detail.

We need to look first at the title for this part as a whole—"collective behavior." As the previous essays may have made clear, there is no neat line between collective activity and the forming of collective images or consciousness. While in some branches of philosophy a split between mind and action is accepted, it would be anathema to writers as diverse as Rousseau, Durkheim, and Freud. Writers who today emphasize collective behavior often explain what they are doing in terms of a procedure of research; behavior is, they say, directly observable, while collective personality or consciousness is not. Researchers on crowds, for instance, start with the tangible actions crowds perform, and work from these actions toward more general notions. (Two books of special interest which follow this procedure are Louis Chevalier, *Laboring Classes and Dangerous Classes,* and George Rude, *The Crowd in History.*) But the difficulty with empirical work of this sort is that often the observer carries certain assumptions in his head about what he is seeing; these assumptions about the nature of behavior lead him to discard much data as irrelevant or unimportant without his being aware he is doing so. It is useful, therefore, to look at the analytic status of the terms we use to label behavior; the complexities of two of these terms, "role" and "crowd," may serve as a guide to the kinds of problems which arise.

The term "role" in contemporary social science is usually defined in the following way: it is "situation-specific" behavior. By this is meant "behavior which is appropriate for a particular social situation." For instance, crying as such could not be described as a role, but crying at a funeral could be; it is behavior which is expected in those circumstances.

This definition neatly disguises the complexities of the concept of role. The word itself has a theatrical meaning, and much of the thinking about roles in the past has taken this theatrical connotation seriously. When people are acting in a conventional manner, when they are acting according to what society defines as appropriate behavior for a given set of circumstances, they are also behaving like stage actors. The reason is, so classical ideas of role have argued, that they are engaged in imitations; people learn to act appropriately in a situation by imitating the way other people have acted in it; this is analogous to stage actors, who learn to behave as if they were someone else. The word "mime" first meant to behave according to what a particular situation suggests you ought to be, and mimetic theory classically meant the theory of impersonation. Recall from the Hobbes reading his emphasis on the necessity of imagining what most social situations are like, since our actual experience is so limited; when we do in fact move into a new situation, Hobbes says, we imitate the image we have in fantasy of how people in such a situation are supposed to act. Thus, Hobbes says, we "become actors of ourselves"—imitators of a life we "create first in dreams."

Because of the mimetic, imitative element, a social role thus contains hidden within it something theatrical. And from the writings of Plato onward, two moral conclusions have been drawn from this hidden connection of society and theater. One is that human beings are improved by their capacities to playact, the other is that they are degraded by these capacities. Imitative activity can be seen as a mode of either improvement or inauthenticity, or as a means of either learning to participate in society or learning to be a slave to social convention.

In Plato, these contrasting views appear, respectively, in the *Laws* and the *Republic*. The image of an actor in the *Laws* is not quite focused as a contemporary reader would expect, because here Plato associates the ability to playact with the intrusion of the gods upon the life of man. Dramatic activity, and more generally the imitative capacities of play, put human beings in touch with the sublime; in surrendering himself to dramatic behavior, man becomes a puppet in the hands of the gods. The association of dramatic activity with religion has, of course, survived antiquity as a central tenet of Catholicism; in many other religions, dramatic ritual is seen as the only way to raise oneself up to contact with the sublime. In the *Republic,* Plato speaks in terms today more easily recognizable. Imitation of others is condemned as a form of inauthenticity, and role-playing is portrayed as a form of social corruption.

These conflicting views about the morality of role-playing can be expressed in wholly secular terms. The debate on these terms cropped up, for instance, in the middle of the eighteenth century, and is presented here in selections from Diderot's *The Paradox of Acting* and Rousseau's *Letter to M. D'Alembert on the Theatre* (the latter being in fact a long treatise of some sixty pages in the original). Diderot argues that acting in social situations, as upon the stage, is a way to improve upon mankind's faulty and erratic natural powers of expression. Rousseau argues that acting in social situations, as upon the stage, blinds the human being to anything but applause for his ability to act as others do; to perform is to conform. Rousseau takes this moral argument a step further, by arguing that certain kinds of environments, like cities where large numbers of strangers meet, are most likely to encourage people to engage in role-playing. Since in large cities people have many opportunities for casual encounters where they can never be found out or tested, the pursuit of reputation through artifice and counterfeit identity becomes rife. Rousseau made a psychological assumption in this *Letter to D'Alembert,* underlined by Lionel Trilling in Trilling's *Sincerity and Authenticity;* it is that roles are not merely masks of the self, but detractions from the self. People come to believe that their mask is their self.

We have seen how St. Augustine attempted to gauge in general terms the moral status of an environment by assessing the effect of the environment upon the emotional life of its members. The debate about roles is a specific instance of that general tendency of thought. If Rousseau is right, selfhood is attenuated and inauthenticated by role-playing; the city is therefore a bad environment; if Diderot is right, a society which encourages conventional behavior encourages people to express themselves more fully and reliably than they would naturally be disposed to do.

It is important to see what happens when a writer working with the concept of roles becomes blind to these complexities. In the selection from the modern sociologist Erving Goffman presented here, roles are treated as "presentations of self" which, if they cause any discomfort or pain, are to be managed by juggling of one's appearances, by appeasement of others, or by enacting of a sense of distance between oneself and the faces one turns to the world. Questions of the moral status of a particular role, of its relation to theatricality, or of inner emotional conflict resolved through creating a social mask—all these classic and complex elements in thinking about roles have little place in Goffman's work. Goffman is describing behavior, not experience.

A more fruitful form of modern inquiry into roles is exemplified by the selection presented here from Lyman and Scott's *The Drama of Social Reality.* They advance the notion that not merely some activity in society is theatrical, but all social relations have elements of theatricality. The notion that society itself is a theater was first derived, under the influence of Plato's *Laws,* by Roman writers; it continued in medieval and renaissance literature as an image of *theatrum mundi.* It is this image which Lyman and Scott seek to bring to life again; they are particularly interested in showing the importance of drama in political affairs, and as the selection from their work presented here makes plain, they have not so much arrived at a completed analysis as laid out the ground rules for a program of inquiry.

11. Plato: The *Laws*   [429–c. 347 B.C.]

ATHENIAN: We also agreed some time ago that those who can command themselves are good, and those who cannot, bad.

CLINIAS: Precisely.

ATHENIAN: Then let us once more consider rather more exactly just what our words mean. Perhaps you will allow me to make the point clearer, if I can, by a parable.

CLINIAS: We are all attention.

ATHENIAN: Well then, we may take it that any human being is one person?

CLINIAS: Of course.

ATHENIAN: But one person who has within himself a pair of unwise and conflicting counselors, whose names are pleasure and pain?

CLINIAS: The fact is as you say.

ATHENIAN: He has, besides, anticipations of the future, and these of two sorts. The common name for both sorts is *expectation,* the special name for anticipation of pain being *fear,* and for anticipation of its opposite, *confidence* ($\theta\acute{\alpha}\rho\rho\text{os}$). And on the top of all, there is *judgment,* to discern which of these states is better or worse, and when judgment takes the form of a public decision of a city, it has the name of *law.*

CLINIAS: I fear I hardly follow you, yet pray proceed with your statement as though I did.

MEGILLUS: I, too, find myself in the same condition.

ATHENIAN: Let us look at the whole matter in some such light as this. We may imagine that each of us living creatures is a puppet made by gods, possibly as a plaything, or possibly with some more serious purpose. That, indeed, is more than we can tell, but one thing is certain. These interior states are, so to say, the cords, or strings, by which we are worked; they are opposed to one another, and pull us with opposite tensions in the direction of opposite actions, and therein lies the division of virtue from vice. In fact, so says our argument, a man must always yield to one of these tensions without resistance, but pull against all the other strings—must yield, that is, to that golden and hallowed drawing of judgment which goes by the name of the public law of the city. The others are hard and ironlike, it soft, as befits gold, whereas they resemble very various substances. So a man must always co-operate with the noble drawing of law, for judgment, though a noble thing, is as gentle and free from violence as noble, whence its drawing needs supporters, if the gold within us is to prevail over the other stuff. In this wise our moral fable of the human puppets will find its fulfillment. . . . while God is the real goal of all beneficent serious endeavor, man, as we said before, has been constructed as a toy for God, and this is, in fact, the finest thing about him. All of us, then, men and women alike, must fall in with our role and spend life in making our *play* as perfect as possible—to the complete inversion of current theory.

CLINIAS: Inversion? In what way?

ATHENIAN: It is the current fancy that our serious work should be done for the sake of our play; thus it is held that war is serious work which ought to be well discharged for the sake of peace. But the truth is that in war we do not find, and we never shall find, either any real play or any real education worth the name, and *these* are the things I count supremely serious for such creatures as ourselves. Hence it is peace in which each of us should spend most of his life and spend it best. What, then, is our right course? We should pass our lives in the playing of games—*certain* games, that is, sacrifice, song, and dance—with the result of ability to gain heaven's grace, and to repel and vanquish an enemy when we have to fight him. What sort of song and dance will effect both results has partly been stated in outline. The path has, so to say, been cut for us, and we should walk in it, in assurance that the poet was right when he said,

> Search, for some thoughts, thine own suggesting mind,
> And others, dictated by heavenly power,
> Shall rise spontaneously in the needful hour.
> For nought unprosperous shall thy ways attend,
> Born with good omens, and with heaven thy friend.

Our nurslings, too, must be of the poet's mind. They must believe that what we have said has been sufficient for its purpose and that, for the rest, they will be visited by promptings, superhuman and divine, as to their sacrifices and dances, suggestions as to the several gods in whose honor, and the several times at which, they are to play their play, win heaven's favor for it, and so live out their lives as what they really are—puppets in the main, though with some touch of reality about them, too.

MEGILLUS: I must say, sir, you have but a poor estimate of our race.

Plato: The *Republic*

This then, Adimantus, is the point we must keep in view. Do we wish our guardians to be good mimics or not? Or is this also a consequence of what we said before, that each one could practice well only one pursuit and not many, but if he attempted the latter, dabbling in many things, he would fail of distinction in all?

Of course it is.

And does not the same rule hold for imitation, that the same man is not able to imitate many things well as he can one?

No, he is not.

Still less, then, will he be able to combine the practice of any worthy pursuit with the imitation of many things and the quality of a mimic, since, unless I mistake, the same men cannot practice well at once even the two forms of imitation that appear most nearly akin, as the writing of tragedy and comedy. Did you not just now call these two imitations?

I did, and you are right in saying that the same men are not able to succeed in both.

Nor yet to be at once good rhapsodists and actors?

True.

But neither can the same men be actors for tragedies and comedies—and all these are imitations, are they not?

Yes, imitations.

And to still smaller coinage than this, in my opinion, Adimantus, proceeds the fractioning of human faculty, so as to be incapable of imitating many things or of doing the things themselves of which the imitations are likenesses.

Most true, he replied.

If, then, we are to maintain our original principle, that our guardians, released from all other crafts, are to be expert craftsmen of civic liberty, and pursue nothing else that does not conduce to this, it would not be fitting for these to do nor yet to imitate anything else. But if they imitate they should from childhood up imitate what is appropriate to them—men, that is, who are brave, sober, pious, free, and all things of that kind—but things unbecoming the free man they should neither do nor be clever at imitating, nor yet any other shameful thing, lest from the imitation they imbibe the reality. Or have you not observed that imitations, if continued from youth far into life, settle down into habits and second nature in the body, the speech, and the thought?

Then, said I, the other kind of speaker, the more debased he is the less will he shrink from imitating anything and everything. He will think nothing unworthy of himself, so that he will attempt, seriously and in the presence of many, to imitate all things, including those we just now mentioned—claps of thunder, and the noise of wind and hail and axles and pulleys, and the notes of trumpets and flutes and Panpipes, and the sounds of all instruments, and the cries of dogs, sheep, and birds—and so his style will depend wholly on imitation in voice and gesture, or will contain but a little of pure narration.

But perhaps, said I, you would affirm it to be ill suited to our polity, because there is no twofold or manifold man among us, since every man does one thing.

It is not suited.

And is this not the reason why such a city is the only one in which we shall find the cobbler a cobbler and not a pilot in addition to his cobbling, and the farmer a farmer and not a judge added to his farming, and the soldier a soldier and not a money-maker in addition to his soldiery, and so of all the rest?

True, he said.

If a man, then, it seems, who was capable by his cunning of assuming every kind of shape and imitating all things should arrive in our city, bringing with himself the poems which he wished to exhibit, we should fall down and worship him as a holy and wondrous and delightful creature, but should say to him that there is no man of that kind among us in our city, nor is it lawful for such a man to arise among us, and we should send him away to another city.

12. Denis Diderot: *The Paradox of Acting* [1713–1784]

Do not people talk in society of a man being a great actor? They do not mean by that that he feels, but that he excels in simulating, though he feels nothing—a part much more difficult than that of the actor: . . . In tribunals, in assemblies, everywhere where a man wishes to make himself master of others' minds, he feigns now anger, now fear, now pity, now love, to bring others into these divers states of feeling. What passion itself fails to do, passion well imitated accomplishes. . . . is it to be believed that an actor on the stage can be deeper, cleverer in feigning joy, sadness, sensibility, admiration, hate, tenderness, than an old courtier? . . .

If the actor were full, really full, of feeling, how could he play the same part twice running with the same spirit and success? Full of fire at the first performance, he would be worn out and cold as marble at the third. But take it that he is an attentive mimic and thoughtful disciple of Nature, then the first time he comes on the stage as Augustus, Cinna, Orosmanes, Agamemnon, or Mahomet, faithful copying of himself and the effects he has arrived at, and constantly observing human nature, will so prevail that his acting, far from losing in force, will gather strength with the new observations he will make from time to time. He will increase or moderate his effects, and you will be more and more pleased with him. If he is himself while he is playing, how is he to stop being himself? If he wants to stop being himself, how is he to catch just the point where he is to stay his hand? . . .

Great poets, great actors, and, I may add, all great copyists of Nature, in whatever art, beings gifted with fine imagination, with broad judgment, with exquisite tact, with a sure touch of taste, are the least sensitive of all creatures. They are too apt for too many things, too busy with observing, considering, and reproducing, to have their inmost hearts affected with any liveliness. To me such an one always has his portfolio spread before him and his pencil in his fingers.

Have you ever thought on the difference between the tears raised by a tragedy of real life and those raised by a touching narrative? You hear a fine piece of recitation; by little and little your thoughts are involved, your heart is touched, and your tears flow. With the tragedy of real life the thing, the feeling and the effect, are all one; your heart is reached at once, you utter a cry, your head swims, and the tears flow. These tears come of a sudden, the others by degrees. And here is the superiority of a true effect of nature over a well-planned scene. It does at one stroke what the scene leads up to by degrees, but it is far more difficult to reproduce its effect; one incident ill given would shatter it. . . . You give a recitation in a drawing-room; your feelings are stirred; your voice fails you; you burst into tears. You have, as you say, felt, and felt deeply. Quite so; but had you made up your mind to that? Not at all. Yet you were carried away, you surprised and touched your hearers, you made a great hit. All this is true enough. But now transfer your easy tone, your simple expression, your every-day bearing, to the stage, and, I assure you, you will be paltry and weak. You may cry to your heart's content, and the audience will only laugh. It will be the tragedy outside a booth at a fair. . . . But, to go back, it must have happened to you a hundred times that at the end of your recitation, in the very midst of the agitation and emotion you have caused in your drawing-room audience, a fresh guest has entered, and wanted to hear you again. You find it impossible, you are weary to the soul. Sensibility, fire, tears, all have left you. . . .

An unhappy, a really unhappy woman, may weep and fail to touch you; worse than that, some trivial disfigurement in her may incline you to laughter; the accent which is apt to her is to your ears dissonant and vexatious; a movement which is habitual to her makes her grief show ignobly and sulkily to you; almost all the violent passions lend themselves to grimaces which a tasteless artist will copy but too faithfully, and which a great actor will avoid. . . .

Not, mark you, that Nature unadorned has not her moments of sublimity; but I fancy that if there is any one sure to give and preserve their sublimity it is the man who can feel it with his passion and his genius, and reproduce it with complete self-possession. . . . You are talking to me of a passing moment in Nature. I am talking to you of a work of Art, planned and composed—a work which is built up by degrees, and which lasts. Take now each of these actors; change the scene in the street as you do on the boards, and show me your personages left successively to themselves, two by two or three by three. Leave them to their own swing; make them full masters of their actions; and you will see what a monstrous discord will result. You will get over this by making them rehearse together. Quite so. And then good-bye to their natural sensibility; and so much the better.

A play is like any well-managed association, in which each

individual sacrifices himself for the general good and effect. And who will best take the measure of the sacrifice? The enthusiast or the fanatic? Certainly not. In society, the man of judgment; on the stage, the actor whose wits are always about him. Your scene in the street has the same relation to a scene on the stage that a band of savages has to a company of civilised men. . . .

The circumstances in which sensibility is as hurtful in society as on the stage are a thousand to one. Take two lovers, both of whom have their declaration to make. Who will come out of it best? Not I, I promise you. I remember that I approached the beloved object with fear and trembling; my heart beat, my ideas grew confused, my voice failed me, I mangled all I said! I cried *yes* for *no;* I made a thousand blunders; I was illimitably inept; I was absurd from top to toe, and the more I saw it, the more absurd I became. Meanwhile, under my very eyes, a gay rival, light-hearted and agreeable, master of himself, pleased with himself, losing no opportunity for the finest flattery, made himself entertaining and agreeable, enjoyed himself; he implored the touch of a hand which was at once given him, he sometimes caught it without asking leave, he kissed it once and again. I the while, alone in a corner, avoiding a sight which irritated me, stifling my sighs, cracking my fingers with grasping my wrists, plunged in melancholy, covered with a cold sweat, I could neither show nor conceal my vexation. . . .

The man of sensibility obeys the impulse of Nature, and gives nothing more or less than the cry of his very heart; the moment he moderates or strengthens this cry he is no longer himself, he is an actor.

The great actor watches appearances; the man of sensibility is his model; he thinks over him, and discovers by after-reflection what it will be best to add or cut away. And so from mere argument he goes to action. . . .

The fact is, that to have sensibility is one thing, to feel is another. One is a matter of soul, the other of judgment. One may feel strongly and be unable to express it; one may alone, or in private life, at the fireside, give expression, in reading or acting, adequate for a few listeners, and give none of any account on the stage. . . .

In the great play, the play of the world, the play to which I am constantly recurring, the stage is held by the fiery souls, and the pit is filled with men of genius. The actors are in other words madmen; the spectators, whose business it is to paint their madness, are sages. And it is they who discern with a ready eye the absurdity of the motley crowd, who reproduce it for you, and who make you laugh both at the unhappy models who have bored you to death and at yourself. It is they who watch you, and who give you the mirth-moving picture of the tiresome wretch and of your own anguish in his clutches.

13. Jean-Jacques Rousseau:
Letter to M. D'Alembert on the Theatre
(*Politics and the Arts*)

What is the talent of the actor? It is the art of counterfeiting himself, of putting on another character than his own, of appearing different than he is, of becoming passionate in cold blood, of saying what he does not think as naturally as if he really did think it, and, finally, of forgetting his own place by dint of taking another's. What is the profession of the actor? It is a trade in which he performs for money, submits himself to the disgrace and the affronts that others buy the right to give him, and puts his person publicly on sale. I beg every sincere man to tell if he does not feel in the depths of his soul that there is something servile and base in this traffic of oneself. You philosophers, who have the pretention of being so far above prejudices, would you not all die of shame if, ignominiously gotten up as kings, you had to take on in the eyes of the public a different role than your own and expose your majesties to the jeers of the populace? What, then, is the spirit that the actor receives from his estate? A mixture of abjectness, duplicity, ridiculous conceit, and disgraceful abasement which renders him fit for all sorts of roles except for the most noble of all, that of man, which he abandons. . . .

When the people is corrupted, the theatre is good for it, and bad for it when it is itself good. . . . It follows from this that, in order to decide if it is proper or not to establish a theatre in a certain town, we must know in the first place if the morals [manners] are good or bad there, . . .

I see immediately that the theatre is a form of amusement; and if it is true that amusements are necessary to man, you will at least admit that they are only permissible insofar as they are necessary, and that every useless amusement is an evil for a being whose life is so short and whose time is so precious. The state of man has its pleasures which are derived from his nature and are born of his labors, his relations, and his needs. And these pleasures, sweeter to the one who tastes them in the measure that his soul is healthier, make whoever is capable of participating in them indifferent to all others. A father, a son, a husband, and a citizen have such cherished duties to fulfil that they are left nothing to give to boredom. The good use of time makes time even more precious, and the better one puts it to use, the less one can find to lose. Thus it is constantly seen that the habit of work renders inactivity intolerable and that a good conscience extinguishes the taste for frivolous pleasures. But it is discontent with one's self, the burden of idleness, the neglect of simple and natural tastes, that makes foreign amusement so necessary. I do not like the need to occupy the heart constantly with the stage as if it were ill at ease inside of us. . . .

This is a question that depends less on the consideration of the theatre than on that of the spectators. . . . In a big city, full of scheming, idle people without religion or principle, whose imagination, depraved by sloth, inactivity, the love of pleasure, and great needs, engenders only monsters and inspires only crimes; in a big city, where morals [manners] and honor are nothing because each, easily hiding his conduct from the public eye, shows himself only by his reputation and is esteemed only for his riches; in a big city, I say, the police can never increase the number of pleasures permitted too much or apply itself too much to making them agreeable in order to deprive individuals of the temptation of seeking more dangerous ones. Since preventing them from occupying themselves is to prevent them from doing harm, two hours a day stolen from the activity of vice prevents the twelfth part of the crimes that would be committed. And all the discussions in cafés and other refuges of the do-nothings and rascals of the place occasioned by plays seen or to be seen are also that much the more gained by family men, either for their daughters' honor or that of their wives, or for their purse or that of their sons.

In a little town, proportionately less activity is unquestionably to be found than in a capital, because the passions are less intense and the needs less pressing, but more original spirits, more inventive industry, more really new things are found there because the people are less imitative; having few models, each draws more from himself and puts more of his own in everything he does; because the human mind, less spread out, less drowned in vulgar opinions, elaborates itself and ferments better in tranquil solitude; because, in seeing less, more is imagined; finally, because less pressed for time, there is more leisure to extend and digest one's ideas. . . . Such is the simplicity of true genius. It is neither scheming nor busybodyish; it knows not the path of honors and fortune nor dreams of seeking it; it compares itself to no one; all its resources are within itself; indifferent to insult and hardly conscious of praise, if it is aware of itself, it does not assign itself a place and enjoys itself without appraising itself. . . .

Whether we deduce from the nature of the theatre in general its best possible forms, or whether we examine all that the learning of an enlightened age and people has done for the perfection of ours, I believe that we can conclude from these diverse considerations that the moral effect of the theatre can never be good or salutary in itself, since, in reckoning only its advantages, we find no kind of real utility without drawbacks which outweigh it. Now, as a consequence of its very lack of utility, the theatre, which can do nothing to improve morals [manners], can do much toward changing them. In encouraging all our penchants, it gives a new ascendency to those which dominate us. The continual emotion which is felt in the theatre excites us, enervates us, enfeebles us, and makes us less able to resist our passions.

14. Erving Goffman: "Role Distance," in *Encounters*   [1922–]

In sociology there are few concepts more commonly used than 'role', few that are accorded more importance, and few that waver so much when looked at closely. . . . *Role* consists of the activity the incumbent would engage in were he to act solely in terms of the normative demands upon someone in his position. Role in this normative sense is to be distinguished from *role performance* or role enactment, which is the actual conduct of a particular individual while on duty in his position. (Accordingly, it is a position that can be entered, filled, and left, not a role, for a role can only be performed; but no student seems to hold to these consistencies, nor will I.) . . .

The individual's role enactment occurs largely through a cycle of face-to-face social situations with *role others,* that is, relevant audiences. These various kinds of role others for an individual in role, when taken together, have recently been termed a *role-set.* The role-set for a doctor, for example, contains colleagues, nurses, patients, and hospital administrators. The norms relating the individual to performers of one of the roles in his role-set will have a special and non-conflictful relation to one another—more so than the norms relating the individual to different kinds of role others. The overall role associated with a position falls into *role sectors* or subroles, each having to do with a particular kind of role other. Doctor-nurse is a role sector of the doctor role; doctor-patient, another.

Social changes in a role can be traced by the loss or gain to the role-set of types of role other. However, even within the special sector of a role relating the performer to one type of role other, the activities involved may themselves fall into different, somewhat independent parcels or bundles, and through time these may also be reduced or added to, a bundle at a time. In any case, we ought not to be embarrassed by the fact that what is handled from one kind of position in one organization may be apportioned to two or three kinds of positions in another organization. We need only claim to know how a role is likely to be broken up should it come to be divided—the points of cleavage—and what roles are likely to be combined at times of organizational retrenchment.

The elementary unit of role analysis, as Linton was at pains to point out, is not the individual but the individual enacting his bundle of obligatory activity. The system or pattern borrows only a part of the individual, and what he does or is at other times and places is not the first concern. The role others for whom he performs similarly represent only slices of these others. Presumably his contribution and their contribution, differentiated and interdependent, fit together into a single assemblage of activity, this *system* or pattern being the real concern of role analysis.

The role perspective has definite implications of a social-psychological kind. In entering the position, the incumbent finds that he must take on the whole array of action encompassed by the corresponding role, so role implies a social determinism and a doctrine about socialization. We do not take on items of conduct one at a time but rather a whole harness load of them and may anticipatorily learn to be a horse even while being pulled like a wagon. Role, then, is the basic unit of socialization. It is through roles that tasks in society are allocated and arrangements made to enforce their performance. . . .

It is important to note that in performing a role the individual must see to it that the impressions of him that are conveyed in the situation are compatible with role-appropriate personal qualities effectively imputed to him: a judge is supposed to be deliberate and sober; a pilot, in a cockpit, to be cool; a book-keeper to be accurate and neat in doing his work. These personal qualities, effectively imputed and effectively claimed, combine with a position's title, when there is one, to provide a basis of *self-image* for the incumbent and a basis for the image that his role others will have of him. A self, then, virtually awaits the individual entering a position; he need only conform to the pressures on him and he will find a *me* ready-made for him. In the language of Kenneth Burke, doing is being.

It can be useful to distinguish between the *regular performance* of a role and a *regular performer* of a role. If, for example, a funeral parlor is to stay in business, then the role of the director, of the immediately bereaved, and of the deceased must be performed regularly; but, of these regularly performed roles, only the director will be a regular performer. The immediately bereaved may play the same role on a few other occasions, but certainly the role of the deceased is played but once by any one individual. We can now see that to speak in common-sense terms of an 'irregular' performer is to refer to someone performing only a few times what is usually performed by a regular performer.

A concept that is often employed in the discussion of roles is that of *commitment*. I propose to restrict this term to questions of impersonally enforced structural arrangements. An individual becomes committed to something when, because of the fixed and interdependent character of many institutional arrangements, his doing or being this something irrevocably conditions other important possibilities in his life, forcing him to take courses of action, causing other persons to build up their activity on the basis of his continuing in his current undertakings, and rendering him vulnerable to unanticipated consequences of these undertakings. He thus becomes locked into a position and coerced into living up to the promises and sacrifices built into it. Typically, a person will become deeply committed only to a role he regularly performs, and it is left to gallants, one-shot gamblers, and the foolhardy to become committed to a role they do not perform regularly.

The self-image available for anyone entering a particular

position is one of which he may become affectively and cognitively enamored, desiring and expecting to see himself in terms
of the enactment of the role and the self-identification emerging
from this enactment. I will speak here of the individual becoming *attached* to his position and its role, adding only that in the
case of larger social units—groups, not positions—attachment
is more likely to have a selfless component. . . .

Although the classic conceptions of position and role can
deal adequately with many difficulties, there remain some issues
that are less easy to resolve. . . . An individual's position,
defining position as it tends to be used, is a matter of life
chances—the likelihood of his undergoing certain fateful experiences, certain trials, tribulations, and triumphs. His position
in some sphere of life is his 'situation' there, in the sense
employed by existentialists: the image that he and others come
to have of him; the pleasures and anxieties he is likely to
experience; the contingencies he meets in face-to-face interaction with others; the relationships he is likely to form; his
probable alignment and stand on public issues, leading various
kinds of persons in various connections to oppose him or support him. I include also the obligations and expectations that
very often come to guide his action relative to specified others.
. . . Role may now be defined, in this corrected version, as the
typical response of individuals in a particular position. Typical
role must of course be distinguished from the actual role performance of a concrete individual in a given position. Between
typical response and actual response we can usually expect
some difference, if only because the position of an individual, in
the terms now used, will depend somewhat on the varying fact
of how he perceives and defines his situation. . . .

The individual stands in a double relationship to attributes
that are, or might be, imputed to him. Some attributes he will
feel are rightfully his, others he will not; some he will be pleased
and able to accept as part of his self-definition, others he will
not. There is some relationship between these two variables—
between what is right and what is pleasing—in that the individual often feels that pleasing imputations regarding himself are in addition rightful, and unpleasing imputations are,

incidentally, undeserved and illegitimate. But this happy relationship between the two variables does not always hold. . . .

This 'effectively' expressed pointed separateness between the individual and his putative role I shall call *role distance*. A shorthand is involved here: the individual is actually denying not the role but the virtual self that is implied in the role for all accepting performers.

In any case, the term 'role distance' is not meant to refer to all behavior that does not directly contribute to the task core of a given role but only to those behaviors that are seen by someone present as relevant to assessing the actor's attachment to his particular role and relevant in such a way as to suggest that the actor possibly has some measure of disaffection from, and resistance against, the role. Thus, for example, a four-year-old halfway through a triumphant performance as a merry-go-round rider may sometimes go out of play, dropping from his face and manner any confirmation of his virtual self, yet may indulge in this break in role without apparent intent, the lapse reflecting more on his capacity to sustain any role than on his feelings about the present one. Nor can it be called role distance if the child rebels and totally rejects the role, stomping off in a huff, for the special facts about self that can be conveyed by holding a role off a little are precisely the ones that cannot be conveyed by throwing the role over.

At seven and eight, the child not only dissociates himself self-consciously from the kind of horseman a merry-go-round allows him to be but also finds that many of the devices that younger people use for this are now beneath him. He rides no-hands, gleefully chooses a tiger or a frog for a steed, clasps hands with a mounted friend across the aisle. He tests limits, and his antics may bring negative sanction from the adult in charge of the machine. And he is still young enough to show distance by handling the task with bored, nonchalant competence, a candy bar languidly held in one hand.

At eleven and twelve, maleness for boys has become a real responsibility, and no easy means of role distance seems to be available on merry-go-rounds. It is necessary to stay away or to exert creative acts of distancy, as when a boy jokingly treats his wooden horse as if it were a racing one: he jogs himself up and down, leans far over the neck of the horse, drives his heels mercilessly into its flanks, and uses the reins for a lash to get more speed, brutally reining in the horse when the ride is over. He is just old enough to achieve role distance by defining the whole undertaking as a lark, a situation for mockery.

Adults who choose to ride a merry-go-round display adult techniques of role distance. One adult rider makes a joke of tightening the safety belt around him; another crosses his arms, giving popcorn with his left hand to the person on his right and a coke with his right hand to the person on his left. A young lady riding sidesaddle tinkles out, 'It's cold,' and calls to her watching boy friend's boy friend, 'Come on, don't be chicken.' A dating couple riding adjacent horses hold hands to bring sentiment, not daring, to the situation. Two double-dating couples employ their own techniques: the male in front sits backwards and takes a picture of the other male rider taking a picture of him. And, of course, some adults, riding close by their threatened two-and-a-half-year-old, wear a face that carefully demonstrates that they do not perceive the ride as an event in itself, their only present interest being their child.

And finally there is the adult who runs the machine and takes the tickets. Here, often, can be found a fine flowering of role distance. Not only does he show that the ride itself is not—as a ride—an event to him, but he also gets off and on and around the moving platform with a grace and ease that can only be displayed by safely taking what for children and even adults would be chances.

Some general points can be made about merry-go-round role distance. First, while the management of a merry-go-round horse in our culture soon ceases to be a challenging 'developmental task', the task of expressing that it is not continues for a long time to be a challenge and remains a felt necessity. A full twist must be made in the iron law of etiquette: the act through which one can afford to try to fit into the situation is an act that can be styled to show that one is somewhat out of place. One enters the situation to the degree that one can demonstrate that one does not belong.

A second general point about role distance is that immediate audiences figure very directly in the display of role distance. Merry-go-round horsemen are very ingenuous and may frankly wait for each time they pass their waiting friends before playing through their gestures of role distance. Moreover, if persons above the age of twelve or so are to trust themselves to making a lark of it, they almost need to have a friend along on the next horse, since persons who are 'together' seem to be able to hold off the socially defining force of the environment much more than a person alone.

A final point: two different means of establishing role distance seem to be found. In one case the individual tries to isolate himself as much as possible from the contamination of the situation, as when an adult riding along to guard his child makes an effort to be completely stiff, affectless, and preoccupied. In the other case the individual cooperatively projects a childish self, meeting the situation more than halfway, but then withdraws from this castoff self by a little gesture signifying that the joking has gone far enough. In either case the individual can slip the skin the situation would clothe him in.

15. Stanford M. Lyman and Marvin B. Scott:
The Drama of Social Reality   [1933-]

"Theory" is derived from the Greek term for "theatre." This derivation suggests that the method appropriate to theorizing was, from the beginning, dramatistic. The early Greek theorists were called *theoria,* a term referring to (1) an envoy sent to consult an oracle; (2) a body of state ambassadors delegated by one city-state to attend the sacral festivals and games of another city-state; and (3) a spectator at the games and, by extension, a traveler who visits foreign places to learn about foreign practices, customs, and laws. To theorize meant, then, to see the world, to report on the world, and, more significantly, to elucidate the seen but unnoticed features of that world. The *theoria* who visited an oracle undertook a search for divine communication and an interpretation of that message. The ambassadors to the festivals and games were charged with noticing what was going on, grasping the meanings in use, and perceiving the implications thereof. As travelers, *theoria* were like modern ethnologists, describing exotic practices and trying to understand their meaning. Thus, oracles, festivals, and games constituted performances that were deemed significant for uncovering *truth*.

The sought-after truth was *aletheia* (literally, "unhiddenness"), the truth that was hidden from view but available to those who would take up the attitude of a seer or *theoria*. Implicit in this view is the idea that the everyday world provides situations from which truth might be extracted by those who would take the trouble to look with the attitude appropriate to witnessing human and divine performances: wonder, astonishment, and naive puzzlement.

To the Greeks, then, human affairs arose, were carried out, and might be conceived as the outcome of action. A theory of human affairs is thus a theory of action. And, as the Greek philosophers knew, a reification of action through repetition and textualization is found in drama. Drama, whose Greek root *dran* meant "to act," is an imitation or a *mimesis* of ordinary acting. Moreover, drama—by providing an opportunity for an audience (*theoria*) to discover the hidden truths (*aletheia*) that it both reifies and universalizes—is the primordial "social science." Drama enacts man's relationship to man, which is fundamental to every social science.

Dramatic performances typically convey their meanings by speech. So also the drama of human existence seems to require speech (communication in the broadest sense). And, by extension, the science of human affairs is largely a study of "performative utterances." Although they may be analytically separated, action and speech are inextricably intertwined in everyday affairs. In speech, man manifests the clarification, motivation, exculpation, and justification for action, and his own identity as well. Sociological analysis, thus, must treat the texts of ordinary performances. Social scientists who theorize within the framework of performance theory must behave, in the first instance, like an *audience* at a drama; they must pay special attention to the nature, order, meaning, and consequences of gesture and speech and locate their scientific attitude in the attentiveness the philosophical spectator gives to the daily drama of human existence.

Social reality, then, is realized theatrically. Otherwise put, reality is a drama, life is theatre, and the social world is inherently dramatic. . . .

Power must be translated into authority if control over others is to be maintained without constant recourse to brute force. The study of this transformation process is a fundamental aspect of political sociology. Usually it is discussed as "the *problem* of authority," or—in times of general political unrest and widespread disenchantment with prevailing systems of governance—as "the *crisis* of authority." Authority, in turn, is a particular and complex form of impression management, designed, as it is, to legitimate the right of the few to rule over and decide the fate of the many. If we take as an assumption that there is no natural or necessary right of some individuals to dominate others, then the particular way in which any individual or collectivity establishes this right is through an efficacious social construction. Typically, this construction takes the form of a *myth* that identifies the ruling group and justifies its right to rule. These efficacious social constructions are basic and essential dramas. They guarantee lasting power for as long as the myth continues to persuade, mollify, or overawe its audiences.

According to Plato, rulership must be exercised by men of exceptional knowledge and superior wisdom. The highest virtue is knowledge, and through the proper employment of that knowledge, the objective good can be discovered and established. . . . From a dramaturgical point of view, however, there still remains the problem of demonstrating one's fitness for office. It is one thing to have knowledge or wisdom, quite another to *indicate* that one has it so that others will recognize it and accord one the rights and perquisites that go with it. Plato does not address this particular problem directly, but, in the manner of the presentation of his general theses, he reveals a method not presented in the argument itself: The *Republic* is written in the form of a dramatic debate.

Socrates, the man of wisdom, is confronted by a chorus of antagonists who not only match wits and wisdom with him, but also tease, threaten, and attempt to trip him up. Socrates himself is not without guile, subtlety, and humor. At various times he employs sarcasm, irony, and a multitude of metaphors. Thus, while celebrating the cause of reason and logic, he reenforces his case with those elementary forms of *rhetoric* that make the difference between pure rationality and its dramatic display. There is a hidden message in this form of presentation: namely, that for a Socrates to be recognized as a rightful ruler, a philosopher-king, he must so develop the presentational strategies of his argument that he will be taken to be that to which he aspires. Presentation of rationality also requires a presentation of self.

Divine sanction found its principal institutionalization in theocracy and those kingdoms organized around the divine right of hereditary monarchs. A fine example of this myth is that presented by John Calvin (1509–1567). According to his interpretation of the doctrine of predestination, certain individuals are preordained for salvation, others for eternal damnation. In this world there is then a spiritual aristocracy composed of the saved, and it is from this group that temporal rulers should be chosen or guided. . . .

There still remains, however, the question of knowing how to recognize the proper civil authority. Calvin asserts that this authority is charged with a divine mission but not subject to popular approval. Magistracy is ordained by God, according to Calvin, and magistrates should be faithful to God's will since they are His deputies on earth. But how does one know the magistrate? Calvin gives the germ of an answer when he notes that "among the elect we regard the call as a testimony of election. Then we hold justification another sign of its manifestation. . . ." Thus did Calvin hint at the dramaturgical elements that adumbrate his theocracy. A ruler must experience a "call" and test that experience by a "justification" in his fortune. Presumably the political arena provides opportunity for "justification" in the competition for office. And in a system wherein the office goes to that person who demonstrates most effectively that he is being "called" to serve, a premium is placed on efficacious displays of piety, prophetic performance, and priestly characteristics. . . .

In a third myth, leadership is acknowledged in men who display exceptional courage or unusual heroics. One of the more significant statements made in behalf of the hero as leader is to be found in the writings of Thomas Carlyle (1795–1881). For Carlyle (*On Heroes, Hero-Worship and the Heroic in History*), "Universal History, the history of what man has accomplished in this world, is at bottom the History of the Great Men who have worked there. They were the leaders of men, these great ones; the modellers, patterns, and in a wide sense creators, of whatsoever the general mass of men contrived to do or attain; all things that we see standing accomplished in the world are properly the outer material result, the practical realization and embodiment, of Thoughts that dwelt in the Great Men sent into the world; the soul of the whole world's history, it may justly be considered, were the history of these." . . .

Quite obviously the heroic myth lends itself most clearly to the dramaturgical *praxis*. The hero is neither born nor trained for his role. He appears. He acts. He is recognized. He is acclaimed. He is crowned. History and coincidence must be so arranged or so fortunate that the moment for demonstrating heroism occurs when and where the would-be hero is in a position to make the most of it. Since the script of history is not written in advance—or, if it is, the text is not available to everyone—the appearance of the hero may be accidental or arise out of that remarkable coincidence that brings together the right moment with the right man.

What does a hero do to demonstrate that he is indeed heroic? Joseph Campbell has provided an inventory of roles he might assume and in doing so has cast at least one of the characters in the drama of history that must occur for the hero to appear and be recognized as such. Campbell observes that the hero may be a warrior, lover, emperor, tyrant, redeemer, or saint. These roles invite a parallel inventory of scenarios and role-sets to match them. Thus, the warrior requires a battle; the lover, a desirable woman; the emperor, an unorganized population; the tyrant, rebellious or oppressed subjects; the redeemer, a people who are lost and in need of redemption; and the saint, a situation calling for piety.

Heroism as a performance requires more than a deed of valor, daring, sacrifice, or piety. For heroism is demonstrated in the *manner* in which the deed is performed. Central to heroism, then, is the management and display of appropriate character. One element of this appropriate character is "coolness" or "poise" in the face of fateful or consequential action. The scenes wherein heroism can be displayed are also precisely those in which its opposite might be revealed. As an individual senses that the moment for heroic action is about to occur, his emotional reserves may falter, his courage fail, and—in the very physical presentation of his being—he may give himself away. . . . In short, then, the trials by which heroism is proved are also character contests. Those who enter them must be willing to overcome the nerve of failure in order to indicate no failure of nerve. . . .

A most interesting myth of legitimacy that arose together with deterministic science and the rise of rationalism is the thesis of the "general will." Associated with the philosophy of Jean-Jacques Rousseau (1712–1778)—who transformed earlier ideas of the coercive but necessary state presented by Hobbes and Locke into an acceptable thesis of subjugation—the argument links surrender of individual wills (necessary for the cessation of the "war of all against all") to an emergence of a "general will" that is at once derivative of but superior to the sum of those wills. . . .

Knowledge of the "general will"—as opposed to the "will of everyone"—is attributed to the sovereign. And this knowledge is the fundamental justification for authority. Indeed, once having been established, the sovereign's right to rule is inalienable, according to Rousseau, and may not be challenged: . . . Thus he who can demonstrate or stage in a convincing manner that he is possessed of the general will can lay claim to political authority.

The dramaturgical elements of popular sovereignty are not difficult to discern. The method of election is itself a contest, requiring each candidate to present himself before the public in such a manner as to secure their support. Campaigns are dramas composed of several acts: the first is the selection of the candidate from among contenders within the political organization (e.g., political parties or factions); the second is the contest for public support bringing opposed parties or factions into direct competition; the third is the election itself, which sets in motion the mechanisms leading to a yet unknown outcome; and the last act includes the scenes of victory and defeat and requires skillful employment of the art of impression management for both the winner and the loser. . . .

A perceptive sense of the artistic requirements of democratic politics has been presented by Gore Vidal, a contemporary novelist-essayist-dramatist whose perspective comes as close to that of a modern Machiavelli as a democracy is likely to produce. Speaking of the American politician in the middle of the twentieth century, Vidal observes that he must conform to certain conventions:

> He must be gregarious (or seem to be), candid (but never give the game away), curious about people (otherwise, he would find his work unendurable). An American politician must not seem too brainy. He must put on no airs. He must smile often but at the same time appear serious. Most disagreeable of all, according to one ancient United States Senator, wise with victory, "is when you got to let some s.o.b. look you straight in the eye and think he's making a fool of you. Oh that is gall and wormwood to the spirit." Above all, a politician must not sound clever or wise or proud.

As Vidal notes, "politics is improvisation. To the artful dodger rather than the true believer goes the prize." He goes on to advise the politician on dramatics, in terms that openly compare the politician to the actor and implicitly suggest that the problems of Machiavelli's prince are in fact of the same kind as those that trouble democratic leaders.

II.
Crowds

Whereas role-playing is a broad category of behavior—a universal one if the writers of the *theatrum mundi* tradition are to be believed—the crowd is a specific social situation which should promote only a well-defined and constricted pattern of behavior. A crowd brings a large number of people together in one place; it brings them together for a temporary period; usually most of the people in the crowd are strangers to one another. Thus the social-psychological question crowd life poses is: What kind of emotional transactions arise in an impersonal, ephemeral situation?

Le Bon's answer was that this situation permits an enormously passionate and potentially destructive pattern of behavior to arise; the crowd is an opportunity for release of the unconscious energies society normally curbs. In this section we see Le Bon's theme expanded in the work of the modern political theorist Elias Canetti. Canetti tries to make concrete many of the ideas Le Bon described as general "tendencies"; Canetti deals with the fear of being physically touched, for instance, arguing that only in crowds of strangers does the individual escape from it, and then showing the violence to which the freedom to touch other people may lead the crowd as a whole. Le Bon is challenged by the cultural historian Walter Benjamin, whose work was done in Germany between the two world wars. Benjamin conceived of impersonal crowds as emotionally empty and blank on the surface; this is a familiar enough theme, but what makes Benjamin's work distinctive is that he then tried to penetrate that surface and understand what kind of emotional life transpires below it. In the investigation he made of the poet Baudelaire's imagery of crowds, for instance, he looked at the way a seemingly blank crowd could encourage people to strike poses, as though posing against a blank stage backdrop; such a figure was Baudelaire's *flâneur.* The idea is one we have already encountered in Rousseau, whose *Letter to D'Alembert* condemns exactly this kind of posturing as the theatrical vice of the city.

The crowd is, of course, the urban scene *par excellence.* For this reason, much of the work on the psychological qualities of urban life has focused on crowds; the city as a whole has not been the focus so much as this particular social situation in it. (Some typical writing in this vein is, in English, Georg Simmel's classic article, "The Metropolis and Mental Life," Lyn Lofland's recent study, *A World of Strangers;* in French and as yet untranslated, Maurice Halbwachs, *La Memoire collective,* and in German and also untranslated, Alexander Mitscherlich, *Die Unwirtlichkeit unserer Städte.*) Similarly, the idea of collective personality has been applied to city life in terms of a particular crowd type: the stranger.

The selections by Alfred Schutz and Georg Simmel on "the stranger" are both sketches of such a collective person. Schutz conceives of him as a migrant to an unfamiliar group, and Schutz's aim is to discover what is the unconscious or unspoken knowledge a group has of itself which the stranger is forced to make conscious and to learn. Elsewhere in his writings, Schutz describes the passage of a stranger into a group as constituting in the stranger's mind a passage from what seems a crowd to what becomes a community. Simmel, by contrast, wants to understand "the stranger" as the representative collective personality of a crowd in and of itself, removed from time and change.

Both these applications of collective-personality theory raise the problem of stereotyping. It is a real problem in social psychology, not just a self-evident vice, because stereotyping has advantages as well as defects and they aren't easily separable. The disadvantage of images like "the stranger" is that the images may call to the observer's attention obvious features of feeling and behavior, but don't get at what's complicated—in a word, what's interesting. Common characteristics between people are usually perceived in terms of what is immediately obvious about them; the less obvious, the less easily generalizable. On the other hand, to get a sense of what is problematic and complicated in a person, you have to start with standards of obvious and not-obvious; stereotyping is one way to create such a standard. Without the stereotype, the person may seem a world unto himself, and so the investigator would have lifted the subject out of a social context.

Any scheme for classifying people runs into the problem of stereotyping to some degree, but collective-personality images have a special difficulty in this regard, for in this pattern of analysis, both social conditions and their emotional effects have to be held constant in order for the collective image to appear; if there is historical change in the conditions, or variations in emotional response to whatever the social conditions at a particular moment are, then the collective image easily goes out of focus. It is for this reason that many social-psychological theorists have concluded that the construction of character types is of limited analytic value, the more detailed and narrowly focused one's vision of a social group is. The same could be said of the concept of "role" in its purely behavioral form.

16. Elias Canetti: *Crowds and Power*   [1905–]

THE FEAR OF BEING TOUCHED

There is nothing that man fears more than the touch of the unknown. He wants to *see* what is reaching towards him, and to be able to recognize or at least classify it. Man always tends to avoid physical contact with anything strange. In the dark, the fear of an unexpected touch can mount to panic. Even clothes give insufficient security: it is easy to tear them and pierce through to the naked, smooth, defenceless flesh of the victim.

All the distances which men create round themselves are dictated by this fear. They shut themselves in houses which no-one may enter, and only there feel some measure of security. The fear of burglars is not only the fear of being robbed, but also the fear of a sudden and unexpected clutch out of the darkness.

The repugnance to being touched remains with us when we go about among people; the way we move in a busy street, in restaurants, trains or buses, is governed by it. Even when we are standing next to them and are able to watch and examine them closely, we avoid actual contact if we can. If we do not avoid it, it is because we feel attracted to someone; and then it is we who make the approach.

The promptness with which apology is offered for an unintentional contact, the tension with which it is awaited, our violent and sometimes even physical reaction when it is not forthcoming, the antipathy and hatred we feel for the offender, even when we cannot be certain who it is—the whole knot of shifting and intensely sensitive reactions to an alien touch— proves that we are dealing here with a human propensity as deep-seated as it is alert and insidious; something which never leaves a man when he has once established the boundaries of his personality. Even in sleep, when he is far more unguarded, he can all too easily be disturbed by a touch.

It is only in a crowd that man can become free of this fear of being touched. That is the only situation in which the fear changes into its opposite. The crowd he needs is the dense crowd, in which body is pressed to body; a crowd, too, whose psychical constitution is also dense, or compact, so that he no longer notices who it is that presses against him. As soon as a man has surrendered himself to the crowd, he ceases to fear its touch. Ideally, all are equal there; no distinctions count, not even that of sex. The man pressed against him is the same as himself. He feels him as he feels himself. Suddenly it is as though everything were happening in one and the same body. This is perhaps one of the reasons why a crowd seeks to close in on itself: it wants to rid each individual as completely as possible of the fear of being touched. The more fiercely people press together, the more certain they feel that they do not fear each other. This reversal of the fear of being touched belongs to the nature of crowds. The feeling of relief is most striking where the density of the crowd is greatest.

The open and the closed crowd

The crowd, suddenly there where there was nothing before, is a mysterious and universal phenomenon. A few people may have been standing together—five, ten or twelve, not more; nothing has been announced, nothing is expected. Suddenly everywhere is black with people and more come streaming from all sides as though streets had only one direction. Most of them do not know what has happened and, if questioned, have no answer; but they hurry to be there where most other people are. There is a determination in their movement which is quite different from the expression of ordinary curiosity. It seems as though the movement of some of them transmits itself to the others. But that is not all; they have a goal which is there before they can find words for it. This goal is the blackest spot where most people are gathered.

This is the extreme form of the spontaneous crowd and

much more will have to be said about it later. In its innermost core it is not quite as spontaneous as it appears, but, except for these 5, 10 or 12 people with whom actually it originates, it is everywhere spontaneous. As soon as it exists at all, it wants to consist of *more* people: the urge to grow is the first and supreme attribute of the crowd. It wants to seize everyone within reach; anything shaped like a human being can join it. The natural crowd is the *open* crowd; there are no limits whatever to its growth; it does not recognize houses, doors or locks and those who shut themselves in are suspect. "Open" is to be understood here in the fullest sense of the word; it means open everywhere and in any direction. The open crowd exists so long as it grows; it disintegrates as soon as it stops growing.

For just as suddenly as it originates, the crowd disintegrates. In its spontaneous form it is a sensitive thing. The openness which enables it to grow is, at the same time, its danger. A foreboding of threatening disintegration is always alive in the crowd. It seeks, through rapid increase, to avoid this for as long as it can; it absorbs everyone, and, because it does, must ultimately fall to pieces.

In contrast to the open crowd which can grow indefinitely and which is of universal interest because it may spring up anywhere, there is the *closed* crowd.

The closed crowd renounces growth and puts the stress on permanence. The first thing to be noticed about it is that it has a boundary. It establishes itself by accepting its limitation. It creates a space for itself which it will fill. This space can be compared to a vessel into which liquid is being poured and whose capacity is known. The entrances to this space are limited in number, and only these entrances can be used; the boundary is respected whether it consists of stone, of solid wall, or of some special act of acceptance, or entrance fee. Once the space is completely filled, no one else is allowed in. Even if there is an overflow, the important thing is always the dense crowd in the closed room; those standing outside do not really belong.

The boundary prevents disorderly increase, but it also makes it more difficult for the crowd to disperse and so postpones its dissolution. In this way the crowd sacrifices its chance of growth, but gains in staying power. It is protected from outside influences which could become hostile and dangerous and it sets its hope on *repetition*. It is the expectation of reassembly which enables its members to accept each dispersal. The building is waiting for them; it exists for their sake and, so long as it is there, they will be able to meet in the same manner. The space is theirs, even during the ebb, and in its emptiness it reminds them of the flood.

THE DISCHARGE

The most important occurrence within the crowd is the *discharge*. Before this the crowd does not actually exist; it is the discharge which creates it. This is the moment when all who belong to the crowd get rid of their differences and feel equal.

These differences are mainly imposed from outside; they are distinctions of rank, status and property. Men as individuals are always conscious of these distinctions; they weigh heavily on them and keep them firmly apart from one another. A man stands by himself on a secure and well defined spot, his every gesture asserting his right to keep others at a distance. He stands there like a windmill on an enormous plain, moving expressively; and there is nothing between him and the next mill. All life, so far as he knows it, is laid out in distances—the house in which he shuts himself and his property, the positions he holds, the rank he desires—all these serve to create distances, to confirm and extend them. Any free or large gesture of approach towards another human being is inhibited. Impulse and counter impulse ooze away as in a desert. No man can get near another, nor reach his height. In every sphere of life, firmly established hierarchies prevent him touching anyone more exalted than himself, or descending, except in appearance, to anyone lower. In different societies the distances are differently balanced against each other, the stress in some lying on birth, in others on occupation or property.

I do not intend to characterize these hierarchies in detail here, but it is essential to know that they exist everywhere and everywhere gain a decisive hold on men's minds and determine their behaviour to each other. But the satisfaction of being higher in rank than others does not compensate for the loss of freedom of movement. Man petrifies and darkens in the distances he has created. He drags at the burden of them, but cannot move. He forgets that it is self-inflicted, and longs for liberation. But how, alone, can he free himself? Whatever he does, and however determined he is, he will always find himself among others who thwart his efforts. So long as they hold fast to *their* distances, he can never come any nearer to them.

Only together can men free themselves from their burdens of distance; and this, precisely, is what happens in a crowd. During the discharge distinctions are thrown off and all feel *equal*. In that density, where there is scarcely any space between, and body presses against body, each man is as near the other as he is to himself; and an immense feeling of relief ensues. It is for the sake of this blessed moment, when no one is greater or better than another, that people become a crowd.

But the moment of discharge, so desired and so happy, contains its own danger. It is based on an illusion; the people who suddenly feel equal have not really become equal; nor will they *feel* equal for ever. They return to their separate houses, they lie down on their own beds, they keep their possessions and their names. They do not cast out their relations nor run away from their families. Only true conversion leads men to give up their old associations and form new ones. Such associations, which by their very nature are only able to accept a limited number of members, have to secure their continuance by rigid rules. Such groups I call crowd crystals. Their function will be described later.

But the crowd, as such, disintegrates. It has a presentiment of this and fears it. It can only go on existing if the process of discharge is continued with new people who join it. Only the growth of the crowd prevents those who belong to it creeping back under their private burdens.

DESTRUCTIVENESS

The destructiveness of the crowd is often mentioned as its most conspicuous quality, and there is no denying the fact that it can be observed everywhere, in the most diverse countries and civilizations. It is discussed and disapproved of, but never really explained.

The crowd particularly likes destroying houses and objects: breakable objects like window panes, mirrors, pictures and crockery; and people tend to think that it is the fragility of these objects which stimulates the destructiveness of the crowd. It is true that the noise of destruction adds to its satisfaction; the banging of windows and the crashing of glass are the robust sounds of fresh life, the cries of something new-born. It is easy to evoke them and that increases their popularity. Everything shouts together; the din is the applause of objects. There seems to be a special need for this kind of noise at the beginning of events, when the crowd is still small and little or nothing has happened. The noise is a promise of the reinforcements the crowd hopes for, and a happy omen for deeds to come. But it would be wrong to suppose that the ease with which things can be broken is the decisive factor in the situation. Sculptures of solid stone have been mutilated beyond recognition; Christians have destroyed the heads and arms of Greek Gods and reformers and revolutionaries have hauled down the statues of Saints, sometimes from dangerous heights, though often the stone they wanted to destroy has been so hard that they have achieved only half their purpose.

The destruction of representational images is the destruction of a hierarchy which is no longer recognized. It is the violation of generally established and universally visible and valid distances. The solidity of the images was the expression of their permanence. They seem to have existed for ever, upright and immovable; never before had it been possible to approach them with hostile intent. Now they are hauled down and broken to pieces. In this act the discharge accomplishes itself.

THE ATTRIBUTES OF THE CROWD

Before I try to undertake a classification of crowds it may be useful to summarize briefly their main attributes. The following four traits are important.

1. *The crowd always wants to grow.* There are no natural boundaries to its growth. Where such boundaries have been artificially created—e.g. in all institutions which are used for the preservation of closed crowds—an eruption of the crowd is always possible and will, in fact, happen from time to time. There are no institutions which can be absolutely relied on to prevent the growth of the crowd once and for all.

2. *Within the crowd there is equality.* This is absolute and indisputable and never questioned by the crowd itself. It is of fundamental importance and one might even define a crowd as a state of absolute equality. A head is a head, an arm is an arm, and differences between individual heads and arms are irrelevant. It is for the sake of this equality that people become a crowd and they tend to overlook anything which might detract from it. All demands for justice and all theories of equality ultimately derive their energy from the actual experience of equality familiar to anyone who has been part of a crowd.

3. *The crowd loves density.* It can never feel too dense. Nothing must stand between its parts or divide them; everything must be the crowd itself. The feeling of density is strongest in the moment of discharge. One day it may be possible to determine this density more accurately and even to measure it.

4. *The crowd needs a direction.* It is in movement and it moves towards a goal. The direction, which is common to all its members, strengthens the feeling of equality. A goal outside the individual members and common to all of them drives underground all the private differing goals which are fatal to the crowd as such. Direction is essential for the continuing existence of the crowd. Its constant fear of disintegration means that it will accept *any* goal. A crowd exists so long as it has an unattained goal.

There is, however, another tendency hidden in the crowd, which appears to lead to new and superior kinds of formation. The nature of these is often not predictable.

Each of these four attributes will be found in any crowd to a greater or lesser degree. How a crowd is to be classified will depend on which of them predominates in it.

I have discussed open and closed crowds and explained

that these terms refer to their growth. The crowd is open so long as its growth is not impeded; it is closed when its growth is limited.

Another distinction is that between *rhythmic* and *stagnating* crowds. This refers to the next two attributes, *equality* and *density;* and to both of them simultaneously.

The *stagnating* crowd lives for its discharge. But it feels certain of this and puts it off. It desires a relatively long period of density to prepare for the moment of discharge. It, so to speak, warms itself at its density and delays as long as possible with the discharge. The process here starts not with equality, but with density; and equality then becomes the main goal of the crowd, which in the end it reaches. Every shout, every utterance in common is a valid expression of this equality.

In the *rhythmic* crowd, on the other hand (for example the crowd of the dance), density and equality coincide from the beginning. Everything here depends on movement. All the physical stimuli involved function in a predetermined manner and are passed on from one dancer to another. Density is embodied in the formal recurrence of retreat and approach; equality is manifest in the movements themselves. And thus, by the skilful enactment of density and equality, a crowd feeling is engendered. These rhythmic formations spring up very quickly and it is only physical exhaustion which brings them to an end.

The next pair of concepts—the *slow* and the *quick* crowd —refer exclusively to the nature of the goal. The conspicuous crowds which are the ones usually mentioned and which form such an essential part of the modern life—the political, sporting and warlike crowds we see daily—are all *quick* crowds. Very different from these are the religious crowds whose goal is a heaven, or crowds formed of pilgrims. Their goal is distant, the way to it long, and the true formation of the crowd is relegated to a far off country or to another world. Of these slow crowds we actually see only the tributaries, for the end they strive after is invisible and not to be attained by the unbelieving. The slow crowd gathers slowly and only sees itself as permanent in a far distance. . . .

STAGNATION

The *stagnating* crowd is closely compressed; it is impossible for it to move really freely. Its state has something passive in it; it waits. It waits for a head to be shown it, or for words, or it watches a fight. What really matters to it is *density*. The pressure which each member feels around him will also be felt as the measure of the strength of the formation of which he is now part. The more people who flow into that formation, the stronger the pressure becomes; feet have nowhere to move, arms are pinned down and only heads remain free, to see, and to hear; every impulse is passed directly from body to body. Each individual knows that there must be a number of people there, but, because they are so closely jammed together, they are felt to be one. This kind of density allows itself time; its effects are constant over a certain period; it is amorphous and not subject to a practised and familiar rhythm. For a long time nothing happens, but the desire for action accumulates and increases until it bursts forth with enhanced violence.

The *patience* of a stagnating crowd becomes less astonishing if one realizes fully the importance this feeling of density has for it. The denser it is, the more people it attracts. Its density is the measure of its size, but is also the stimulus to further growth; the densest crowd grows fastest. Stagnation before the discharge is an exhibition of this density; the longer a crowd remains stagnant, the longer it feels and manifests its density.

For the individuals who compose such a crowd the period of stagnation is a period of marvels; laid down are all the strings and weapons with which at other times they arm themselves against each other; they touch one another, but do not feel confined; a clutch is a clutch no longer; they do not fear each other. Before they set forth, in whatever direction this will be, they want to make sure that they will remain together when they do. They want to grow closer together beforehand and, to do this, they need to be undisturbed. The stagnating crowd is not quite sure of its unity and therefore keeps still for as long as possible.

But this patience has its limits. The discharge must come sometime. Without it, it would be impossible to say that there really was a crowd. The outcry which used to be heard at public executions when the head of the malefactor was held up by the executioner, and the outcry heard today at sporting occasions, are the *voice* of the crowd. But the outcry must be spontaneous. Rehearsed and regularly repeated shouts are no proof that the crowd has achieved a life of its own. They may lead to it, but they may also be only external, like the drill of a military unit. Contrasted with them, the spontaneous and never quite predictable outcry of a crowd is unmistakable, and its effect enormous. It can express emotions of any kind; *which* emotions often matters less than their strength and variety and the freedom of their sequence. It is they which give the crowd its "feeling" space.

They can also, however, be so violent and concentrated that they immediately tear the crowd apart. This is what happens at public executions; one and the same victim can be killed only once. If he happens to be someone thought inviolable, there will, up to the very last moment, be some doubt as to whether he can in fact be killed; and this doubt will accentuate the inherent stagnation of the crowd. All the sharper and more effective, then, will be the sight of the severed head. The succeeding outcry will be terrible, but it will be the last outcry of this particular crowd. We may say that, in this case, the crowd pays for the lengthened period of stagnant expectation, which it will have enjoyed intensely, with its own immediate death.

Our modern arrangements for sport are more practical. The spectators can *sit:* universal patience is made visible to itself. They are free to stamp their feet, but they stay in the same place; they are free to clap their hands. A definite time is allowed for the occasion, and in general, they can count on its not being shortened. For this time, at least, they will remain together. Within it, however, anything may happen. No-one can know whether, or when, or on which side, goals will be shot; and, apart from these longed-for occurrences, there are many other lesser events which can lead to vociferous eruptions, many occasions on which the crowd will hear its own voice.

The final disintegration and scattering of this crowd is made somewhat less painful by being determined in advance. It is known, too, that the beaten side will have an opportunity of taking its revenge; everything is not over for good. The crowd can really feel comfortable at a match; first it can jam the entrances and then it can settle down in the seats. It can shout as opportunity arises and, even when everything is over, it can hope for similar occasions in the future.

Stagnant crowds of a much more passive kind form in *theatres*. Ideally, actors play to full houses; the desired number of spectators is fixed from the start. People arrive on their own. There may be small aggregations in front of the box-office, but people find their way separately into the auditorium. They are taken to their seats. Everything is fixed: the play they are going to see, the actors who will perform, the time the curtain will rise, and the spectators themselves in their seats. Late-comers are received with slight hostility. There they all sit, like a well-drilled herd, still and infinitely patient. But everyone is very well aware of his own separate existence. He has paid for his seat and he notices who sits next to him. Till the play starts, he leisurely contemplates the rows of assembled heads. They awaken in him an agreeable but not too pressing feeling of density. The equality of the spectators really consists only in the fact that they are all exposed to the same performance. But their spontaneous reactions to it are limited. Even their applause has its prescribed times; in general people clap only when they are supposed to. The strength of the applause is the only clue to the extent to which they have become a crowd; it is the only measure of this, and is valued accordingly by the actors.

Stagnation in the theatre has become so much a rite that individuals feel only gentle external pressure, which does not stir them too deeply and scarcely ever gives them a feeling of inner unity and togetherness. But one should not underestimate the extent of their real and shared expectation, nor forget that it persists during the whole of the performance. People rarely leave a theatre before the end of the play; even when disappointed they sit it through, which means that, for that period anyway, they stay together.

17. Walter Benjamin: "On Some Motifs in Baudelaire," in *Illuminations*   [1892–1940]

The crowd—no subject was more entitled to the attention of nineteenth-century writers. It was getting ready to take shape as a public in broad strata who had acquired facility in reading. It became a customer; it wished to find itself portrayed in the contemporary novel, as the patrons did in the paintings of the Middle Ages. The most successful author of the century met this demand out of inner necessity. To him, crowd meant—almost in the ancient sense—the crowd of the clients, the public. Victor Hugo was the first to address the crowd in his titles: *Les Misérables, Les Travailleurs de la mer.* In France, Hugo was the only writer able to compete with the serial novel. As is generally known, Eugène Sue was the master of this genre, which began to be the source of revelation for the man in the street. In 1850 an overwhelming majority elected him to Parliament as representative of the city of Paris. It is no accident that the young Marx chose Sue's *Les Mystères de Paris* for an attack. He early recognized it as his task to forge the amorphous mass, which was then being wooed by an aesthetic socialism, into the iron of the proletariat. Engels' description of these masses in his early writings may be regarded as a prelude, however modest, to one of Marx's themes. In his book *The Condition of the Working Class in England,* Engels writes: "A city like London, where one can roam about for hours without reaching the beginning of an end, without seeing the slightest indication that open country is nearby, is really something very special. This colossal centralization, this agglomeration of three and a half million people on a single spot has multiplied the strength of these three and a half million inhabitants a hundred-fold. . . . But the price that has been paid is not discovered until later. Only when one has tramped the pavements of the main streets for a few days does one notice that these Londoners have had to sacrifice what is best in human nature in order to create all the wonders of civilization with which their city teems, that a hundred creative faculties that lay dormant in them remained inactive and were suppressed. . . . There is something distasteful about the very bustle of the streets, something that is abhorrent to human nature itself. Hundreds of thousands of people of all classes and ranks of society jostle past one another; are they not all human beings with the same characteristics and potentialities, equally interested in the pursuit of happiness? . . . And yet they rush past one another as if they had nothing in common or were in no way associated with one another. Their only agreement is a tacit one: that everyone should keep to the right of the pavement, so as not to impede the stream of people moving in the opposite direction. No one even bothers to spare a glance for the others. The greater the number of people that are packed into a tiny space, the more repulsive and offensive becomes the brutal indifference, the unfeeling concentration of each person on his private affairs."

This description differs markedly from those to be found in minor French masters, such as Gozlan, Delvau, or Lurine. It lacks the skill and ease with which the *flâneur* moves among the crowd and which the journalist eagerly learns from him. Engels is dismayed by the crowd; he responds with a moral reaction, and an aesthetic one as well; the speed with which people rush past one another unsettles him. The charm of his description lies in the intersecting of unshakable critical integrity with an old-fashioned attitude. The writer came from a Germany that was still provincial; he may never have faced the temptation to lose himself in a stream of people. When Hegel went to Paris for the first time not long before his death, he wrote to his wife: "When I walk through the streets, people look just as they do in Berlin; they wear the same clothes and the faces are about the same—the same aspect, but in a large crowd." To move in this crowd was natural for a Parisian. No matter how great the distance which an individual cared to keep from it, he still was colored by it and, unlike Engels, was not able to view it from without. As regards Baudelaire, the masses were anything but external to him; indeed, it is easy to trace in his works his defensive reaction to their attraction and allure.

The masses had become so much a part of Baudelaire that it is rare to find a description of them in his works. His most important subjects are hardly ever encountered in descriptive form. As Dujardin so aptly put it, he was "more concerned with implanting the image in the memory than with adorning and elaborating it." It is futile to search in *Les Fleurs du mal* or in *Spleen de Paris* for any counterpart to the portrayals of the city which Victor Hugo did with such mastery. Baudelaire describes neither the Parisians nor their city. Forgoing such descriptions enables him to invoke the ones in the form of the other. His crowd is always the crowd of a big city, his Paris is invariably overpopulated. It is this that makes him so superior to Barbier, whose descriptive method caused a rift between the masses and the city. In *Tableaux parisiens* the secret presence of a crowd is demonstrable almost everywhere. When Baudelaire takes the dawn as his theme, the deserted streets emanate something of that "silence of a throng" which Hugo senses in nocturnal Paris. As Baudelaire looks at the plates in the anatomical works for sale on the dusty banks of the Seine, the mass of the departed takes the place of the singular skeletons on these pages. In the figures of the *danse macabre,* he sees a compact mass on the move. The heroism of the wizened old women whom the cycle "Les petites vieilles" follows on their rounds, consists in their standing apart from the crowd, unable to keep its pace, no longer participating with their thoughts in the present. The mass was the agitated veil; through it Baudelaire saw Paris. The presence of the mass determines one of the most famous components of *Les Fleurs du mal*.

In the sonnet "À une passante" the crowd is nowhere named in either word or phrase. And yet the whole happening hinges on it, just as the progress of a sailboat depends on the wind.

La rue assourdissante autour de moi hurlait.
Longue, mince, en grand deuil, douleur majestueuse,
Une femme passa, d'une main fastueuse
Soulevant, balançant le feston et l'ourlet;

Agile et noble, avec sa jambe de statue.
Moi, je buvais, crispé comme un extravagant,
Dans son oeil, ciel livide où germe l'ouragan,
La douceur qui fascine et le plaisir qui tue.

Un éclair . . . puis la nuit!—Fugitive beauté
Dont le regard m'a fait soudainement renaître,
Ne te verrai-je plus que dans l'éternité?

Ailleurs, bien loin d'ici! Trop tard! *Jamais* peut-être!
Car j'ignore où tu fuis, tu ne sais où je vais,
O toi que j'eusse aimée, ô toi qui le savais!*

In a widow's veil, mysteriously and mutely borne along by the crowd, an unknown woman comes into the poet's field of vision. What this sonnet communicates is simply this: Far from experiencing the crowd as an opposed, antagonistic element, this very crowd brings to the city dweller the figure that fascinates. The delight of the urban poet is love—not at first sight, but at last sight. It is a farewell forever which coincides in the poem with the moment of enchantment. Thus the sonnet supplies the figure of shock, indeed of catastrophe. But the nature of the poet's emotions has been affected as well. What makes his body contract in a tremor—*crispe comme un extravagant,* Baudelaire says—is not the rapture of a man whose every fiber is suffused with *eros;* it is, rather, like the kind of sexual shock that can beset a lonely man. The fact that "these verses could only have been written in a big city," as Thibaudet put it, is not very meaningful. They reveal the stigmata which life in a

---

* The deafening street was screaming all around me.
  Tall, slender, in deep mourning—majestic grief—
  A woman made her way, with fastidious hand
  Raising and swaying festoon and hem;

  Agile and noble, with her statue's limbs.
  And there was I, who drank, contorted like a madman,
  Within her eyes—that livid sky where hurricane is born—
  Gentleness that fascinates, pleasure that kills.

  A lightning-flash . . . then night!—O fleeting beauty
  Whose glance all of a sudden gave me new birth,
  Shall I see you again only in eternity?

  Far, far from here! Too late! or maybe, *never?*
  For I know not where you flee, you know not where I go,
  O you I would have loved (O you who knew it too!)

metropolis inflicts upon love. Proust read the sonnet in this light, and that is why he gave his later echo of the woman in mourning, which appeared to him one day in the form of Albertine, the evocative caption "La Parisienne." "When Albertine came into my room again, she wore a black satin dress. It made her pale, and she resembled the type of the fiery and yet pale Parisian woman, the woman who is not used to fresh air and has been affected by living among masses and possibly in an atmosphere of vice, the kind that can be recognized by a certain glance which seems unsteady if there is no rouge on her cheeks." This is the look—even as late as Proust—of the object of a love which only a city dweller experiences, which Baudelaire captured for poetry, and of which one might not infrequently say that it was spared, rather than denied, fulfillment.

A story by Poe which Baudelaire translated may be regarded as the classic example among the older versions of the motif of the crowd. It is marked by certain peculiarities which, upon closer inspection, reveal aspects of social forces of such power and hidden depth that we may count them among those which alone are capable of exerting both a subtle and a profound effect upon artistic production. The story is entitled "The Man of the Crowd." Set in London, its narrator is a man who, after a long illness, ventures out again for the first time into the hustle and bustle of the city. In the late afternoon hours of an autumn day he installs himself behind a window in a big London coffeehouse. He looks over the other guests, pores over advertisements in the paper, but his main focus of interest is the throng of people surging past his window in the street. "The latter is one of the principal thoroughfares of the city, and had been very much crowded during the whole day. But, as the darkness came on, the throng momently increased; and by the time the lamps were well lighted, two dense and continuous tides of population were rushing past the door. At this particular period of the evening I had never before been in a similar situation, and the tumultuous sea of human heads filled me, therefore, with a delicious novelty of emotion. I gave up, at length, all care of things within the hotel, and became absorbed in contemplation of the scene without." Important as it is, let us disregard the narrative to which this is the prelude and examine the setting.

The appearance of the London crowd as Poe describes it is as gloomy and fitful as the light of the gas lamps overhead. This applies not only to the riffraff that is "brought forth from its den" as night falls. The employees of higher rank, "the upper clerks of staunch firms," Poe describes as follows: "They had all slightly bald heads, from which the right ears, long used to penholding, had an odd habit of standing off on end. I observed that they always removed or settled their hats with both hands, and wore watches, with short gold chains of a substantial and ancient pattern." Even more striking is his description of the crowd's movements. "By far the greater number of those who went by had a satisfied business-like demeanour, and seemed to be thinking only of making their way through the press. Their brows were knit, and their eyes rolled quickly; when pushed against by fellow-wayfarers they evinced no symptom of impatience, but adjusted their clothes and hurried on. Others, still a numerous class, were restless in their movements, had flushed faces, and talked and gesticulated to themselves, as if feeling in solitude on account of the very denseness of the company around. When impeded in their progress, these people suddenly ceased muttering, but redoubled their gesticulations, and awaited, with an absent and overdone smile upon the lips, the course of the persons impeding them. If jostled, they bowed profusely to the jostlers, and appeared overwhelmed with confusion." One might think he was speaking of half-drunken wretches. Actually, they were "noblemen, merchants, attorneys, tradesmen, stock-jobbers."

Poe's manner of presentation cannot be called realism. It shows a purposely distorting imagination at work, one that removes the text far from what is commonly advocated as the model of social realism. Barbier, perhaps one of the best examples of this type of realism that come to mind, describes things in a less eccentric way. Moreover, he chose a more transparent subject: the oppressed masses. Poe is not concerned with these; he deals with "people," pure and simple. For him, as for Engels, there was something menacing in the spectacle they presented. It is precisely this image of big-city crowds that became decisive for Baudelaire. If he succumbed to the force by which he was drawn to them and, as a *flâneur,* was made one of them, he was nevertheless unable to rid himself of a sense of their essentially inhuman make-up. He becomes their accomplice even as he dissociates himself from them. He becomes deeply involved with them, only to relegate them to oblivion with a single glance of contempt. There is something compelling about this ambivalence where he cautiously admits to it. Perhaps the charm of his "Crépuscule du soir," so difficult to account for, is bound up with this.

Baudelaire saw fit to equate the man of the crowd, whom Poe's narrator follows throughout the length and breadth of nocturnal London, with the *flâneur.* It is hard to accept this view. The man of the crowd is no *flâneur.* In him, composure has given way to manic behavior. Hence he exemplifies, rather, what had to become of the *flâneur* once he was deprived of the milieu to which he belonged. If London ever provided it for him, it was certainly not the setting described by Poe. In comparison, Baudelaire's Paris preserved some features that dated back to the happy old days. Ferries were still crossing the Seine at points that would later be spanned by the arch of a bridge. In the year of Baudelaire's death it was still possible for some entrepreneur to cater to the comfort of the well-to-do with a fleet of five hundred sedan chairs circulating about the city. Arcades where the *flâneur* would not be exposed to the sight of carriages that did not recognize pedestrians as rivals were enjoying undiminished popularity. There was the pedestrian who would let himself be jostled by the crowd, but there was also the *flâneur* who demanded elbow room and was unwilling to forgo the life of a gentleman of leisure. Let the many attend to their daily affairs; the man of leisure can indulge in the perambulations of the *flâneur* only if as such he is already out of place. He is as much out of place in an atmosphere of complete leisure as in the feverish turmoil of the city. London has its man of the crowd. His counterpart, as it were, is the boy Nante [Ferdinand], of the street corner, a popular figure in Berlin before the

March Revolution of 1848; the Parisian *flâneur* might be said to stand midway between them.

How the man of leisure looks upon the crowd is revealed in a short piece by E. T. A. Hoffman, the last that he wrote, entitled "The Cousin's Corner Window." It antedates Poe's story by fifteen years and probably is one of the earliest attempts to capture the street scene of a large city. The differences between the two pieces are worth noting. Poe's narrator observes from behind the window of a public coffeehouse, whereas the cousin is installed at home. Poe's observer succumbs to the fascination of the scene, which finally lures him outside into the whirl of the crowd. Hoffmann's cousin, looking out from his corner window, is immobilized as a paralytic; he would not be able to follow the crowd even if he were in the midst of it. His attitude toward the crowd is, rather, one of superiority, inspired as it is by his observation post at the window of an apartment building. From this vantage point he scrutinizes the throng; it is market day, and they all feel in their element. His opera glasses enable him to pick out individual genre scenes. The employment of this instrument is thoroughly in keeping with the inner disposition of its user. He would like, as he admits, to initiate his visitor into the "principles of the art of seeing." This consists of an ability to enjoy *tableaux vivants*—a favorite pursuit of the Biedermeier period. Edifying sayings provide the interpretation. One can look upon the narrative as an attempt which was then due to be made. But it is obvious that the conditions under which it was made in Berlin prevented it from being a complete success. If Hoffmann had ever set foot in Paris or London, or if he had been intent upon depicting the masses as such, he would not have focused on a market place; he would not have portrayed the scene as being dominated by women; he would perhaps have seized on the motifs that Poe derives from the swarming crowds under the gas lamps. Actually, there would have been no need for these motifs in order to bring out the uncanny elements that other students of the physiognomy of the big city have felt. A thoughtful observation by Heine is relevant here: "Heine's eyesight," wrote a correspondent in a letter to Varnhagen in 1838, "caused him acute trouble in the spring.

On the last such occasion I was walking down one of the boulevards with him. The magnificence, the life of this in its way unique thoroughfare roused me to boundless admiration, something that prompted Heine this time to make a significant point in stressing the horror with which this center of the world was tinged."

Fear, revulsion, and horror were the emotions which the big-city crowd aroused in those who first observed it. For Poe it has something barbaric; discipline just barely manages to tame it. Later, James Ensor tirelessly confronted its discipline with its wildness; he liked to put military groups in his carnival mobs, and both got along splendidly—as the prototype of totalitarian states, in which the police make common cause with the looters. Valéry, who had a fine eye for the cluster of symptoms called "civilization," has characterized one of the pertinent facts. "The inhabitant of the great urban centers," he writes, "reverts to a state of savagery—that is, of isolation. The feeling of being dependent on others, which used to be kept alive by need, is gradually blunted in the smooth functioning of the social mechanism. Any improvement of this mechanism eliminates certain modes of behavior and emotions." Comfort isolates; on the other hand, it brings those enjoying it closer to mechanization. The invention of the match around the middle of the nineteenth century brought forth a number of innovations which have one thing in common: one abrupt movement of the hand triggers a process of many steps. This development is taking place in many areas. One case in point is the telephone, where the lifting of a receiver has taken the place of the steady movement that used to be required to crank the older models. Of the countless movements of switching, inserting, pressing, and the like, the "snapping" of the photographer has had the greatest consequences. A touch of the finger now sufficed to fix an event for an unlimited period of time. The camera gave the moment a posthumous shock, as it were. Haptic experiences of this kind were joined by optic ones, such as are supplied by the advertising pages of a newspaper or the traffic of a big city. Moving through this traffic involves the individual in a series of shocks and collisions. At dangerous intersections, nervous impulses flow through him in rapid succession, like the energy from a battery. Baudelaire speaks of a man who plunges into the crowd as into a reservoir of electric energy. Circumscribing the experience of the shock, he calls this man "a *kaleidoscope* equipped with consciousness." Whereas Poe's passers-by cast glances in all directions which still appeared to be aimless, today's pedestrians are obliged to do so in order to keep abreast of traffic signals. Thus technology has subjected the human sensorium to a complex kind of training. There came a day when a new and urgent need for stimuli was met by the film. In a film, perception in the form of shocks was established as a formal principle. That which determines the rhythm of production on a conveyor belt is the basis of the rhythm of reception in the film.

Marx had good reason to stress the great fluidity of the connection between segments in manual labor. This connection appears to the factory worker on an assembly line in an independent, objectified form. Independently of the worker's volition, the article being worked on comes within his range of action and moves away from him just as arbitrarily. "It is a common characteristic of all capitalist production . . . ," wrote Marx, "that the worker does not make use of the working conditions. The working conditions make use of the worker; but it takes machinery to give this reversal a technically concrete form." In working with machines, workers learn to co-ordinate "their own movements with the uniformly constant movements of an automaton." These words shed a peculiar light on the absurd kind of uniformity with which Poe wants to saddle the crowd—uniformities of attire and behavior, but also a uniformity of facial expression. Those smiles provide food for thought. They are probably the familiar kind, as expressed in the phrase "keep smiling"; in that context they function as a mimetic shock absorber. "All machine work," it is said in the above context, "requires early drilling of the worker." This drill must be differentiated from practice. Practice, which was the sole determinant in craftsmanship, still had a function in manufacturing. With it as the basis, "each particular area of production finds its appropriate technical form in *experience* and *slowly* perfects it." To be sure, it quickly crystallizes it, "as soon as a certain degree of maturity has been attained." On the other hand, this same manufacturing produces "in every handicraft it seizes a class of so-called unskilled laborers which the handicraft system strictly excluded. In developing the greatly simplified specialty to the point of virtuosity at the cost of the work capacity as a whole, it starts turning the lack of any development into a specialty. In addition to ranks we get the simple division of workers into the skilled and the unskilled." The unskilled worker is the one most deeply degraded by the drill of the machines. His work has been sealed off from experience; practice counts for nothing there. What the Fun Fair achieves with its Dodgem cars and other similar amusements is nothing but a taste of the drill to which the unskilled laborer is subjected in the factory—a sample which at times was for him the entire menu; for the art of being off center, in which the little man could acquire training in places like the Fun Fair, flourished concomitantly with unemployment. Poe's text makes us understand the true connection between wildness and discipline. His pedestrians act as if they had adapted themselves to the machines and could express themselves only automatically. Their behavior is a reaction to shocks. "If jostled, they bowed profusely to the jostlers."

18. Alfred Schutz: "The Stranger," in *Collected Papers*   [1899–1959]

The present paper intends to study in terms of a general theory of interpretation the typical situation in which a stranger finds himself in his attempt to interpret the cultural pattern of a social group which he approaches and to orient himself within it. For our present purposes the term "stranger" shall mean an adult individual of our times and civilization who tries to be permanently accepted or at least tolerated by the group which he approaches. The outstanding example for the social situation under scrutiny is that of the immigrant, and the following analyses are, as a matter of convenience, worked out with this instance in view. . . .

As a convenient starting point we shall investigate how the cultural pattern of group life presents itself to the common sense of a man who lives his everyday life within the group among his fellow-men. . . . The knowledge of the man who acts and thinks within the world of his daily life is not homogeneous; it is (1) incoherent, (2) only partially clear, and (3) not at all free from contradictions.

1. It is incoherent because the individual's interests which determine the relevance of the objects selected for further inquiry are themselves not integrated into a coherent system. They are only partially organized under plans of any kind, such as plans of life, plans of work and leisure, plans for every social role assumed. But the hierarchy of these plans changes with the situation and with the growth of the personality; interests are shifted continually and entail an uninterrupted transformation of the shape and density of the relevance lines. Not only the selection of the objects of curiosity but also the degree of knowledge aimed at changes.

2. Man in his daily life is only partially—and we dare say exceptionally—interested in the clarity of his knowledge, i.e., in full insight into the relations between the elements of his world and the general principles ruling those relations. He is satisfied that a well-functioning telephone service is available to him and, normally, does not ask how the apparatus functions in detail and what laws of physics make this functioning possible. He buys merchandise in the store, not knowing how it is produced, and pays with money, although he has only a vague idea of what money really is. He takes it for granted that his fellow-man will understand his thought if expressed in plain language and will answer accordingly, without wondering how this miraculous performance may be explained. Furthermore, he does not search for the truth and does not quest for certainty. All he wants is information on likelihood and insight into the chances

or risks which the situation at hand entails for the outcome of his actions. That the subway will run tomorrow as usual is for him almost of the same order of likelihood as that the sun will rise. If by reason of a special interest he needs more explicit knowledge on a topic, a benign modern civilization holds ready for him a chain of information desks and reference libraries.

3. His knowledge, finally, is not consistent. At the same time he may consider statements as equally valid which in fact are incompatible with one another. As a father, a citizen, an employee, and a member of his church he may have the most different and the least congruent opinions on moral, political, or economic matters. This inconsistency does not necessarily originate in a logical fallacy. Men's thinking is distributed over subject matters located within different and differently relevant levels, and they are not aware of the modifications they would have to make in passing from one level to another. . . .

The system of knowledge thus acquired—incoherent, inconsistent, and only partially clear, as it is—takes on for the members of the in-group the appearance of a *sufficient* coherence, clarity, and consistency to give anybody a reasonable chance of understanding and of being understood. Any member born or reared within the group accepts the ready-made standardized scheme of the cultural pattern handed down to him by ancestors, teachers, and authorities as an unquestioned and unquestionable guide in all the situations which normally occur within the social world. The knowledge correlated to the cultural pattern carries its evidence in itself—or, rather, it is taken for granted in the absence of evidence to the contrary. It is a knowledge of trustworthy *recipes* for interpreting the social world and for handling things and men in order to obtain the best results in every situation with a minimum of effort by avoiding undesirable consequences. The recipe works, on the one hand, as a precept for actions and thus serves as a scheme of expression: whoever wants to obtain a certain result has to proceed as indicated by the recipe provided for this purpose. On the other hand, the recipe serves as a scheme of interpretation: whoever proceeds as indicated by a specific recipe is supposed to intend the correlated result. Thus it is the function of the cultural pattern to eliminate troublesome inquiries by offering ready-made directions for use, to replace truth hard to attain by comfortable truisms, and to substitute the self-explanatory for the questionable.

This "thinking as usual," as we may call it, . . . may be maintained as long as some basic assumptions hold true, namely: (1) that life and especially social life will continue to be the same as it has been so far; that is to say, that the same problems requiring the same solutions will recur and that, therefore, our former experiences will suffice for mastering future situations; (2) that we may rely on the knowledge handed down to us by parents, teachers, governments, traditions, habits, etc., even if we do not understand its origin and its real meaning; (3) that in the ordinary course of affairs it is sufficient to know something *about* the general type or style of events we may encounter in our life-world in order to manage or control them; and (4) that neither the systems of recipes as schemes of interpretation and expression nor the underlying basic assumptions just mentioned are our private affair, but that they are likewise accepted and applied by our fellow-men.

If only one of these assumptions ceases to stand the test, thinking-as-usual becomes unworkable. Then a "crisis" arises which, according to W. I. Thomas' famous definition, "interrupts the flow of habit and gives rise to changed conditions of consciousness and practice"; or, as we may say, it overthrows precipitously the actual system of relevances. The cultural pattern no longer functions as a system of tested recipes at hand; it reveals that its applicability is restricted to a specific historical situation.

Yet the stranger, by reason of his personal crisis, does not share the above-mentioned basic assumptions. He becomes essentially the man who has to place in question nearly everything that seems to be unquestionable to the members of the approached group.

To him the cultural pattern of the approached group does not have the authority of a tested system of recipes, and this, if for no other reason, because he does not partake in the vivid historical tradition by which it has been formed. To be sure, from the stranger's point of view, too, the culture of the approached group has its peculiar history, and this history is even accessible to him. But it has never become an integral part of his biography, as did the history of his home group. Only the ways in which his fathers and grandfathers lived become for everyone elements of his own way of life. Graves and reminiscences can neither be transferred nor conquered. The stranger, therefore, approaches the other group as a newcomer in the true meaning of the term. At best he may be willing and able to share the present and the future with the approached group in vivid and immediate experience; under all circumstances, however, he remains excluded from such experiences of its past. Seen from the point of view of the approached group, he is a man without a history. . . .

The discovery that things in his new surroundings look quite different from what he expected them to be at home is frequently the first shock to the stranger's confidence in the validity of his habitual "thinking as usual." Not only the picture which the stranger has brought along of the cultural pattern of the approached group but the whole hitherto unquestioned scheme of interpretation current within the home group becomes invalidated. It cannot be used as a scheme of orientation within the new social surroundings. For the members of the approached group *their* cultural pattern fulfills the functions of such a scheme. But the approaching stranger can neither use it simply as it is nor establish a general formula of transformation between both cultural patterns permitting him, so to speak, to convert all the co-ordinates within one scheme of orientation into those valid within the other—and this for the following reasons.

First, any scheme of orientation presupposes that everyone who uses it looks at the surrounding world as grouped around himself who stands at its center. He who wants to use a map successfully has first of all to know his standpoint in two respects: its location on the ground and its representation on the map. Applied to the social world this means that only members of the in-group, having a definite status in its hierarchy and also being aware of it, can use its cultural pattern as a natural and trustworthy scheme of orientation. The stranger, however, has to face the fact that he lacks any status as a member of the social group he is about to join and is therefore unable to get a starting-point to take his bearings. He finds himself a border case outside the territory covered by the scheme of orientation current within the group. He is, therefore, no longer permitted to consider himself as the center of his social environment, and this fact causes again a dislocation of his contour lines of relevance.

Second, the cultural pattern and its recipes represent only for the members of the in-group a unit of coinciding schemes of interpretation as well as of expression. For the outsider, however, this seeming unity falls to pieces. The approaching stranger has to "translate" its terms into terms of the cultural pattern of his home group, provided that, within the latter, interpretive equivalents exist at all. If they exist, the translated terms may be understood and remembered; they can be recognized by recurrence; they are at hand but not in hand. Yet, even then, it is obvious that the stranger cannot assume that his interpretation of the new cultural pattern coincides with that current with the members of the in-group. On the contrary, he has to reckon with fundamental discrepancies in seeing things and handling situations.

Only after having thus collected a certain knowledge of the interpretive function of the new cultural pattern may the stranger start to adopt it as the scheme of his own expression. The difference between the two stages of knowledge is familiar to any student of a foreign language and has received the full attention of psychologists dealing with the theory of learning. It is the difference between the passive understanding of a language and its active mastering as a means for realizing one's own acts and thoughts. . . .

For those who have grown up within the cultural pattern, not only the recipes and their possible efficiency but also the typical and anonymous attitudes required by them are an unquestioned "matter of course" which gives them both security and assurance. In other words, these attitudes by their very anonymity and typicality are placed not within the actor's stratum of relevance which requires explicit knowledge *of* but in the region of mere acquaintance in which it will do to put one's trust. This interrelation between objective chance, typicality, anonymity, and relevance seems to be rather important. . . .

For the approaching stranger, however, the pattern of the approached group does not guarantee an objective chance for success but rather a pure subjective likelihood which has to be checked step by step, that is, he has to make sure that the solutions suggested by the new scheme will also produce the desired effect for him in his special position as outsider and newcomer who has not brought within his grasp the whole system of the cultural pattern but who is rather puzzled by its inconsistency, incoherence, and lack of clarity. He has, first of all, to use the term of W. I. Thomas, to *define* the situation. Therefore, he cannot stop at an approximate acquaintance with the new pattern, trusting in his vague knowledge *about* its general style and structure but needs an explicit knowledge *of* its elements, inquiring not only into their *that* but into their *why*. Consequently, the shape of his contour lines of relevance by necessity differs radically from those of a member of the in-group as to situations, recipes, means, ends, social partners, etc. Keeping in mind the above-mentioned interrelationship between relevance, on the one hand, and typicality and anonymity, on the other, it follows that he uses another yardstick for anonymity and typicality of social acts than the members of the in-group. For to the stranger the observed actors within the approached group are not—as for their co-actors—of a certain presupposed anonymity, namely, mere performers of typical functions, but individuals. On the other hand, he is inclined to take mere individual traits as typical ones. Thus he constructs a social world of pseudo-anonymity, pseudo-intimacy, and pseudo typicality. Therefore, he cannot integrate the personal types constructed by him into a coherent picture of the approached group and cannot rely on his expectation of their response. And even less can the stranger himself adopt those typical and anonymous attitudes which a member of the in-group is entitled to expect from a partner in a typical situation. Hence the stranger's lack of feeling for distance, his oscillating between remoteness and intimacy, his hesitation and uncertainty, and his distrust in every matter which seems to be so simple and uncomplicated to those who rely on the efficiency of unquestioned recipes which have just to be followed but not understood. . . .

These facts explain two basic traits of the stranger's attitude toward the group to which nearly all sociological writers dealing with this topic have rendered special attention, namely, (1) the stranger's objectivity and (2) his doubtful loyalty.

1. The stranger's objectivity cannot be sufficiently explained by his critical attitude. To be sure, he is not bound to worship the "idols of the tribe" and has a vivid feeling for the incoherence and inconsistency of the approached cultural pattern. But this attitude originates far less in his propensity to judge the newly approached group by the standards brought from home than in his need to acquire full knowledge *of* the elements of the approached cultural pattern and to examine for this purpose with care and precision what seems self-explanatory to the in-group. The deeper reason for his objectivity, however, lies in his own bitter experience of the limits of the "thinking as usual," which has taught him that a man may loose his status, his rules of guidance, and even his history and that the normal way of life is always far less guaranteed than it seems. Therefore, the stranger discerns, frequently with a grievous clear-sightedness, the rising of a crisis which may menace the whole foundation of the "relatively natural conception of the world," while all those symptoms pass unnoticed by the members of the in-group, who rely on the continuance of their customary way of life.

2. The doubtful loyalty of the stranger is unfortunately very frequently more than a prejudice on the part of the approached group. This is especially true in cases in which the stranger proves unwilling or unable to substitute the new cultural pattern entirely for that of the home group. Then the stranger remains what Park and Stonequist have aptly called a "marginal man," a cultural hybrid on the verge of two different patterns of group life, not knowing to which of them he belongs. But very frequently the reproach of doubtful loyalty originates

in the astonishment of the members of the in-group that the stranger does not accept the total of its cultural pattern as the natural and appropriate way of life and as the best of all possible solutions of any problem. The stranger is called ungrateful, since he refuses to acknowledge that the cultural pattern offered to him grants him shelter and protection. But these people do not understand that the stranger in the state of transition does not consider this pattern as a protecting shelter at all but as a labyrinth in which he has lost all sense of his bearings. . . .

Strangeness and familiarity are not limited to the social field but are general categories of our interpretation of the world. If we encounter in our experience something previously unknown and which therefore stands out of the ordinary order of our knowledge, we begin a process of inquiry. We first define the new fact; we try to catch its meaning; we then transform step by step our general scheme of interpretation of the world in such a way that the strange fact and its meaning become compatible and consistent with all the other facts of our experience and their meanings. If we succeed in this endeavor, then that which formerly was a strange fact and a puzzling problem to our mind is transformed into an additional element of our warranted knowledge. We have enlarged and adjusted our stock of experiences.

What is commonly called the process of social adjustment which the newcomer has to undergo is but a special case of this general principle. The adaptation of the newcomer to the in-group which at first seemed to be strange and unfamiliar to him is a continuous process of inquiry into the cultural pattern of the approached group. If this process of inquiry succeeds, then this pattern and its elements will become to the newcomer a matter of course, an unquestionable way of life, a shelter, and a protection. But then the stranger is no stranger any more, and his specific problems have been solved.

19. Georg Simmel: "The Stranger," in *The Sociology of Georg Simmel* [1858–1918]

If wandering is the liberation from every given point in space, and thus the conceptional opposite to fixation at such a point, the sociological form of the "stranger" presents the unity, as it were, of these two characteristics. This phenomenon too, however, reveals that spatial relations are only the condition, on the one hand, and the symbol, on the other, of human relations. The stranger is thus being discussed here, not in the sense often touched upon in the past, as the wanderer who comes today and goes tomorrow, but rather as the person who comes today and stays tomorrow. He is, so to speak, the *potential* wanderer: although he has not moved on, he has not quite overcome the freedom of coming and going. He is fixed within a particular spatial group, or within a group whose boundaries are similar to spatial boundaries. But his position in this group is determined, essentially, by the fact that he has not belonged to it from the beginning, that he imports qualities into it, which do not and cannot stem from the group itself.

The unity of nearness and remoteness involved in every human relation is organized, in the phenomenon of the stranger, in a way which may be most briefly formulated by saying that in the relationship to him, distance means that he, who is close by, is far, and strangeness means that he, who also is far, is actually near. For, to be a stranger is naturally a very positive relation; it is a specific form of interaction. The inhabitants of Sirius are not really strangers to us, at least not in any sociologically relevant sense: they do not exist for us at all; they are beyond far and near. The stranger, like the poor and like sundry "inner enemies," is an element of the group itself. His position as a full-fledged member involves both being outside it and confronting it. The following statements, which are by no means intended as exhaustive, indicate how elements which increase distance and repel, in the relations of and with the stranger produce a pattern of coordination and consistent interaction.

Throughout the history of economics the stranger everywhere appears as the trader, or the trader as stranger. As long as economy is essentially self-sufficient, or products are exchanged within a spatially narrow group, it needs no middleman: a trader is only required for products that originate outside the group. Insofar as members do not leave the circle in order to buy these necessities—in which case *they* are the "strange" merchants in that outside territory—the trader *must* be a stranger, since nobody else has a chance to make a living.

This position of the stranger stands out more sharply if he settles down in the place of his activity, instead of leaving it again: in innumerable cases even this is possible only if he can live by intermediate trade. Once an economy is somehow closed, the land is divided up, and handicrafts are established that satisfy the demand for them, the trader, too, can find his existence. For in trade, which alone makes possible unlimited combinations, intelligence always finds expansions and new territories, an achievement which is very difficult to attain for the original producer with his lesser mobility and his dependence upon a circle of customers that can be increased only slowly. Trade can always absorb more people than primary production; it is, therefore, the sphere indicated for the stranger, who intrudes as a supernumerary, so to speak, into a group in which the economic positions are actually occupied—the classical example is the history of European Jews. The stranger is by nature no "owner of soil"—soil not only in the physical, but also in the figurative sense of a life-substance which is fixed, if not in a point in space, at least in an ideal point of the social environment. Although in more intimate relations, he may develop all kinds of charm and significance, as long as he is considered a stranger in the eyes of the other, he is not an "owner of soil." Restriction to intermediary trade, and often (as though sublimated from it) to pure finance, gives him the specific character of *mobility*. If mobility takes place within a closed group, it embodies that synthesis of nearness and distance which constitutes the formal position of the stranger. For, the fundamentally mobile person comes in contact, at one time or another, with every individual, but is not organically connected, through established ties of kinship, locality, and occupation, with any single one.

Another expression of this constellation lies in the objectivity of the stranger. He is not radically committed to the unique ingredients and peculiar tendencies of the group, and therefore approaches them with the specific attitude of "objectivity." But objectivity does not simply involve passivity and detachment; it is a particular structure composed of distance and nearness, indifference and involvement. I refer to the discussion (in the chapter on "Superordination and Subordination") of the dominating positions of the person who is a stranger in the group; its most typical instance was the practice of those Italian cities to call their judges from the outside, because no native was free from entanglement in family and party interests.

With the objectivity of the stranger is connected, also, the phenomenon touched upon above, although it is chiefly (but not exclusively) true of the stranger who moves on. This is the fact that he often receives the most surprising openness—confidences which sometimes have the character of a confessional and which would be carefully withheld from a more closely related person. Objectivity is by no means non-participation (which is altogether outside both subjective and objective interaction), but a positive and specific kind of participation—just as the objectivity of a theoretical observation does not refer to the mind as a passive *tabula rasa* on which things inscribe their qualities, but on the contrary, to its full activity that operates according to its own laws, and to the elimination, thereby, of accidental dislocations and emphases, whose individual and subjective differences would produce different pictures of the same object.

Objectivity may also be defined as freedom: the objective individual is bound by no commitments which could prejudice his perception, understanding, and evaluation of the given. The freedom, however, which allows the stranger to experience and treat even his close relationships as though from a bird's-eye view, contains many dangerous possibilities. In uprisings of all sorts, the party attacked has claimed, from the beginning of things, that provocation has come from the outside, through emissaries and instigators. Insofar as this is true, it is an exaggeration of the specific role of the stranger: he is freer, practically and theoretically; he surveys conditions with less prejudice; his criteria for them are more general and more objective ideals; he is not tied down in his action by habit, piety, and precedent.

Finally, the proportion of nearness and remoteness which gives the stranger the character of objectivity, also finds practical expression in the more *abstract nature* of the relation to him. That is, with the stranger one has only certain *more general* qualities in common, whereas the relation to more organically connected persons is based on the commonness of specific differences from merely general features. In fact, all somehow personal relations follow this scheme in various patterns. They are determined not only by the circumstance that certain common features exist among the individuals, along with individual differences, which either influence the relationship or remain outside of it. For, the common features themselves are basically determined in their effect upon the relation by the question whether they exist only between the participants in this particular relationship, and thus are quite general in regard to this relation, but are specific and incomparable in regard to everything outside of it—or whether the participants feel that these features are common to them because they are common to a group, a type, or mankind in general. In the case of the second alternative, the effectiveness of the common features becomes diluted in proportion to the size of the group composed of members who are similar in this sense. Although the commonness functions as their unifying basis, it does not make *these* particular persons interdependent on one another, because it could as easily connect everyone of them with all kinds of individuals other than the members of his group. This too, evidently, is a way in which a relationship includes both nearness and distance at the same time: to the extent to which the common features are general, they add, to the warmth of the relation founded on them, an element of coolness, a feeling of the contingency of precisely *this* relation—the connecting forces have lost their specific and centripetal character.

In the relation to the stranger, it seems to me, this constellation has an extraordinary and basic preponderance over the individual elements that are exclusive with the particular relationship. The stranger is close to us, insofar as we feel between him and ourselves common features of a national, social, occupational, or generally human, nature. He is far from us, insofar as these common features extend beyond him or us, and connect us only because they connect a great many people.

A trace of strangeness in this sense easily enters even the most intimate relationships. In the stage of first passion, erotic relations strongly reject any thought of generalization: the lovers think that there has never been a love like theirs; that nothing can be compared either to the person loved or to the feelings for that person. An estrangement—whether as cause or as consequence it is difficult to decide—usually comes at the moment when this feeling of uniqueness vanishes from the relationship. A certain skepticism in regard to its value, in itself and for them, attaches to the very thought that in their relation, after all, they carry out only a generally human destiny; that they experience an experience that has occurred a thousand times before; that, had they not accidentally met their particular partner, they would have found the same significance in another person.

Something of this feeling is probably not absent in any relation, however close, because what is common to two is never common to them alone, but is subsumed under a general idea which includes much else besides, many *possibilities* of commonness. No matter how little these possibilities become real and how often we forget them, here and there, nevertheless, they thrust themselves between us like shadows, like a mist which escapes every word noted, but which must coagulate into a solid bodily form before it can be called jealousy. In some cases, perhaps the more general, at least the more unsurmountable, strangeness is not due to different and ununderstandable matters. It is rather caused by the fact that similarity, harmony, and nearness are accompanied by the feeling that they are not really the unique property of this particular relationship: they are something more general, something which potentially prevails between the partners and an indeterminate number of others, and therefore gives the relation, which alone was realized, no inner and exclusive necessity.

On the other hand, there is a kind of "strangeness" that rejects the very commonness based on something more general which embraces the parties. The relation of the Greeks to the Barbarians is perhaps typical here, as are all cases in which it is precisely general attributes, felt to be specifically and purely human, that are disallowed to the other. But "stranger," here, has no positive meaning; the relation to him is a non-relation; he is not what is relevant here, a member of the group itself.

As a group member, rather, he is near and far *at the same time,* as is characteristic of relations founded only on generally human commonness. But between nearness and distance, there arises a specific tension when the consciousness that only the quite general is common, stresses that which is not common. In the case of the person who is a stranger to the country, the city, the race, etc., however, this non-common element is once more nothing individual, but merely the strangeness of origin, which is or could be common to many strangers. For this reason, strangers are not really conceived as individuals, but as strangers of a particular type: the element of distance is no less general in regard to them than the element of nearness.

This form is the basis of such a special case, for instance, as the tax levied in Frankfort and elsewhere upon medieval Jews. Whereas the *Beede* [tax] paid by the Christian citizen changed with the changes of his fortune, it was fixed once for all for every single Jew. This fixity rested on the fact that the Jew had his social position as a *Jew,* not as the individual bearer of certain objective contents. Every other citizen was the owner of a particular amount of property, and his tax followed its fluctuations. But the Jew as a taxpayer was, in the first place, a

Jew, and thus his tax situation had an invariable element. This same position appears most strongly, of course, once even these individual characterizations (limited though they were by rigid invariance) are omitted, and all strangers pay an altogether equal head-tax.

In spite of being inorganically appended to it, the stranger is yet an organic member of the group. Its uniform life includes the specific conditions of this element. Only we do not know how to designate the peculiar unity of this position other than by saying that it is composed of certain measures of nearness and distance. Although some quantities of them characterize all relationships, a *special* proportion and reciprocal tension produce the particular, formal relation to the "stranger."

PART THREE

DEVELOPMENTAL CONCEPTS: THE FAMILY, THE LIFE CYCLE

I.
An Historian's Argument

The last section ended with a problem. Images like "the stranger" may presume a fixed environment which creates a fixed emotional situation. Another mode of inquiry has tried to work with categories of social-psychological experience in a more historical and developmental way. We shall focus on two schools which have dealt with social-psychological change. One derives from Freud, and is concerned with studying psychological changes over the course of a person's lifetime in relation to his shifting experiences in society. The other school derives from Marx, and is concerned with the changing character of social institutions, specifically the family, and how its history has shaped the psychological processes within the family. The Freudian-derived school addresses itself to a theory of the "life cycle," while the Marxian-derived school addresses itself to a theory of the gradual "privatization" of the family.

The clearest way to approach the work of these two schools is to understand their relationship to each other. The modern French historian Philippe Ariès has tried to show that the subject matter of the life-cycle psychologists and the Marxian analysts of the family is bound together, for, Ariès argues, as the family became an increasingly private and socially withdrawn institution in modern times, people began to perceive the stages of life, and especially childhood and adolescence, in new terms, Childhood became more drawn out and elaborate than in the medieval era, when the child from the age of five or six was considered an incipient adult. The psychological notions people had about the stages of childhood became ideas of metamorphosis from one kind of creaturehood (childhood) to another (adolescence) to another (adulthood). Ariès believes that the more the family became a nonproductive, purely psychological union, unlike the households of the Middle Ages, which were units of work and kinship combined, the more this private union produced a kind of internal division of labor. Life became psychologically segmented into stages as it became socially more privatized.

While Ariès' argument is congenial to the Marxist school, it sits uneasily with many social psychologists who believe the life cycle is biologically based; the latter are prone to think the stages of life are perceived in different terms, in different kinds of historical situations, rather than determined by history itself. Whatever the final verdict may be on the truth of Ariès' argument, its intellectual value is great, for here is a socially and psychologically unified picture of what the term "development" means.

20. Philippe Ariès: *Centuries of Childhood* [1914–]

The historian who studies iconographic documents in the hope of discovering the tremor of life which he can feel in his own existence, is surprised at the scarcity, at least until the sixteenth century, of interior and family scenes. He has to hunt for them with a magnifying-glass and interpret them with the aid of hypotheses. On the other hand he promptly makes the acquaintance of the principal character in this iconography, a character as essential as the chorus in the classical theatre: the crowd—

not the massive, anonymous crowd of our overpopulated cities, but the assembly of neighbours, women and children, numerous but not unknown to one another (a familiar throng rather similar to that which can be seen today in the *souks* of Arab towns or the *cours* of Mediterranean towns in the evening). It is as if everyone had come out instead of staying at home: there are scenes depicting streets and markets, games and crafts, soldiers and courtiers, churches and tortures. In the street, in the fields, outside, in public, in the midst of a collective society —that is where the artist chooses to set the events or people he wishes to depict.

The idea of isolating individual or family portraits gradually emerged. But the importance which we have given to these early attempts should not blind us to the fact that they were rare and timid to begin with. For a long time—until the seventeenth century, when the iconography of the family became extremely rich—the important thing was the representation of public life. This representation doubtless corresponds to a profound reality. Life in the past, until the seventeenth century, was lived in public. We have given a good many examples of the ascendancy of society. The traditional ceremonies which accompanied marriage and which were regarded as more important than the religious ceremonies (which for a long time were entirely lacking in solemnity), the blessing of the marriage bed; the visit paid by the guests to the newly-married pair when they were already in bed; the rowdyism during the wedding night, and so on—afford further proof of society's rights over the privacy of the couple. What objection could there be when in fact privacy scarcely ever existed, when people lived on top of one another, masters and servants, children and adults, in houses open at all hours to the indiscretions of callers? The density of society left no room for the family. Not that the family did not exist as a reality: it would be paradoxical to deny that it did. But it did not exist as a concept.

We have studied the birth and development of this concept of the family from the fifteenth century to the eighteenth. We have seen how, until the eighteenth century, it failed to destroy the old sociability; admittedly it was limited to the well-to-do-classes, those of the notabilities, rural or urban, aristocratic or middle-class, artisans or merchants. Starting in the eighteenth century, it spread to all classes and imposed itself tyrannically on people's consciousness. The evolution of the last few centuries has often been presented as the triumph of individualism over social constraints, with the family counted among the latter. But where is the individualism in these modern lives, in which all the energy of the couple is directed to serving the interests of a deliberately restricted posterity? Was there not greater individualism in the gay indifference of the prolific fathers of the ancien regime? Admittedly the modern family no longer has the same material reality as under the ancien regime, when it was identified with an estate and a reputation. Except in cases whose importance is constantly diminishing, the problem of the transmission of property takes second place to that of the children's welfare, and that welfare is no longer necessarily seen in loyalty to a professional tradition. The family has become an exclusive society in which its members are happy to stay and which they enjoy evoking, as General de Martange did in his letters as early as the end of the eighteenth century. The whole evolution of our contemporary manners is unintelligible if one neglects this astonishing growth of the concept of the family. It is not individualism which has triumphed, but the family.

But this family has advanced in proportion as sociability has retreated. It is as if the modern family had sought to take the place of the old social relationships (as these gradually defaulted), in order to preserve mankind from an unbearable moral solitude. Starting in the eighteenth century, people began defending themselves against a society whose constant intercourse had hitherto been the source of education, reputation and wealth. Henceforth a fundamental movement would destroy the old connections between masters and servants, great and small, friends or clients. It was a movement which was sometimes retarded by the inertia of geographical or social isolation. It would be quicker in Paris than in other towns, quicker in the middle classes than in the lower classes. Everywhere it reinforced private life at the expense of neighbourly relationships, friendships, and traditional contacts. The history of modern manners can be reduced in part to this long effort to break away from others, to escape from a society whose pressure had become unbearable. The house lost the public character which it had in certain cases in the seventeenth century, in favour of the club and the café, which in their turn have become less crowded. Professional and family life have stifled that other activity which once invaded the whole of life: the activity of social relations.

* One is tempted to conclude that sociability and the concept of the family were incompatible, and could develop only at each other's expense.

In the Middle Ages, at the beginning of modern times, and for a long time after that in the lower classes, children were mixed with adults as soon as they were considered capable of doing without their mothers or nannies, not long after a tardy weaning (in other words, at about the age of seven). They immediately went straight into the great community of men, sharing in the work and play of their companions, old and young alike. The movement of collective life carried along in a single torrent all ages and classes, leaving nobody any time for solitude and privacy. In these crowded, collective existences there was no room for a private sector. The family fulfilled a function; it ensured the transmission of life, property and names; but it did not penetrate very far into human sensibility. Myths such as courtly and precious love denigrated marriage, while realities such as the apprenticeship of children loosened the emotional bond between parents and children. Medieval civilization had forgotten the *paideia* of the ancients and knew nothing as yet of modern education. That is the main point: it had no idea of education. Nowadays our society depends, and knows that it depends, on the success of its educational system. It has a system of education, a concept of education, an awareness of its importance. New sciences such as psycho-analysis, pediatrics and psychology devote themselves to the problems of childhood, and their findings are transmitted to parents by way of a mass of popular literature. Our world is obsessed by the physical, moral and sexual problems of childhood.

This preoccupation was unknown to medieval civilization, because there was no problem for the Middle Ages: as soon as he had been weaned, or soon after, the child became the natural companion of the adult. The age groups of Neolithic times, the Hellenistic *paideia,* presupposed a difference and a transition between the world of children and that of adults, a transition made by means of an initiation or an education. Medieval civilization failed to perceive this difference and therefore lacked this concept of transition.

The great event was therefore the revival, at the beginning of modern times, of an interest in education. This affected a certain number of churchmen, lawyers and scholars, few in number in the fifteenth century, but increasingly numerous and influential in the sixteenth and seventeeth centuries when they merged with the advocates of religious reform. For they were primarily moralists rather than humanists: the humanists remained attached to the idea of a general culture spread over the whole of life and showed scant interest in an education confined to children. These reformers, these moralists, whose influence on school and family we have observed in this study, fought passionately against the anarchy (or what henceforth struck them as the anarchy) of medieval society, where the Church, despite its repugnance, had long ago resigned itself to it and urged the faithful to seek salvation far from this pagan world, in some monastic retreat. A positive moralization of society was taking place: the moral aspect of religion was gradually triumphing in practice over the sacred or eschatological aspect. This was how these champions of a moral order were led to recognize the importance of education. We have noted their influence on the history of the school, and the transformation of the free school into the strictly disciplined college. Their writings extended from Gerson to Port-Royal, becoming increasingly frequent in the sixteenth and seventeenth centuries. The religious orders founded at that time, such as the Jesuits or the Oratorians, became teaching orders, and their teaching was no longer addressed to adults like that of the preachers or mendicants of the Middle Ages, but was essentially meant for children and young people. This literature, this propaganda, taught par-

ents that they were spiritual guardians, that they were responsible before God for the souls, and indeed the bodies too, of
their children.

Henceforth it was recognized that the child was not ready
for life, and that he had to be subjected to a special treatment, a
sort of quarantine, before he was allowed to join the adults.

This new concern about education would gradually install
itself in the heart of society and transform it from top to
bottom. The family ceased to be simply an institution for the
transmission of a name and an estate—it assumed a moral and
spiritual function, it moulded bodies and souls. The care expended on children inspired new feelings, a new emotional
attitude, to which the iconography of the seventeenth century
gave brilliant and insistent expression: the modern concept of
the family. Parents were no longer content with setting up only
a few of their children and neglecting the others. The ethics of
the time ordered them to give all their children, and not just the
eldest—and in the late seventeenth century even the girls—a
training for life. It was understood that this training would be
provided by the school. Traditional apprenticeship was replaced
by the school, an utterly transformed school, an instrument of
strict discipline, protected by the law-courts and the police-
courts. The extraordinary development of the school in the
seventeenth century was a consequence of the new interest
taken by parents in their children's education. The moralists
taught them that it was their duty to send their children to
school very early in life: 'Those parents', states a text of 1602,
'who take an interest in their children's education (*liberos
erudiendos*) are more worthy of respect than those who just
bring them into the world. They give them not only life but a
good and holy life. That is why those parents are right to send
their children at the tenderest age to the market of true wisdom
(in other words to college) where they will become the archi-
tects of their own fortune, the ornaments of their native land,
their family and their friends.'

Family and school together removed the child from adult
society. The school shut up a childhood which had hitherto
been free within an increasingly severe disciplinary system,

which culminated in the eighteenth and nineteenth centuries in the total claustration of the boarding-school. The solicitude of family, Church, moralists and administrators deprived the child of the freedom he had hitherto enjoyed among adults. It inflicted on him the birch, the prison cell—in a word, the punishments usually reserved for convicts from the lowest strata of society. But this severity was the expression of a very different feeling from the old indifference: an obsessive love which was to dominate society from the eighteenth century on. It is easy to see why this invasion of the public's sensibility by childhood should have resulted in the now better-known phenomenon of Malthusianism or birth-control. The latter made its appearance in the eighteenth century just when the family had finished organizing itself around the child, and raised the wall of private life between the family and society.

The modern family satisfied a desire for privacy and also a craving for identity: the members of the family were united by feeling, habit and their way of life. They shrank from the promiscuity imposed by the old sociability. It is easy to understand why this moral ascendancy of the family was originally a middle-class phenomenon: the nobility and the lower class, at the two extremities of the social ladder, retained the old idea of etiquette much longer and remained more indifferent to outside pressures. The lower classes retained almost down to the present day the liking for crowds. There is therefore a connection between the concept of the family and the concept of class. Several times in the course of this study we have seen them intersect. For centuries the same games were common to the different classes; but at the beginning of modern times a choice was made among them: some were reserved for people of quality, the others were abandoned to the children and the lower classes. The seventeenth-century charity schools, founded for the poor, attracted the children of the well-to-do just as much; but after the eighteenth century the middle-class families ceased to accept this mixing and withdrew their children from what was to become a primary-school system, to place them in the *pensions* and the lower classes of the colleges, over which they established a monopoly. Games and schools, originally common to the whole of society, henceforth formed part of a class system. It was all as if a rigid, polymorphous social body had broken up and had been replaced by a host of little societies, the families, and by a few massive groups, the classes; families and classes brought together individuals related to one another by their moral resemblance and by the identity of their way of life, whereas the old unique social body embraced the greatest possible variety of ages and classes. For these classes were all the more clearly distinguished and graded for being close together in space. Moral distances took the place of physical distances. The strictness of external signs of respect and of differences in dress counterbalanced the familiarity of communal life. The valet never left his master, whose friend and accomplice he was, in accordance with an emotional code to which we have lost the key today, once we have left adolescence behind; the haughtiness of the master matched the insolence of the servant and restored, for better or for worse, a hierarchy which excessive familiarity was perpetually calling in question.

People lived in a state of contrast; high birth or great wealth rubbed shoulders with poverty, vice with virtue, scandal with devotion. Despite its shrill contrasts, this medley of colours caused no surprise. A man or woman of quality felt no embarrassment at visiting in rich clothes the poor wretches in the prisons, the hospitals or the streets, nearly naked beneath their rags. The juxtaposition of these extremes no more embarrassed the rich than it humiliated the poor. Something of this moral atmosphere still exists today in southern Italy. But there came a time when the middle class could no longer bear the pressure of the multitude or the contact of the lower class. It seceded: it withdrew from the vast polymorphous society to organize itself separately, in a homogeneous environment, among its families, in homes designed for privacy, in new districts kept free from all lower-class contamination. The juxtaposition of inequalities, hitherto something perfectly natural, became intolerable to it: the revulsion of the rich preceded the shame of the poor. The quest for privacy and the new desires for comfort which it aroused (for there is a close connection between comfort and privacy) emphasized even further the contrast between the material ways of life of the lower and middle classes. The old society concentrated the maximum number of ways of life into the minimum of space and accepted, if it did not impose, the bizarre juxtaposition of the most widely different classes. The new society, on the contrary, provided each way of life with a confined space in which it was understood that the dominant features should be respected, and that each person had to resemble a conventional model, an ideal type, and never depart from it under pain of excommunication.

The concept of the family, the concept of class, and perhaps elsewhere the concept of race, appear as manifestations of the same intolerance towards variety, the same insistence on uniformity.

II.
The Private Family

In Ariès' view, "the private family" is a group phenomenon which all the members of the family experience. There is a more refined form of privatization, however. This is the shutting away only of some members of the family, so that the people who are constrained to stay at home are less free and are subservient to those whose lives are not wholly family-centered. The classic Marxian analyses of privatization explore this latter form. As the family withdrew from economic or political activity, a particular form of inequality arose in the family, an inequality based on sexual differences, an inequality expressing itself as different family roles for each sex. Thus the study of privatization in the family and the study of sex roles came to be joined in the literature on the family.

For a time, during the 1940s and 1950s, this joining together of the subjects of privatization and sex role was regarded as a simple factual error. It was thought that the subservience of women to men was relatively constant throughout literate and pre-literate societies, and so, it was reasoned, sexual imbalance was a consequence of the structure of "society" as such. This comfortably inegalitarian argument (you can't do anything about sexual inequality because it is inevitable) has by now been discarded as factually itself in error. Works like Amaury de Reincourt's *Sex and Power in History* or a wide variety of modern ethnography show societies in which sexual equality existed, societies also in which the family group played a strong public role in both politics and economic production.

Thus the classic arguments about privatization and sexual inequality are being taken seriously once more. As a preface to the Marxian writings which form the core of this argument, John Stuart Mill's classic defense of sexual equality, *The Subjection of Women,* is presented. Mill argues that the origin of sexual inequalities does lie far back in human history, but that if the family were regarded as similar to other modern kinds of human associations, like business, which are based on contracts, this sexual inequality could be ended. Mill sees no conflict between sexual equality and private property rights, for the right of contract, the basis of private property, is also the source of human freedom. Mill's view of the ideal and equal family is that of a voluntary association organized around a clearly articulated code of rights and duties which can be changed at the will of either partner.

The Marxian analysts of the family do, of course, see a conflict between the ideal of human equality and rights of property. The seminal work of this school is Friedrich Engels' *The Origin of the Family, Private Property, and the State;* the selection presented here focuses on the condition of the private family and sexual inequality in the time Engels was writing—the late nineteenth century—and leaves out most of the anthropological research and speculation Engels did on the family in early antiquity. Engels, along with the French sociologist La Playe, was one of the first to treat the family as an historically variant social institution, and no matter what decision one takes about the correctness of his views, the originality of his work makes *The Origin . . .* an enduring classic of family studies. A modern compliment to Engels is presented in the essay by Max Horkheimer on "Authority and the Family." Horkheimer takes one step more in the correlation between withdrawal of the family from the public sphere and the subjection of women; he shows that by this means the bourgeois, private family created images and experiences of authority which make the capitalistic social structure as a whole seem legitimate. Horkheimer was one of the founders of what is known as the Frankfurt School, an association of social scientists formed in Germany between the wars, displaced to the United States, and later re-formed again in Germany after World War II. Among the younger members of this school were Walter Benjamin, whose essay on crowds has already been presented, and Herbert Marcuse, one of whose essays appears at the end of this volume. The Frankfurt School, especially during the interwar years, when Horkheimer wrote this essay, wanted to join the established principles of Marxism to the then newly appearing principles of psychoanalysis.

The reader who would like to pursue the issue of privatization further might find it helpful to compare the pictures of family life in Fielding's *Tom Jones,* written in the middle of the eighteenth century, to those in Flaubert's *Madame Bovary,* published a century later, to those in Thomas Mann's *Buddenbrooks,* published at the beginning of the present century. A history of the Frankfurt School appears in Martin Jay's *The Dialectical Imagination.* Perhaps the most intelligent contemporary writing in the Engels/Horkheimer tradition is Juliet Mitchell's *Woman's Estate.*

As a postscript to the issue of privatization, the editor has added part of an essay of his own which raises the question of whether the private family in its classic bourgeois form has come to an end.

21. John Stuart Mill: *The Subjection of Women*   [1806–1873]

The laws of most countries are far worse than the people who execute them, and many of them are only able to remain laws by being seldom or never carried into effect. If married life were all that it might be expected to be, looking to the laws alone, society would be a hell upon earth. Happily there are both feelings and interests which in many men exclude, and in most, greatly temper, the impulses and propensities which lead to tyranny: and of those feelings, the tie which connects a man with his wife affords, in a normal state of things, incomparably the strongest example. The only tie which at all approaches to it, that between him and his children, tends, in all save exceptional cases, to strengthen, instead of conflicting with, the first. Because this is true; because men in general do not inflict, nor women suffer, all the misery which could be inflicted and suffered if the full power of tyranny with which the man is legally invested were acted on; the defenders of the existing form of the institution think that all its iniquity is justified, and that any complaint is merely quarrelling with the evil which is the price paid for every great good. But the mitigations in practice, which are compatible with maintaining in full legal force this or any other kind of tyranny, instead of being any apology for despotism, only serve to prove what power human nature possesses of reacting against the vilest institutions, and with what vitality the seeds of good as well as those of evil in human character diffuse and propagate themselves. Not a word can be said for despotism in the family which cannot be said for political despotism. Every absolute king does not sit at his window to enjoy the groans of his tortured subjects, nor strips them of their last rag and turns them out to shiver in the road. The despotism of Louis XVI was not the despotism of Philippe le Bel, or of Nadir Shah, or of Caligula; but it was bad enough to justify the French Revolution, and to palliate even its horrors. If an appeal be made to the intense attachments which exist between wives and their husbands, exactly as much may be said of domestic slavery. It was quite an ordinary fact in Greece and Rome for slaves to submit to death by torture rather than betray their masters. In the proscriptions of the Roman civil wars it was remarked that wives and slaves were heroically faithful, sons very commonly treacherous. Yet we know how cruelly many Romans treated their slaves. But in truth these intense individual feelings nowhere rise to such a luxuriant height as under the most atrocious institutions. It is part of the irony of life, that the strongest feelings of devoted gratitude of which human nature seems to be susceptible, are called forth in human beings towards those who, having the power entirely to crush their earthly existence, voluntarily refrain from using that power. How great a place in most men this sentiment fills, even in religious devotion, it would be cruel to inquire. We daily see how much their gratitude to Heaven appears to be stimulated by the contemplation of fellow-creatures to whom God has not been so merciful as he has to themselves.

Whether the institution to be defended is slavery, political absolutism, or the absolutism of the head of a family, we are always expected to judge of it from its best instances; and we are presented with pictures of loving exercise of authority on one side, loving submission to it on the other—superior wisdom ordering all things for the greatest good of the dependents, and surrounded by their smiles and benedictions. All this would be very much to the purpose if anyone pretended that there are no such things as good men. Who doubts that there may be great goodness, and great happiness, and great affection, under the absolute government of a good man? Meanwhile, laws and institutions require to be adapted, not to good men, but to bad. Marriage is not an institution designed for a select few. Men are not required, as a preliminary to the marriage ceremony, to prove by testimonials that they are fit to be trusted with the exercise of absolute power. The tie of affection and obligation to a wife and children is very strong with those whose general social feelings are strong, and with many who are little sensible to any other social ties; but there are all degrees of sensibility and insensibility to it, as there are all grades of goodness and wickedness in men, down to those whom no ties will bind, and on whom society has no action but through its *ultima ratio,* the penalties of the law. In every grade of this descending scale are men to whom are committed all the legal powers of a husband. . . .

In domestic as in political tyranny, the case of absolute monsters chiefly illustrates the institution by showing that there is scarcely any horror which may not occur under it if the despot pleases, and thus setting in a strong light what must be the terrible frequency of things only a little less atrocious. Absolute fiends are as rare as angels, perhaps rarer: ferocious savages, with occasional touches of humanity, are however very frequent: and in the wide interval which separates these from any worthy representatives of the human species, how many are the forms and gradations of animalism and selfishness, often under an outward varnish of civilisation and even cultivation, living at peace with the law, maintaining a creditable appearance to all who are not under their power, yet sufficient often to make the lives of all who are so, a torment and a burthen to them! It would be tiresome to repeat the commonplaces about the unfitness of men in general for power, which, after the political discussions of centuries, everyone knows by heart, were it not that hardly anyone thinks of applying these maxims to the case in which above all others they are applicable, that of power, not placed in the hands of a man here and there, but offered to every adult male, down to the basest and most ferocious. It is not because a man is not known to have broken any of the Ten Commandments, or because he maintains a respectable character in his dealings with those whom he cannot compel to have intercourse with him, or because he does not fly out into violent bursts of ill-temper against those who are not obliged to bear with him, that it is possible to surmise of what sort his conduct will be in the unrestraint of home. Even the commonest men reserve the violent, the sulky, the undisguisedly seflish side of their character for those who have no power to withstand it. The relation of superiors to dependents is the nursery of these vices of character, which, wherever else they exist, are an overflowing from that source. A man who is morose or violent to his equals, is sure to be one who has lived among inferiors, whom he could frighten or worry into submission. If the family in its best forms is, as it is often said to be, a school of sympathy, tenderness, and loving forgetfulness of self, it is still oftener, as respects its chief, a school of wilfulness, overbearingness, unbounded selfish indulgence, and a double-dyed and idealised selfishness, of which sacrifice itself is only a particular form: the care for the wife and children being only care for them as parts of the man's own interests and belongings, and their individual happiness being immolated in every shape to his smallest preferences. What better is to be looked for under the existing form of the institution? We know that the bad propensities of human nature are only kept within bounds when they are allowed no scope for their indulgence. We know that from impulse and habit, when not from deliberate purpose, almost everyone to whom others yield, goes on encroaching upon them, until a point is reached at which they are compelled to resist. Such being the common tendency of human nature; the almost unlimited power which present social institutions give to the man over at least one human being—the one with whom he resides, and whom he has always present—this power seeks out and evokes the latent germs of selfishness in the remotest corners of his nature—fans its faintest sparks and smouldering embers—offers to him a licence for the indulgence of those points of his original character which in all other relations he would have found it necessary to repress and conceal, and the repression of which would in time have become a second nature. I know that there is another side to the question. I grant that the wife, if she cannot effectually resist, can at least retaliate; she, too, can make the man's life extremely uncomfortable, and by that power is able to carry many points which she ought, and many which she ought not, to prevail in. But this instrument of self-protection—which may be called the power of the · scold, or the shrewish sanction—has the fatal defect, that it avails most against the least tyrannical superiors, and in favour of the least deserving dependents. It is the weapon of irritable and self-willed women; of those who would make the worst use of power if they themselves had it, and who generally turn this power to a bad use. The amiable cannot use such an instrument, the highminded disdain it. And on the other hand, the husbands against whom it is used most effectively are the gentler and more inoffensive; those who cannot be induced, even by provocation, to resort to any very harsh exercise of authority. The wife's power of being disagreeable generally only establishes a counter-tyranny, and makes victims in their turn chiefly of those husbands who are least inclined to be tyrants.

What is it, then, which really tempers the corrupting effects of the power, and makes it compatible with such amount of good as we actually see? Mere feminine blandishments, though of great effect in individual instances, have very little effect in modifying the general tendencies of the situation; for their power only lasts while the woman is young and attractive, often only while her charm is new, and not dimmed by familiarity; and on many men they have not much influence at any time. The real mitigating causes are, the personal affection which is the growth of time in so far as the man's nature is susceptible of it and the woman's character sufficiently congenial with his to excite it; their common interests as regards the children, and their general community of interest as concerns third persons (to which however there are very great limitations); the real importance of the wife to his daily comforts and enjoyments, and the value he consequently attaches to her on his personal account, which, in a man capable of feeling for others, lays the foundation of caring for her on her own; and lastly, the influence naturally acquired over almost all human beings by those near to their persons (if not actually disagreeable to them): who, both by their direct entreaties, and by the insensible contagion of their feelings and dispositions, are often able, unless counteracted by some equally strong personal influence, to obtain a degree of command over the conduct of the superior, altogether excessive and unreasonable. Through these various means, the wife frequently exercises even too much power over the man; she is able to affect his conduct in things in which she may not be qualified to influence it for good—in which her influence may be not only unenlightened, but employed on the morally wrong side; and in which he would act better if left to his own prompting. But neither in the affairs of families nor in those of states is power a compensation for the loss of freedom. Her power often gives her what she has no right to, but does not enable her to assert her own rights. A Sultan's favourite slave has slaves under her, over whom she tyrannises; but the desirable thing would be that she should neither have slaves nor be a slave. By entirely sinking her own existence in her husband; by having no will (or persuading him that she has no will) but his, in anything which regards their joint relation, and by making it the business of her life to work upon his sentiments, a wife may gratify herself by influencing, and very probably perverting, his conduct, in those of his external relations which she has never qualified herself to judge of, or in which she is herself wholly influenced by some personal or other partiality or prejudice. Accordingly, as things now are, those who act most kindly to their wives, are quite as often made worse, as better, by the wife's influence, in respect to all interests extending beyond the family. She is taught that she has no business with things out of that sphere; and accordingly she seldom has any honest and conscientious opinion on them; and therefore hardly ever meddles with them for any legitimate purpose, but generally for an interested one. She neither knows nor cares which is the right side in politics, but she knows what will bring in money or invitations, give her husband a title, her son a place, or her daughter a good marriage.

But how, it will be asked, can any society exist without government? In a family, as in a state, some one person must be the ultimate ruler. Who shall decide when married people differ in opinion? Both cannot have their way, yet a decision one way or the other must be come to.

It is not true that in all voluntary association between two people, one of them must be absolute master: still less that the law must determine which of them it shall be. The most frequent case of voluntary association, next to marriage, is partnership in business: and it is not found or thought necessary to enact that in every partnership, one partner shall have entire control over the concern, and the others shall be bound to obey his orders. No one would enter into partnership on terms which would subject him to the responsibilities of a principal, with only the powers and privileges of a clerk or agent. If the law dealt with other contracts as it does with marriage, it would ordain that one partner should administer the common business as if it was his private concern; that the others should have only delegated powers; and that this one should be designated by some general presumption of law, for example as being the eldest. The law never does this: nor does experience show it to be necessary that any theoretical inequality of power should exist between the partners, or that the partnership should have any other conditions than what they may themselves appoint by their articles of agreement. Yet it might seem that the exclusive power might be conceded with less danger to the rights and interests of the inferior, in the case of partnership than in that of marriage, since he is free to cancel the power by withdrawing from the connexion. The wife has no such power, and even if she had, it is almost always desirable that she should try all measures before resorting to it.

It is quite true that things which have to be decided every day, and cannot adjust themselves gradually, or wait for a compromise, ought to depend on one will; one person must have their sole control. But it does not follow that this should always be the same person. The natural arrangement is a division of powers between the two; each being absolute in the executive branch of their own department, and any change of system and principle requiring the consent of both. The division neither can nor should be pre-established by the law, since it must depend on individual capacities and suitabilities. If the two persons chose, they might pre-appoint it by the marriage contract, as pecuniary arrangements are now often pre-appointed. There would seldom be any difficulty in deciding such things by mutual consent, unless the marriage was one of those unhappy ones in which all other things, as well as this, become subjects of bickering and dispute. The division of rights would naturally follow the division of duties and functions; and that is already made by consent, or at all events not by law, but by general custom, modified and modifiable at the pleasure of the persons concerned.

22. Friedrich Engels: *The Origin of the Family, Private Property, and the State* [1820–1895]

As wealth increased, it, on the one hand, gave the man a more important status in the family than the woman, and, on the other hand, created a stimulus to utilize this strengthened position in order to overthrow the traditional order of inheritance in favour of his children. But this was impossible as long as descent according to mother right prevailed. This had, therefore, to be overthrown, and it was overthrown; and it was not so difficult to do this as it appears to us now. For this revolution— one of the most decisive ever experienced by mankind—need not have disturbed one single living member of a gens. All the members could remain what they were previously. The simple decision sufficed that in future the descendants of the male members should remain in the gens, but that those of the females were to be excluded from the gens and transferred to that of their father. The reckoning of descent through the female line and the right of inheritance through the mother were hereby overthrown and male lineage and right of inheritance from the father instituted. As to how and when this revolution was effected among the civilized peoples we know nothing. It falls entirely within prehistoric times. . . .

The overthrow of mother right was the *world-historic defeat of the female sex.* The man seized the reins in the house also; the woman was degraded, enthralled, the slave of the man's lust, a mere instrument of breeding children. This lowered position of women, especially manifest among the Greeks of the Heroic and still more of the Classical Age, has become gradually embellished and dissembled and, in part, clothed in a milder form, but by no means abolished.

The first effect of the sole rule of the men that was now established is shown in the intermediate form of the family which now emerges, the patriarchal family. . . . The essential features are the incorporation of bondsmen and the paternal power; the Roman family, accordingly, constitutes the perfected type of this form of the family. The word *familia* did not originally signify the ideal of our modern philistine, which is a compound of sentimentality and domestic discord. Among the Romans, in the beginning, it did not even refer to the married couple and their children, but to the slaves alone. . . . The expression was invented by the Romans to describe a new social organism, the head of which had under him wife and children and a number of slaves, under Roman paternal power, with power of life and death over them all. . . . To which Marx adds: "The modern family contains in embryo not only slavery (*servitus*) but serfdom also, since from the very beginning it is connected with agricultural services. It contains within itself *in miniature* all the antagonisms which later develop on a wide scale within society and its state." . . .

The *Monogamian* Family. As already indicated, this arises out of the pairing family in the transition period from the middle to the upper stage of barbarism, its final victory being one of the signs of the beginning of civilization. It is based on the supremacy of the man; its express aim is the begetting of children of undisputed paternity, this paternity being required in order that these children may in due time inherit their father's wealth as his natural heirs. The monogamian family differs from pairing marriage in the far greater rigidity of the marriage tie, which can now no longer be dissolved at the pleasure of either party. Now, as a rule, only the man can dissolve it and cast off his wife. The right of conjugal infidelity remains his even now, sanctioned, at least, by custom (the *Code Napoléon* expressly concedes this right to the husband as long as he does not bring his concubine into the conjugal home), and is exercised more and more with the growing development of society. Should the wife recall the ancient sexual practice and desire to revive it, she is punished more severely than ever before. . . .

Thus, monogamy does not by any means make its appearance in history as the reconciliation of man and woman, still less as the highest form of such a reconciliation. On the contrary, it appears as the subjection of one sex by the other, as the proclamation of a conflict between the sexes entirely unknown hitherto in prehistoric times. In an old unpublished manuscript, the work of Marx and myself in 1846, I find the following: "The first division of labour is that between man and woman for child breeding." And today I can add: The first class antagonism which appears in history coincides with the development of the antagonism between man and woman in monogamian marriage, and the first class oppression with that of the female sex by the male. Monogamy was a great historical advance, but at the same time it inaugurated, along with slavery and private wealth, that epoch, lasting until today, in which every advance is likewise a relative regression, in which the well-being and development of the one group are attained by the misery and repression of the other. It is the cellular form of civilized society, in which we can already study the nature of the antagonisms and contradictions which develop fully in the latter. . . .

Bourgeois marriage of our own times is of two kinds. In Catholic countries the parents, as heretofore, still provide a suitable wife for their young bourgeois son, and the consequence is naturally the fullest unfolding of the contradiction inherent in monogamy—flourishing hetaerism on the part of the husband, and flourishing adultery on the part of the wife. The Catholic Church doubtless abolished divorce only because it was convinced that for adultery, as for death, there is no cure whatsoever. In Protestant countries, on the other hand, it is the rule that the bourgeois son is allowed to seek a wife for himself from his own class, more or less freely. Consequently, marriage can be based on a certain degree of love which, for decency's sake, is always assumed, in accordance with Protestant hypocrisy. In this case, hetaerism on the part of the man is less actively pursued, and adultery on the woman's part is not so much the rule. Since, in every kind of marriage, however, people remain what they were before they married, and since the citizens of Protestant countries are mostly philistines, this Protestant monogamy leads merely, if we take the average of the best cases, to a wedded life of leaden boredom, which is described as domestic bliss. The best mirror of these two ways of marriage is the novel; the French novel for the Catholic style, and the German novel for the Protestant. In both cases "he gets it": in the German novel the young man gets the girl; in the French, the husband gets the cuckold's horns. Which of the two is in the worse plight is not always easy to make out. For the dullness of the German novel excites the same horror in the French bourgeois as the "immorality" of the French novel excites in the German philistine, although lately, since "Berlin is becoming a metropolis," the German novel has begun to deal a little less timidly with hetaerism and adultery, long known to exist there.

In both cases, however, marriage is determined by the class position of the participants, and to that extent always remains marriage of convenience. In both cases, this marriage of convenience often enough turns into the crassest prostitution—sometimes on both sides, but much more generally on the part of the wife, who differs from the ordinary courtesan only in that she does not hire out her body, like a wageworker, on piecework, but sells it into slavery once for all. And Fourier's words hold good for all marriages of convenience: "Just as in grammar two negatives make a positive, so in the morals of marriage, two prostitutions make one virtue." Sex love in the relation of husband and wife is and can become the rule only among the oppressed classes, that is, at the present day, among the proletariat, no matter whether this relationship is officially sanctioned or not. But here all the foundations of classical monogamy are removed. Here, there is a complete absence of all property, for the safeguarding and inheritance of which monogamy and male domination were established. Therefore, there is no stimulus whatever here to assert male domination. What is more, the means, too, are absent; bourgeois law, which protects this domination, exists only for the propertied classes and their dealings with the proletarians. It costs money, and therefore, owing to the worker's poverty, has no validity in his attitude towards his wife. Personal and social relations of quite a different sort are the decisive factors here. Moreover, since large-scale industry has transferred the woman from the house to the labour market and the factory, and makes her, often enough, the breadwinner of the family, the last remnants of male domination in the proletarian home have lost all foundation—except, perhaps, for some of that brutality towards women which became firmly rooted with the establishment of monogamy. Thus, the proletarian family is no longer monogamian in the strict sense, even in cases of the most passionate love and strictest faithfulness of the two parties, and despite all spiritual and worldly benedictions which may have been received. The two eternal adjuncts of monogamy—hetaerism and adultery—therefore, play an almost negligible role here; the woman has regained, in fact, the right of separation, and when the man and woman cannot get along they prefer to part. In short, proletarian marriage is monogamian in the etymological sense of the word, but by no means in the historical sense. . . .

Today, in the great majority of cases the man has to be the earner, the breadwinner of the family, at least among the propertied classes, and this gives him a dominating position which requires no special legal privileges. In the family, he is the bourgeois; the wife represents the proletariat. In the industrial world, however, the specific character of the economic oppression that weighs down the proletariat stands out in all its sharpness only after all the special legal privileges of the capitalist class have been set aside and the complete juridical equality of both classes is established. The democratic republic does not abolish the antagonism between the two classes; on the contrary, it provides the field on which it is fought out. And, similarly, the peculiar character of man's domination over woman in the modern family, and the necessity, as well as the manner, of establishing real, social equality between the two, will be brought out into full relief only when both are completely equal before the law. It will then become evident that the first premise for the emancipation of women is the reintroduction of the entire female sex into public industry; and that this again demands that the quality possessed by the individual family of being the economic unit of society be abolished. . . .

Since sex love is by its very nature exclusive—although this exclusiveness is fully realized today only in the woman—then marriage based on sex love is by its very nature monogamy. We have seen how right Bachofen was when he regarded the advance from group marriage to individual marriage chiefly as the work of the women; only the advance from pairing marriage to monogamy can be placed to the men's account, and, historically, this consisted essentially in a worsening of the position of women and in facilitating infidelity on the part of the men. With the disappearance of the economic considerations which compelled women to tolerate the customary infidelity of the men—the anxiety about their own livelihood and even more about the future of their children—the equality of woman thus achieved will, judging from all previous experience, result far more effectively in the men becoming really monogamous than in the women becoming polyandrous.

23. Max Horkheimer: "Authority and the Family," in *Critical Theory*   [1895–]

The role of coercion, which marks not only the origin but also the development of all States, can indeed be hardly overestimated when we try to explain social life in history up to the present. The coercion does not consist simply in punishment for those who violate the imposed order of things. It consists also in the hunger of a man and his family which over and over again drives him to accept the existing conditions for work, among which must be numbered his good behavior in most areas of life. But in the course of development the cruelty and publicity of punishment could be reduced, at least in certain economically well-off periods. In addition, threats of punishment have become increasingly differentiated and intellectualized, so that, in part at least, terror has changed into fear and fear into caution. And as in periods of economic growth and increased social wealth some functions of punishment could be taken over by its positive counterpart, the hope of reward, so too the lords and sentinels who originally, in keeping with primitive traits of the psychic apparatus, were supplemented by an army of spirits and demons, were partially replaced by a divinity or a world of ideas, conceived in brighter or darker colors according to the spirit of the age. All this already means that naked coercion cannot by itself explain why the subject classes have borne the yoke so long in times of cultural decline, when property relationships, like existing ways of life in general, had obviously reduced social forces to immobility and the economic apparatus was ready to yield a better method of production. The historian must here study the whole culture, although knowledge of material conditions is, of course, the basis of understanding. . . .

One function of the entire cultural apparatus at any given period has been to internalize in men of subordinate position the idea of a necessary domination of some men over others, as determined by the course of history down to the present time. As a result and as a continually renewed condition of this cultural apparatus, the belief in authority is one of the driving forces, sometimes productive, sometimes obstructive, of human history. . . .

Submission to the categorical imperative of duty has been from the beginning a conscious goal of the bourgeois family. In the Renaissance, humanistic education was a benefit which seemed a happy beginning of a new age, even if with few exceptions such an education extended only to the children of Italian princes. But in the countries which assumed economic leadership once the sea route to East India was discovered, childhood became increasingly grim and oppressive.

In the developmental history of the family from the absolutist to the liberalist period, a new factor in habituation to authority emerges even more strongly. No longer is it obedience that is immediately demanded, but, on the contrary, the application of reason. Anyone who looks at the world soberly will see that the individual must adapt and subordinate himself. Such education to realism, too, the goal of every good pedagogy in the more developed phases of bourgeois society, was anticipated in the Protestant conception of the family. It is present in

> the very essence of Lutheranism, which looks upon the physical superiority of man as the expression of a superior relationship willed by God, and a stable order as the chief end of all social organizations. The house-father represents the law, and possesses unlimited power over others; he is the breadwinner, the pastor, and the priest of his household.

The naturally given fact of the father's physical strength is regarded in Protestantism as also a moral fact to be respected. Because the father is *de facto* stronger, he is also *de jure* stronger. The child is not only to take the father's superiority into account; he is also to have esteem for it. In this kind of familial situation, with its determinative influence on the child's education, we find anticipated in large measure the structure of authority as it existed outside the family. According to the latter, the prevailing differences in conditions of life, which the individual finds in the world, are simply to be accepted; he must make his way within that framework and not rebel against it. To recognize facts means to accept them. Distinctions established by nature are willed by God, and, in bourgeois society, wealth and poverty seem naturally determined. When the child respects in his father's strength a moral relationship and thus learns to love what his reason recognizes to be a fact, he is experiencing his first training for the bourgeois authority relationship.

The father thus has a moral claim upon submission to his strength, but not because he proves himself worthy of respect; rather he proves himself worthy by the very fact that he is stronger. At the beginning of the bourgeois age the father's control of his household was doubtless an indispensable condition of progress. The self-control of the individual, the disposition for work and discipline, the ability to hold firmly to certain ideas, consistency in practical life, application of reason, perseverance and pleasure in constructive activity could all be developed, in the circumstances, only under the dictation and guidance of the father whose own education had been won in the school of life. . . .

In the course of history the family has had extremely diverse and numerous roles to play. As compared with periods in which it was the predominant productive community, not only has the family completely lost many of its former functions but even the ones left to it have been affected by changes in society as a whole. In 1911 Müller-Lyer listed as functions of the family the management of the household, the reproduction, rearing, and education of children, the control of population growth and of genetic lines, the development of sociableness, the care of the sick and elderly, the accumulation and hereditary transmission of capital and other property, as well as the determination of choice of occupation. But sociological literature is now full of evidence that the family has already become a problematic form for carrying out the functions listed. . . .

The "free persons" in the modern family can indeed no longer be sold by the father, and the grown-up son and his children are not now subject to the supreme authority of the grandfather. But the fact that in the average bourgeois family the husband possesses the money, which is power in the form of substance, and determines how it is to be spent, makes wife, sons, and daughters even in modern times "his," puts their lives in large measure into his hands, and forces them to submit to his orders and guidance. As in the economy of recent centuries direct force has played an increasingly smaller role in coercing men into accepting a work situation, so too in the family rational considerations and free obedience have replaced slavery and subjection. But the relationship in question is that of the isolated and helpless individual who must bow to circumstances whether they be corrupt or reasonable. The despair of women and children, the deprivation of any happiness in life, the material and psychic exploitation consequent upon the economically based hegemony of the father have weighed mankind down no less in recent centuries than in antiquity, except for very limited periods, regions, and social strata.

The spiritual world into which the child grows in consequence of such dependence, as well as the fantasies with which he peoples the real world, his dreams and wishes, his ideas and judgments, are all dominated by the thought of man's power over man, of above and below, of command and obedience. This scheme is one of the forms understanding takes in this period, one of its transcendental functions. The necessity of a division and hierarchy of mankind, resting on natural, accidental, and irrational principles, is so familiar and obvious to the child that he can experience the earth and universe, too, and even the other world, only under this aspect; it is the pregiven mold into which every new impression is poured. The ideologies of merit and accomplishment, harmony and justice, can continue to have a place in this picture of the world because the fact that the reification of social categories contradicts them does not emerge into consciousness. According to the structure, property relationships are stable and eternal; they do not manifest the fact that they are in truth the objects of social activity and revolution, and therefore they are not prejudicial to the appropriateness claimed by the social structure. Yet because of these contradictions the bourgeois child, unlike the child of ancient society, develops an authority-oriented character which, according to his social class and individual lot in life, has in greater or lesser degree a calculating, fawning, and moralizing or rationalizing aspect. To yield to his father because the latter has the money is, in his eyes, the only reasonable thing to do, independently of any consideration of the father's human qualities. Such a consideration even proves to be fruitless, at least in the later stages of bourgeois society. . . .

As long as there is no decisive change in the basic structure of social life and in the modern culture which rests on that structure, the family will continue to exercise its indispensable function of producing specific, authority-oriented types of character. The family is an important element in the patterned unity which marks the present period of history. All the self-consistent political, moral, and religious movements which have aimed at strengthening and renewing this unity, have been quite aware of the fundamental role of the family as creator of the authority-oriented cast of mind and have regarded it as a prime duty to strengthen the family and all its social presuppositions, such as the outlawing of extra-marital sexual relations, propaganda for having and rearing children, and the restricting of women to the domestic sphere. . . .

Even in the golden age of the bourgeois order, it must be remembered, there was a renewal of social life, but it was achieved at the cost of great sacrifice for most individuals. In that situation, the family was a place where the suffering could be given free expression and the injured individual found a retreat within which he could put up some resistance. In the economy man was being reduced to a mere function of one or other economic factor: wealth or technically demanding physical or mental work. The same process of reduction to subpersonal status was going on within the family in so far as the father was becoming the money-earner, the woman a sexual object or a domestic servant, and the children either heirs of the family possessions or living forms of social security who would later make up with interest for all the effort expended on them. Within the family, however, unlike public life, relationships were not mediated through the market and the individual members were not competing with each other. Consequently the individual always had the possibility there of living not as a mere function but as a human being. In civic life, even when common concerns were not mediated by a contract, as in the case of natural catastrophes, wars, or the suppression of revolutions, they always had an essentially negative character, being mainly concerned with the warding off of dangers. But common concerns took a positive form in sexual love and especially in maternal care. The growth and happiness of the other are willed in such unions. A felt opposition therefore arises between them and hostile reality outside. To this extent, the family not only educates for authority in bourgeois society; it also cultivates the dream of a better condition for mankind. In the yearning of many adults for the paradise of their childhood, in the way a mother can speak of her son even though he has come into conflict with the world, in the protective love of a wife for her husband, there are ideas and forces at work which admittedly are not dependent on the existence of the family in its present form and, in fact, are even in danger of shrivelling up in such a milieu, but which, nevertheless, in the bourgeois system of life rarely have any place but the family where they can survive at all. . . .

To the extent that any principle besides that of subordination prevails in the modern family, the woman's maternal and sisterly love is keeping alive a social principle dating from before historical antiquity, a principle which Hegel conceives "as the law of the ancient gods, 'the gods of the underworld,' " that is, of prehistory.

Because it still fosters human relations which are determined by the woman, the present-day family is a source of strength to resist the total dehumanization of the world and contains an element of antiauthoritarianism. But it must also be recognized that because of her dependence woman herself has been changed. She is, in large measure, socially and legally under the authority of the male and is seen in relation to him, thus experiencing in her person the law that prevails in this anarchic society. In the process her own development is lastingly restricted. The male and, concretely, the male as formed by existing circumstances dominates her in a double way: societal life is essentially managed by men, and the man is at the head of the family. . . .

The familial role of the woman strengthens the authority of the status quo in two ways. Being dependent on her husband's position and earnings, she is also circumscribed by the fact that the head of the family adapts himself to the situations he meets and under no circumstances rebels against the powers that be but does his utmost to better his position. Profound economic and even physiological interests link the woman to her husband's ambition. Before all else, however, her concern is with her own and her children's economic security. The introduction of the franchise for women was a gain for conservative forces even in states where a strengthening of labor groups had been expected.

The sense of economic and social responsibility for wife and child, which necessarily becomes an essential trait of the male in the bourgeois world, is one of the most important elements in the functioning of the family as a conservative force in that society. When accommodation to existing authority relationships becomes advisable for husband and father out of love for his family, then the very thought of rebellion causes him the most agonizing conflicts of conscience. The struggle against certain historical conditions ceases to be a matter simply of personal courage and becomes the sacrifice of persons dear to him. The existence of many states in the modern period is closely bound up with such inhibitions and their continuance. If these restraints ceased or even lessened in intensity, such states would immediately be endangered. Furthermore, it is not only concern for his family but also the constant spoken or tacit urging of his wife that chains the husband to the status quo. In their upbringing by the mother the children, too, experience directly the influence of a mind dedicated to the prevailing order of things, although, on the other hand, love for a mother who is dominated by the father can also sow in the children the seeds of a lasting spirit of rebellion.

It is not only in this direct way, however, that the woman exercises her function of strengthening authority. Her whole position in the family results in an inhibiting of important psychic energies which might have been effective in shaping the world. Monogamy as practiced in bourgeois male-dominated society presupposes the devaluation of purely sensuous pleasure. As a result, not only is the sexual life of the spouses surrounded with mystery as far as the children are concerned, but every sensuous element is strictly banished from the son's tenderness for his mother. She and his sisters have the right to pure feelings and unsullied reverence and esteem from him. The forced separation, expressly represented by the mother and especially by the father, of idealistic dedication and sexual desire, tender mindfulness and simple self-interest, heavenly interiority and earthly passion forms one psychic root of an existence rent by contradictions. Under the pressure of such a family situation the individual does not learn to understand and respect his mother in her concrete existence, that is, as this particular social and sexual being. Consequently he is not only educated to repress his socially harmful impulses (a feat of immense cultural significance), but, because this education takes the problematic form of camouflaging reality, the individual also loses for good the disposition of part of his psychic energies. Reason and joy in its exercise are restricted; the suppressed inclination towards the mother reappears as a fanciful and sentimental susceptibility to all symbols of the dark, maternal, and protective powers because the woman bows to the law of the patriarchal family, she becomes an instrument for maintaining authority in this society. Hegel refers with enthusiasm to Antigone's final words in Sophocles' play: "If this seems good of the gods, / Suffering, we may be made to know our error." When she thus renounces all opposition, she simultaneously accepts the principle of male-dominated bourgeois society: bad luck is your own fault. . . .

In the bourgeois golden age there was a fruitful interaction between family and society, because the authority of the father was based on his role in society, while society was renewed by the education for authority which went on in the patriarchal family. Now, however, the admittedly indispensable family is becoming a simple problem of technological manipulation by government. The totality of relationships in the present age, the universal web of things, was strengthened and stabilized by one particular element, namely, authority, and the process of strengthening and stabilization went on essentially at the particular, concrete level of the family. The family was the "germ cell" of bourgeois culture and it was, like the authority in it, a living reality. This dialectical totality of universality, particularity, and individuality proves now to be a unity of antagonistic forces, and the disruptive element in the culture is making itself more strongly felt than the unitive.

24. Richard Sennett: "Destructive *Gemeinschaft*"   [1943–]

When we think of our great-grandparents' experiences of physical love, we are most likely to think about the inhibitions and repressions. Victorian bourgeois prudery was so extreme it occasionally acquired an almost surreal quality; a common practice, for instance, was to cover the legs of grand pianos with leggings, because a bare leg as such was thought "provocative." This prudery lay at the root of a number of psychopathologies especially acute at the time—not only hysterias, but also what the Victorians called "complaints," which among women were manifested by such symptoms as uncontrollable vomiting at the sight of menstrual blood and among men by such symptoms as acute attacks of anxiety after the discovery of an ejaculation occurring during sleep. Certainly no one today could possibly hope for a return to such repression. Yet it is important to see the rationale behind this sexual repression and even to comprehend a certain dignity among bourgeois men and women in these Puritanical struggles with themselves. A code of eroticism ruled nineteenth-century bourgeois consciousness, an eroticism composed of three elements.

The first of these elements was the belief that states of feeling and signs of character manifest themselves involuntarily. Hence, what is deeply felt or deeply rooted in character is beyond the power of the will to shape or hide: emotion appears unbidden, and at moments of vulnerability emotion is a betrayal. The involuntary expression of emotion received its greatest theoretical elaboration in Charles Darwin's *The Expression of the Emotions in Man and Animals.* Darwin connected the involuntary betrayal of emotion with the necessities of biology which ruled the human organism. But the same idea had more popular expressions which sought to indicate ways of detecting transitory states of feeling. Thus, depression was supposed to reveal itself by involuntary tension in the cheeks, an episode of masturbation by the sudden growth of a spot of hair on the palms.

Similarly, character traits were to be read through details of appearance. The involuntary expression of character involved a particular system of cognition, as in the practice of phrenology and Bertillion measurement: the shape of the skull, hand, or foot supposedly revealing the presence of certain characterological traits which the criminal, defective, or salacious person could do nothing to disguise. The Bertillion measures of criminality concern millimeters of difference between the cranial shape of the criminal and the law-abider. Because these involuntary clues of personality were like cameos, personality itself was felt to be so difficult to control; one might control most of one's behavior and still some little thing would give away.

In such a culture, anxiety about sexual matters formed part of a larger belief that the expression of all feeling escaped control by the ego. One's only defenses were either to shield oneself as completely as possible, to neutralize one's appearance, as the Victorians did through their clothing, or to attempt to repress feeling itself. For if a transitory emotion is uncontrollably manifest through the most minute clues, one can be secure only if one tries to stop feeling in the first place. Shielding and denial, then, are logical consequences of believing in the *immanence* of the personality; the line between inside and outside is dissolved.

This Victorian belief led to a fetishism of appearances. I use this term more in a Marxian than a Freudian sense, to indicate how the trivia of appearance could be believed to be signs of a whole human being. If the self speaks through minutiae of appearance, then every appearance must be a guide to some characterological state. Thus, it becomes logical to cover the legs of a piano with skirts, because an exposed leg is the sign of lewdness. In the clothing of the Victorian era, this fetishism of appearances was especially strong. A gentleman wearing a drab black broadcloth coat could be distinguished from an ordinary bourgeois wearing a similar garment because the buttons on the gentleman's sleeve could actually button and unbutton. For men this fetishism centered around questions of class; for women it centered around sexual propriety. The differences between the dress of "loose" women and the proper ladies who appeared in *Le Moniteur de la Mode* lay in minor distinctions in the use of color for shawls and hoods, or the length or shortness of gloves. Minute differences between objects speak of vast differences in feeling between those who wear them.

In the sections of the first volume of *Das Kapital* where Marx takes up the subject of fetishized objects, he explains them as a veil modern capitalism draws over production relations, so that the inequities of production, which might be visible if goods were conceived of simply in terms of use, are obscured; these objects seem instead to contain mysterious and enticing psychological qualities. Missing in his analysis, however, is a consideration of the psychological consequences of becoming mystified, of believing in the minutiae of man-made things as personality omens, for the person so mystified. The Victorian bourgeoisie was more than a class laboring under an illusion; it was also a class trying to make sense of its daily experience on the basis of this illusion. People scanned the public world for signs of the private life of others at the same time that each attempted to shield himself from being so read. This double process of searching and shielding was hardly a simple state of equilibrium or a matter of balance between public and private.

Sexual relations in a world conceived in such terms had of necessity to be social relations. Today, having an affair with another person would not be likely to cause someone to call into question his or her capacities as a parent, or—if it were someone sufficiently "liberated"—his or her capacities as husband or wife. For the Victorian bourgeoisie, those connections had to be made. If every act, every feeling, counts in terms of defining the whole person, then emotional experience in one domain carries unavoidable implications about the character of the person acting in another. A violation of morality in one sphere signifies a moral violation in every other; an adulteress cannot be a loving mother, she has betrayed her children in taking a lover, and so on. Again, I wish to call attention not so much to how brutal this repressive code could be as to the premise which produced the repression. The immanence of character in all appearances forced the Victorian to weigh each experience in relation to other experiences to us seemingly quite dissociated. For all the desire to flee the world at large and hide in privatized, isolated places, the Victorians had to measure the acts of the private sphere on the basis of their public implications. . . .

Today the phrase "the private family" seems to connote a single idea, but until the eighteenth century privacy was not associated with family or intimate life, but rather with secrecy and governmental privilege. There have been numerous attempts to explain the union of privacy and family life in the modern period, the most notable and direct being that of Engels. Because of the sterility of human relations in the productive system of capitalism, Engels argued, people concentrated their desires for full emotional relations in a single sphere, the home, and tried to make this sphere privileged, exempt from the emptiness which pervaded office or factory. Engel's idea of privatization supplements the movement which Tönnes perceived in the larger society from *Gemeinschaft* to *Gesellschaft* relations; in sum, the family becomes a miniature *Gemeinschaft* in a largely alien world.

The term privatization has become a cliché today among those who study and write about the family, and has taken on two overtones which obscure its meaning. All too often writings on the private family (an isolated nuclear family in form) assume that privatization can actually work: people who want to go and hide can really do so. This is the assumption of the historian Philippe Ariès and those of his school when they talk about the family withdrawing from the world in modern times. Missing in this account is a recognition that the social forces which divide work from family also invade the family itself. If we do recognize the pervasive power of capitalism, then we must think of the experience of privatization in the nineteenth-century family as an attempt to make the family warm and snug against the outside, but an attempt which constantly failed because the alien world organized personal relations within the house as much as impersonal relations without.

Secondly, the cliché of privatization misleads by suggesting a static condition that of a permanently privatized family. But what happens once the family becomes privatized? After all, this process of privatization has been at work for 200 years, and yet many of those who study it use terms to describe it which apply to fixed emotional states: "isolation," "emotional over-involvement with kin," and the like. "Surely the families of *Emma Bovary, Buddenbrooks,* and *Herzog,* all ostensibly privatized, are not the same.

Let us return for a moment to Engels's view of the pressures creating privatization in the nineteenth century. These are pressures of displacement in one direction: from a work experience more and more empty to family experience forced to provide a full range of emotional relationships, including those which properly belong to, but have been shifted from, the public world of production. What then would generate a contrary pressure, so that the family ultimately failed in its efforts to provide a refuge, failed to become securely privatized? Critical in producing this contrary motion was the idea of personality revealed in external appearances which had crystallized by the 1860s and early 1870s.

In the child-rearing manuals published in the 1860s in

both France and England, a common, almost monotonous theme occurs: for children to grow up with stable characters, they must maintain orderly appearances in the family circle. Not only must the child, whether boy or girl, act consistently through "good habits" and "beneficent rules," but the parents must display good habits and act consistently in front of their children. The reason this advice about family dynamics was given is that the Victorian bourgeoisie feared that if appearances were not routinized in the home, and if spontaneity were not effectively suppressed, then the personality would never crystallize and the child would never grow emotionally strong. This fear is linked to a series of assumptions which we have already examined: since basic personality traits are linked even to the minutiae of external appearances, in order for basic personality traits to be formed appearances must be rigidly controlled.

For all the desire family members had to withdraw from the terrors of the world into a relaxed warm zone, the codes of personality in the last century pushed family relations back into the welter of contradictory impulses of order and immanence which troubled the public world. Between husbands and wives the same pressure for stabilization of behavior existed as governed the relations of parents and children. Love between man and woman depended on the ability of the partners to conform to the rules of what a husband and wife should be. But if adherence to rules of propriety was necessary at home, the realms of work and home were not therefore identical. In the home, changed appearances would threaten the partners' trust in each other, threaten their sense that each knew who the other was. A repressive, rigid routine became the means of certifying that the marriage itself was real—just as the child was thought to grow in a healthy way only if he experienced others in terms he could trust. For the Victorians, trust meant trust to remain the same.

Thus, the privatization the family experienced in the nineteenth century was a consequence of its search for an order in which stable personality could flourish; and yet it involved a belief in immanent personality which thrust the family back out into the very anxieties about order and immanent meaning which ruled public life. *Both* the desire to retreat and the reconstruction of the outer society are elements of privatization. The first would soon have exhausted itself as a desire had not the second so insistently thrust family dynamics back into the public contradiction, so that the family's mission of orderly retreat never seemed accomplished.

For families of the present generation, privatization on these terms has ceased to exist. There is no longer a world alien to the self to which the self refers. For example, to preserve a marriage as a social contract, people today are not willing to observe proprieties of the rigid sort which characterized the last century; if one is obliged to make great sacrifices of immediate feeling and perception about the other partner in the marriage, then the marriage itself soon seems sour. Because so many nineteenth-century people were imprisoned in respectable but loveless marriages, the breaking of rigid codes of correct behavior may well seem all to the good. The problem is that this change in the terms of privatization has not liberated individuals within the family, but paradoxically, has made the family bond more important and more destructive. The reason for this is that when family relations become withdrawals from the world the person has no experiences outside the family which can be used to judge experiences within it. The family comes to seem the terrain on which all emotions are displayed: emotions which are not familial have no reality because the world outside is only instrumental. The movement from privacy to intimacy is a movement from the family as an unsuccessful private institution to the family as a tyrannical, psychologically pure universe.

What is the rationale for conceiving of the family as socially withdrawn and emotionally complete? It is that of the narcissistic mirror. If the family is not a work unit as in the *ancien régime,* if it is not an arrangement involving an arbitrarily rigid set of roles, as in the nineteenth century, then what appears in this "free" psychic network has a reality and purity unsullied by alien contingencies. Once freed from the world, the family will appear to be a disclosure of pure psychological experience. The lessons of such experience will then be taken out beyond the family circle, and psychological transactions in the world will be judged in terms of familial categories, which seem like pure types. . . .

The most profound indicator of the family as an image of a purely psychological and morally dominant condition comes from the realm of ideology. Today our concept of psychological emancipation involves liberation of the self rather than liberation from the self. In ordinary speech we idealize being able to express our feelings openly or feeling free to do so. . . . Social institutions are bad at the moment when they get in the way of free human expression. . . . Liberation of one's feelings is basically a familistic ideal. Liberation from one's feelings is a nonfamilistic ideal. The first refers to the possibility of experience in which anything one wants, any sensation one has, can be received by others; that is, liberation of one's feelings presupposes an accepting environment, one in which interest in whatever one does feel, and appreciation for it, will be shown by others. The model for such an accepting environment is the child displaying himself to an audience of adoring parents. Liberation from one's feelings, on the other hand, refers to the possibility of experience which is impersonal, experience in which the person observes a convention, plays a role, participates in a form; the classic locus of such liberation is the city, its classic name cosmopolitanism. . . .

A society in which liberation of self replaces liberation from the self as an ideal has obliterated any possibilities of self-transcendence from its moral life. Instead of transcending the self, one makes it into a comprehensive standard of reality. One does not balance public against private; instead, one assumes that one *is,* that life is authentic, when one focuses inward, taking moments of self-disclosure in the family to be the reality in which the self is nourished. The outside is vaguely threatening but also simply vague, a reality of necessities, constraints upon the self, bonds to be broken. . . .

This is why a society like ours, celebrating the sheer existence of human feeling, cannot be called privatized. There is no understanding of what it means to harbor an impulse in private. . . . We are prone to convert discretion and tact into signs of domination. Surely the word liberation is itself misleading as a description of the present situation if it connotes a state of progress. A hundred years ago, personality was socialized only by ideas of repression; today it is not socialized at all. These are opposite and equal evils.

III.
Stages in the Life Cycle

If Ariès is correct, the appearance of the private family has created a prolonged childhood divided into different stages; it is this historical change which makes plausible life-cycle analysis. Even if Ariès' view is correct, it is analytically incomplete. In any interpretation of the movement from birth to death in terms of distinct growth stages, two assumptions must be made.

Some process of change must occur in the human being such that once a new development occurs, it cannot be lost; in other words, the effects of it must be cumulative. This is the difference between "growth" and simple change. In the latter case, the sequence of events would be what is sometimes called a "noncorrelative progression." Event A would be followed by B, B by C, but A's only relation to B is that it must come before, B's only relation to C is that it must come before. Noncumulative change is a difficult pattern to ascribe to human beings because it denies both learning mechanisms and memory. If a person is capable of doing something in stage B which he could not do in stage A, it is assumed that he has learned something over time from his experiences in stage A and in this sense carried those experiences forward; if a person in stage C can remember experiences from stages B and A, it is assumed that the two prior stages are still cognitively available in stage C, and in this sense A and B are part of C. Thus the first assumption of a model of the life cycle: events over time have a cumulative meaning.

The second analytic ingredient for a theory of stages of psychological growth is so simple that its importance is often overlooked. This is that the process of accumulation from stage to stage must be tied to biological changes in the human organism. The processes of growth are not abstract "mental" experiences; they are part of general somatic change. Of course this correlation could easily degenerate into physiological determinism; life-cycle theorists try to avoid this by treating each biological stage as a limiting condition on how much, and at what pace, emotional growth accumulates. From this correlation two consequences follow.

First, behavior or sensation can be labeled as immature or regressive. The labels are created by comparing what is possible to experience at a given stage to what is actually experienced, and experiential possibility is defined by the state of one's motor control, sexual development, sheer physical strength, rather than by abstract moral criteria, such as the dictum that, by thirteen, one should be capable of taking communion with God. This biological emphasis on progression and regression is central for psychoanalytic interpretations of growth. Second, the emotional life of human beings must owe its origins not to something unique about man, but to something man shares with other animals. Other animals also feel, learn, and recall in time to their state of physical development. This tying of man's emotional life to the life of other animals appears as a basic premise of Charles Darwin's *The Expression of the Emotions in Man and Animals.*

Since much of the modern writing about life stages of growth developed out of the psychoanalytic movement, it is useful to pin down the particular idea of emotional cumulation on which psychoanalytic thinking draws. This idea is that as the human being develops, he gains ever greater powers of "objectification"; he learns how to distinguish what is like and unlike himself, learns to recognize his own limits, learns conversely to recognize the limits of the burdens other people can place upon him. The first writer to portray objectification as a cumulative process in the life cycle was the eighteenth-century Italian humanist Giambattista Vico. A short excerpt from Vico's *The New Science* is presented here to illustrate his thinking on this subject.

A rather longer selection from Darwin's work is presented to illustrate the origins of the correlation between biological possibility and emotional growth. *The Expression of the Emotions in Man and Animals* is a neglected book, but an important one; it puts the case for correlations between biology and psychology in terms of directly observable animal behavior. Recall the difficulty Freud mentions having, in the passages cited in Part One, in demonstrating the existence of those biological instincts which create a state of war within the human being. Darwin is resolved to create a theory no less sweeping than Freud's, but only out of easily reportable and describable data. Indeed, Freud pays tribute to Darwin throughout his writings as having laid the solid groundwork for biological formulations of psychological processes.

Two major life-cycle theories of psychological growth are presented here, those of Erik H. Erikson and Lawrence Kohlberg. Erikson studied with Freud and has remained within the psychoanalytic tradition. His work on the life cycle is distinctive, however, in that he formulates the process of growth in terms of conflicts which human beings experience in a definable sequence; the actual process of growing is for Erikson a process of working through each of these conflicts. For Erikson, the gaining of psychological strength derives from these experiences of conflict, so that "strength" implies both a power of mastery and a capacity for openness to internal disorder.

As an example of how increased powers of objectification emerge from these conflicts, an excerpt from Ernest G. Schachtel's *Metamorphosis* is presented in which Schachtel explores the development of what he calls "focal attention in children."

And finally, there appears in this section the work of a psychologist who explores the relationship of psychological growth to the development of moral capacities. In one way, Lawrence Kohlberg has converted the idea itself of objectification into a moral Good; in another way, his work harks back to

Mill's belief in the morality of contractual interchange, only now the "contract" becomes a form of psychological mutuality which transcends the formal and legal contracts of society. The reader should know that the editor has interwoven two different articles of Kohlberg's together into one; in the more popular of the two articles Kohlberg had begun to do this himself, and that procedure has simply been extended here.

25. Giambattista Vico: *The New Science* [1668–1744]

The nature of institutions is nothing but their coming into being at certain times and in certain guises. Whenever the time and guise are defined so are the institutions defined that come into being.

The inseparable properties of institutions must be due to the modification or guise with which they are born. By these properties we may therefore verify that the nature or birth is still the nature of the institutions, that how they were born makes them what they still are. . . .

When men are ignorant of the natural causes producing things, and cannot even explain them by analogy with similar things, they attribute their own nature to them. The vulgar, for example, say the magnet loves the iron. The human mind, because of its indefinite nature, wherever it is lost in ignorance makes itself the rule of the universe in respect of everything it does not know. . . . Because of the indefinite nature of the human mind, wherever it is lost in ignorance man makes himself the measure of all things. . . . It is another property of the human mind that whenever men can form no idea of distant and unknown things, they judge them by what is familiar and at hand. . . .

The human mind is naturally inclined by the senses to see itself externally in the body, and only with great difficulty does it come to understand itself by means of reflection. This axiom gives us the universal principle of etymology in all languages: words are carried over from bodies and from the properties of bodies to signify the institutions of the mind and spirit. . . .

There must in the nature of human institutions be a mental language common to all nations, which uniformly grasps the substance of things feasible in human social life and expresses it with as many diverse modifications as these same things may have diverse aspects. . . . This common mental language is proper to our Science, by whose light linguistic scholars will be enabled to construct a mental vocabulary common to all the various articulate languages living and dead. . . .

The nature of children is such that by the ideas and names associated with the first men, women, and things they have known, they afterward apprehend and name all the men, women, and things which have any resemblance or relation to the first. . . . In children memory is most vigorous, and imagination is therefore excessively vivid, for imagination is nothing but extended or compounded memory. This axiom is the principle of the expressiveness of the poetic images that the world formed in its first childhood. . . . The first men, the children, as it were, of the human race, not being able to form intelligible class concepts of things, had a natural need to create poetic characters; that is, imaginative class concepts or universals, to which, as to certain models or ideal portraits, to reduce all the particular species which resembled them. . . .

Children excel in imitation; we observe that they generally amuse themselves by imitating whatever they are able to apprehend. This axiom shows that the world in its infancy was composed of poetic nations, for poetry is nothing but imitation. This axiom will explain the fact that all the arts of the necessary, the useful, the convenient, and even in large part those of human pleasure, were invented in the poetic centuries before the philosophers came; for the arts are nothing but imitations of nature, and in a certain way "real" poems.

26. Charles Darwin: *The Expression of the Emotions in Man and Animals* [1809–1882]

I will begin by giving the three Principles, which appear to me to account for most of the expressions and gestures involuntarily used by man and the lower animals, under the influence of various emotions and sensations. . . . Facts observed both with man and the lower animals will here be made use of; but the latter facts are preferable, as less likely to deceive us. . . .

It appears to me that so many expressions are thus explained in a fairly satisfactory manner, that probably all will hereafter be found to come under the same or closely analogous heads. I need hardly premise that movements or changes in any part of the body,—as the wagging of a dog's tail, the drawing back of a horse's ears, the shrugging of a man's shoulders, or the dilatation of the capillary vessels of the skin,—may all equally well serve for expression. The three Principles are as follows. . . .

I. *The principle of serviceable associated Habits.*—Certain complex actions are of direct or indirect service under certain states of the mind, in order to relieve or gratify certain sensations, desires, &c.; and whenever the same state of mind is induced, however feebly, there is a tendency through the force of habit and association for the same movements to be performed, though they may not then be of the least use. Some actions ordinarily associated through habit with certain states of the mind may be partially repressed through the will, and in such cases the muscles which are least under the separate control of the will are the most liable still to act, causing movements which we recognise as expressive. In certain other cases the checking of one habitual movement requires other slight movements; and these are likewise expressive.

II. *The principle of Antithesis.*—Certain states of the mind lead to certain habitual actions, which are of service, as under our first principle. Now when a directly opposite state of mind is induced, there is a strong and involuntary tendency to the performance of movements of a directly opposite nature, though these are of no use; and such movements are in some cases highly expressive.

III. *The principle of actions due to the constitution of the Nervous System, independently from the first of the Will, and independently to a certain extent of Habit.*—When the sensorium is strongly excited, nerve-force is generated in excess, and is transmitted in certain definite directions, depending on the connection of the nerve-cells, and partly on habit: or the supply of nerve-force may, as it appears, be interrupted. Effects are thus produced which we recognise as expressive. This third principle may, for the sake of brevity, be called that of the direct action of the nervous system.

With respect to our *first Principle,* it is notorious how powerful is the force of habit. The most complex and difficult movements can in time be performed without the least effort or consciousness. . . . That they are inherited we see with horses in certain transmitted paces, such as cantering and ambling, which are not natural to them,—in the pointing of young pointers and the setting of young setters—in the peculiar manner of flight of certain breeds of the pigeon, &c. We have analogous cases with mankind in the inheritance of tricks or unusual gestures. . . . When our minds are much affected, so are the movements of our bodies. . . . Reflex actions, in the strict sense of the term, are due to the excitement of a peripheral nerve, which transmits its influence to certain nerve-cells, and these in their turn excite certain muscles or glands into action; and all this may take place without any sensation or consciousness on our part, though often thus accompanied. . . .

Some actions, which were at first performed consciously, have become through habit and association converted into reflex actions, and are now so firmly fixed and inherited, that they are performed, even when not of the least use, as often as the same causes arise, which originally excited them in us through the volition. . . . When any sensation, desire, dislike, &c., has led during a long series of generations to some voluntary move-ment, then a tendency to the performance of a similar move-ment will almost certainly be excited, whenever the same, or any analogous or associated sensation &c., although very weak, is experienced; notwithstanding that the movement in this case may not be of the least use. Such habitual movements are often, or generally inherited; and they then differ but little from reflex actions. When we treat of the special expressions of man, the latter part of our first Principle, as given at the commencement of this chapter, will be seen to hold good; namely, that when movements, associated through habit with certain states of the mind, are partially repressed by the will, the strictly involuntary muscles, as well as those which are least under the separate control of the will, are liable still to act; and their action is often highly expressive. Conversely, when the will is temporarily or permanently weakened, the voluntary muscles fail before the involuntary. . . .

With respect to the expressive movements due to the prin-ciple of antithesis, it is clear that the will has intervened, though in a remote and indirect manner. So again with the movements coming under our third principle; these, in as far as they are influenced by nerve-force readily passing along habitual chan-nels, have been determined by former and repeated exertions of the will. The effects indirectly due to this latter agency are often combined in a complex manner, through the force of habit and association, with those directly resulting from the excitement of the cerebro-spinal system. This seems to be the case with the increased action of the heart under the influence of any strong emotion. When an animal erects its hair, assumes a threatening attitude, and utters fierce sounds, in order to terrify an enemy, we see a curious combination of movements which were origi-nally voluntary with those that are involuntary. It is, however, possible that even strictly involuntary actions, such as the erec-tion of the hair, may have been affected by the mysterious power of the will. . . .

I have often felt much difficulty about the proper applica-tion of the terms, will, consciousness, and intention. Actions, which were at first voluntary, soon become habitual, and at last hereditary, and may then be performed even in opposition to the will. Although they often reveal the state of the mind, this result was not at first either intended or expected. Even such words as that "certain movements serve as a means of expression" are apt to mislead, as they imply that this was their primary purpose or object. This, however, seems rarely or never to have been the case; the movements having been at first either of some direct use, or the indirect effect of the excited state of the sensorium. An infant may scream either intentionally or instinctively to show that it wants food; but it has no wish or intention to draw its features into the peculiar form which so plainly indicates misery; yet some of the most characteristic expressions exhibited by man are derived from the act of screaming. . . .

I have endeavoured to show in considerable detail that all the chief expressions exhibited by man are the same throughout the world. This fact is interesting, as it affords a new argument in favour of the several races being descended from a single parent-stock, which must have been almost completely human in structure, and to a large extent in mind, before the period at which the races diverged from each other. No doubt similar structures, adapted for the same purpose, have often been independently acquired through variation and natural selection by distinct species; but this view will not explain close similarity between distinct species in a multitude of unimportant details. Now if we bear in mind the numerous points of structure having no relation to expression, in which all the races of man closely agree, and then add to them the numerous points, some of the highest importance and many of the most trifling value, on which the movements of expression directly or indirectly depend, it seems to me improbable in the highest degree that so much similarity, or rather identity of structure, could have been acquired by independent means. Yet this must have been the case if the races of man are descended from several aboriginally distinct species. It is far more probable that the many points of close similarity in the various races are due to inheritance from a single parent-form, which had already assumed a human character.

27. Erik H. Erikson:
"Growth and Crises of the Healthy
Personality"   [1902–]

The Fact-finding Committee of the White House Conference on Childhood and Youth has asked me to repeat here in greater detail a few ideas set forth in another context (Erikson, 1950a). There the matter of the healthy personality emerges, as if accidentally, from a variety of clinical and anthropological considerations. Here it is to become the central theme.

An expert, it is said, can separate fact from theory, and knowledge from opinion. It is his job to know the available techniques by which statements in his field can be verified. If, in this paper, I were to restrict myself to what is, in this sense, *known* about the "healthy personality," I would lead the reader and myself into a very honorable but very uninspiring austerity. In the matter of man's relation to himself and to others, methodological problems are not such as to be either instructive or suggestive in a short treatise.

On the other hand, if I were to write this paper in order to give another introduction to the theory of Freudian psychoanalysis, I would hardly contribute much to an understanding of the healthy personality. For the psychoanalyst knows very much more about the dynamics and cure of the disturbances which he treats daily than about the prevention of such disturbances.

I will, however, start out from Freud's far-reaching discovery that neurotic conflict is not very different in content from the conflicts which every child must live through in his child-

The original version of this paper appeared in *Symposium on the Healthy Personality*, Supplement II; Problems of Infancy and Childhood, Transactions of Fourth Conference, March, 1950, M.J.E. Senn, ed. New York: Josiah Macy, Jr. Foundation.

hood, and that every adult carries these conflicts with him in the recesses of his personality. I shall take account of this fact by stating for each childhood stage what these critical psychological conflicts are. For man, to remain psychologically alive, must resolve these conflicts unceasingly, even as his body must unceasingly combat the encroachment of physical decomposition. However, since I cannot accept the conclusion that just to be alive, or not to be sick, means to be healthy, I must have recourse to a few concepts which are not part of the official terminology of my field. Being interested also in cultural anthropology, I shall try to describe those elements of a really healthy personality which—so it seems to me—are most noticeably absent or defective in neurotic patients and which are most obviously present in the kind of man that educational and cultural systems seem to be striving, each in its own way, to create, to support, and to maintain.

I shall present human growth from the point of view of the conflicts, inner and outer, which the healthy personality weathers, emerging and re-emerging with an increased sense of inner unity, with an increase of good judgment, and an increase in the capacity to do well, according to the standards of those who are significant to him. The use of the words "to do well," of course, points up the whole question of cultural relativity. For example, those who are significant to a man may think he is doing well when he "does some good"; or when he "does well" in the sense of acquiring possessions; or when he is doing well in the sense of learning new skills or new ways of understanding or mastering reality; or when he is not much more than just getting along.

Formulations of what constitutes a healthy personality in an adult are presented in other parts of the Fact-finding Committee's work. If I may take up only one, namely, Marie Jahoda's (1950) definition, according to which a healthy personality *actively masters his environment,* shows a certain *unity of personality,* and is able to *perceive the world and himself correctly,* it is clear that all of these criteria are relative to the child's cognitive and social development. In fact, we may say that childhood is defined by their initial absence and by their gradual development in many complicated steps. I consider it my task to approach this question from the genetic point of view: How does a healthy personality grow or, as it were, accrue from the successive stages of increasing capacity to master life's outer and inner dangers—with some vital enthusiasm to spare?

ON HEALTH AND GROWTH

Whenever we try to understand growth, it is well to remember the *epigenetic principle* which is derived from the growth of organisms *in utero*. Somewhat generalized, this principle states that anything that grows has a *ground plan,* and that out of this ground plan the *parts* arise, each part having its *time* of special ascendancy, until all parts have arisen to form a *functioning whole.* At birth the baby leaves the chemical exchange of the womb for the social exchange system of his society, where his gradually increasing capacities meet the opportunities and limitations of his culture. How the maturing organism continues to unfold, not by developing new organs, but by a prescribed sequence of locomotor, sensory, and social capacities, is described in the child-development literature. Psychoanalysis has given us an understanding of the more idiosyncratic experiences and especially the inner conflicts, which constitute the manner in which an individual becomes a distinct personality. But here, too, it is important to realize that in the sequence of his most personal experiences the healthy child, given a reasonable amount of guidance, can be trusted to obey inner laws of development, laws which create a *succession of potentialities for significant interaction* with those who tend him. While such interaction varies from culture to culture, it must remain within the *proper rate and the proper sequence* which govern the *growth of a personality* as well as that of an organism. Personality can be said to develop according to steps predetermined in the human organism's readiness to be driven toward, to be aware of, and to interact with, a widening social radius, beginning with the dim image of a mother and ending with mankind, or at any rate that segment of mankind which "counts" in the particular individual's life.

It is for this reason that, in the presentation of stages in the development of the personality, we employ an *epigenetic dia-*

gram analogous to one previously employed for an analysis of Freud's psychosexual stages.[1] It is, in fact, the purpose of this presentation to bridge the theory of infantile sexuality (without repeating it here in detail), and our knowledge of the child's physical and social growth within his family and the social structure. An epigenetic diagram looks like this (see Diagram A, p. 214).

The double-lined squares signify both a sequence of stages (I to III) and a gradual development of component parts; in other words the diagram formalizes a *progression through time of a differentiation of parts.* This indicates (1) that each item of the healthy personality to be discussed is *systematically related to all others,* and that they all depend on the *proper development in the proper sequence of each item;* and (2) that each item *exists in some form before "its" decisive and critical time* normally arrives.

If I say, for example, that a *sense of basic trust* is the first component of mental health to develop in life, a *sense of autonomous will* the second, and a *sense of initiative* the third, the purpose of the diagram may become clearer (see Diagram B, p. 214).

This diagrammatic statement, in turn, is meant to express a number of fundamental relations that exist among the three components, as well as a few fundamental facts for each.

Each comes to its ascendance, meets its crisis, and finds its lasting solution (in ways to be described here) *toward the end of the stages* mentioned. All of them exist in the beginning in some form, although we do not make a point of this fact, and we shall not confuse things by calling these components different names at earlier or later stages. A baby may show something like "autonomy" from the beginning, for example, in the particular way in which he angrily tries to wriggle his hand free when tightly held. However, under normal conditions, it is not until the second year that he begins to experience the whole *critical alternative between being an autonomous creature and being a dependent one;* and it is not until then that he is ready for a *decisive encounter* with his environment, an environment which, in turn, feels called upon to convey to him its *particular*

[1] See Part I of the author's *Childhood and Society* (1950a).

Diagram A

	Component 1	Component 2	Component 3
Stage I	I_1	I_2	I_3
Stage II	II_1	II_2	II_3
Stage III	III_1	III_2	III_3

DIAGRAM A

Diagram B

	Component 1	Component 2	Component 3
First Stage (about first year)	BASIC TRUST	Earlier form of AUTONOMY	Earlier form of INITIATIVE
Second Stage (about second and third years)	Later form of BASIC TRUST	AUTONOMY	Earlier form of INITIATIVE
Third Stage (about fourth and fifth years)	Later form of BASIC TRUST	Later form of AUTONOMY	INITIATIVE

DIAGRAM B

ideas and concepts of autonomy and coercion in ways decisively contributing to the character, the efficiency, and the health of his personality in his culture.

It is this *encounter,* together with the resulting crisis, which is to be described for each stage. Each stage becomes a *crisis* because incipient growth and awareness in a significant part function goes together with a shift in instinctual energy and yet causes specific vulnerability in that part. One of the most difficult questions to decide, therefore, is whether or not a child at a given stage is weak or strong. Perhaps it would be best to say that he is always vulnerable in some respects and completely oblivious and insensitive in others, but that at the same time he is unbelievably persistent in the same respects in which he is vulnerable. It must be added that the smallest baby's weakness gives him power; out of his very dependence and weakness he makes signs to which his environment (if it is guided well by a responsiveness based both on instinctive and traditional patterns) is peculiarly sensitive. A baby's presence exerts a consistent and persistent domination over the outer and inner lives of every member of a household. Because these members must reorient themselves to accommodate his presence, they must also grow as individuals and as a group. It is as true to say that babies control and bring up their families as it is to say the converse. A family can bring up a baby only by being brought up by him. His growth consists of a series of challenges to them to serve his newly developing potentialities for social interaction.

Each successive step, then, is a potential crisis because of a radical *change in perspective.* There is, at the beginning of life, the most radical change of all: from intrauterine to extrauterine life. But in postnatal existence, too, such radical adjustments of perspective as lying relaxed, sitting firmly, and running fast must all be accomplished in their own good time. With them, the interpersonal perspective, too, changes rapidly and often radically, as is testified by the proximity in time of such opposites as "not letting mother out of sight" and "wanting to be independent." Thus, *different capacities use different opportunities* to become full-grown components of the ever-new configuration that is the growing personality.

Erik H. Erikson: "The Problem of Ego Identity"

SOCIETAL: EGO AND ENVIRONMENT

I

It has not escaped the reader that the term identity covers much of what has been called the self by a variety of workers, be it in the form of a self-concept (George H. Mead, 1934), a self-system (Harry S. Sullivan, 1946–1947), or in that of fluctuating self-experiences described by Schilder (1934), Federn (1927–1949), and others.* Within psychoanalytic ego psychology, Hartmann, above all, has circumscribed this general area more clearly when in discussing the so-called *libidinal cathexis of the ego in narcissism,* he comes to the conclusion that it is rather a self which is thus being cathected. He advocates a term *"self-representation,"* as differentiated from "object representation" (Hartmann, 1950). This self-representation was, less systematically, anticipated by Freud in his occasional references to the ego's "attitudes toward the self" and to fluctuating cathexes bestowed upon this self in labile states of "self-esteem" (Freud,

---

* I am not yet able to establish the systematic convergencies and divergencies between the work of the so-called "Neo-Freudians" and that which I am trying to formulate. It will be seen, however, that in individuals as well as in groups I prefer to speak of a "sense of identity" rather than of a "character structure" or "basic character." In nations, too, my concepts would lead me to concentrate on the conditions and experiences which heighten or endanger a national sense of identity rather than on a static national character. An introduction to this subject is offered in my book, *Childhood and Society* (1950a). Here it is important to remember that each identity cultivates its own sense of freedom—wherefore a people rarely understands what makes other peoples feel free. This fact is amply exploited by totalitarian propaganda and underestimated in the Western world.

1914). In this paper, we are concerned with the *genetic continuity* of such a self-representation—a continuity which must lastly be ascribed to the work of the ego. No other inner agency could accomplish the selective accentuation of significant identifications throughout childhood and the gradual integration of self-images in anticipation of an identity. It is for this reason that I have called identity, at first, ego identity. But in brashly choosing a name analogous to "ego ideal," I have opened myself to the query as to what the relationship of these two concepts is.

Freud assigned the *internalized perpetuation* of cultural influences to the functions of the "superego or ego ideal" which was to represent the commands and the prohibitions emanating from the environment and its traditions. Let us compare two statements of Freud's which are relevant here. ". . . the superego of the child is not really built up on the model of the parents, but on that of the parents' super-ego; it takes over the same content, it becomes the vehicle of tradition and of all the age-long values which have been handed down in this way from generation to generation. You may easily guess what great help is afforded by the recognition of the super-ego in understanding the social behavior of man, in grasping the problem of delinquency, for example, and perhaps, too, in providing us with some practical hints upon education. . . . Mankind never lives completely in the present; the *ideologies of the super-ego** perpetuate the past, the traditions of the race and the people, which yield but slowly to the influence of the present and to new developments, and, so long as they work through the super-ego, play an important part in man's life" (Freud, 1932, pp. 95–96). Freud, it is to be noted here, speaks of the "ideologies of the super-ego," thus giving the superego ideational content; yet he also refers to it as a "vehicle," i.e., as a part of the psychic system through which ideas work. It would seem that by ideologies of the superego Freud means the superego's specific contributions to the archaic, to the magic in the inner coerciveness of ideologies.

In a second statement Freud acknowledges the social side of the ego ideal. "The ego ideal opens up an important avenue

* [Erikson's] italics.

for the understanding of group psychology. In addition to its individual side, this ideal has a social side; it is also the common ideal of a family, a class or a nation" (1914, p. 101).

It would seem that the terms superego and ego ideal have come to be distinguished by their different relation to phylogenetic and to ontogenetic history. The superego is conceived as a more archaic and thoroughly internalized representative of the evolutionary principle of morality, of man's *congenital proclivity* toward the development of a primitive, categorical conscience. Allied with (ontogenetically) early introjects, the superego remains a rigidly vindictive and punitive inner agency of "blind" morality. The ego ideal, however, seems to be more flexibly bound to the ideals of the particular *historical period* and thus is closer to the ego function of reality testing.

Ego identity (if we were to hold on to this term and to this level of discourse) would in comparison be even closer to *social reality* in that as a subsystem of the ego it would test, select, and integrate the self-representations derived from the psychosocial crises of childhood. It could be said to be characterized by the more or less *actually attained but forever-to-be-revised* sense of the reality of the self within social reality; while the imagery of the ego ideal could be said to represent a set of *to-be-strived-for but forever-not-quite-attainable ideal* goals for the self.

However, in using the word self in the sense of Hartmann's self-representation, one opens the whole controversy to a radical consideration. One could argue that it may be wise in matters of the ego's perceptive and regulative dealings with its self to reserve the designation "ego" for the subject, and to give the designation "self" to the object. The ego, then, as a central organizing agency, is during the course of life faced with a changing self which, in turn, demands to be synthesized with abandoned and anticipated selves. This suggestion would be applicable to the *body ego,* which could be said to be the part of the self provided by the attributes of the organism, and therefore, might more appropriately be called the *body self;* it would also concern the ego ideal as the representative of the ideas, images, and configurations, which serve the persistent comparison with an *ideal self;* and finally, it would apply to what I have called *ego iden-*

tity. What could consequently be called the *self-identity* emerges from all those experiences in which a sense of temporary self-diffusion was successfully contained by a renewed and ever more realistic self-definition and social recognition. *Identity formation thus can be said to have a self-aspect, and an ego aspect.* It is part of the ego in the sense that it represents the ego's synthesizing function on one of its frontiers, namely, the actual social structure of the environment and the image of reality as transmitted to the child during successive childhood crises. (The other frontiers would be the id, and the demands made on the ego by our biological history and structure; the superego and the demands of our more primitively moralistic proclivities; and the ego ideal with its idealized parent images.) Identity, in this connection, has a claim to recognition as the adolescent ego's most important support, in the task of containing the postpubertal id, and in balancing the then newly invoked superego as well as the again overly demanding ego ideal.

Until the matter of ego vs. self is sufficiently defined to permit a terminological decision, I shall use the bare term identity in order to suggest a social function of the ego which results, in adolescence, in a relative psychosocial equilibrium essential to the tasks of young adulthood.

II

The word "psychosocial" so far has had to serve as an emergency bridge between the so-called "biological" formulations of psychoanalysis and newer ones which take the cultural environment into more systematic consideration.

The so-called basic *biological* orientation of psychoanalysis has gradually become a habitual kind of *pseudo biology,* and this especially in the conceptualization (or lack thereof) of man's "environment." In psychoanalytic writings the terms "outer world" or "environment" are often used to designate an uncharted area which is said to be outside merely because it fails to be inside—inside the individual's somatic skin, or inside his psychic systems, or inside his self in the widest sense. Such a vague and yet omni-present "outerness" by necessity assumes a number of ideological connotations, and, in fact, assumes the character of a number of world images: sometimes "the outer world" is conceived of as reality's conspiracy against the infantile wish world; sometimes as the (indifferent or annoying) fact of the existence of other people; and then again as the (at least partially benevolent) presence of maternal care. But even in the recent admission of the significance of the "mother-child relationship," a stubborn tendency persists to treat the mother-child unit as a "biological" entity more or less isolated from its cultural surroundings, which then again become an "environment" of vague supports or of blind pressures and mere "conventions." Thus, step for step, we are encumbered by the remnants of juxtapositions which were once necessary and fruitful enough: for it was important to establish the fact that moralistic and hypocritical social demands are apt to crush the adult and to exploit the child. It was important to conceptualize certain intrinsic antagonisms between the individual's and society's energy households. However, the implicit conclusion that an individual ego could exist against or without a specifically human "environment," i.e., social organization, is senseless; and, far from being "biological" in its orientation, threatens to isolate psychoanalytic theory from the rich ethological and ecological findings of modern biology.

It is again Hartmann (1939) who opens the way to new considerations. His statement that the human infant is born preadapted to an "average expectable environment" implies a more truly biological as well as an inescapably societal formulation. For not even the very best of mother-child relationships could, by themselves, account for that subtle and complex "milieu" which permits a human baby not only to survive but also to develop his potentialities for growth and uniqueness. Man's ecology includes among its dimensions constant natural, historical, and technological readjustment; which makes it at once obvious that only a perpetual social metabolism and a constant (if ever so imperceptible) restructuring of tradition can safeguard for each new generation of infants anything approaching an "average expectability" of environment. Today, when rapid technological changes have taken the lead, the matter of establishing by scientific means and of preserving in flexible forms an "average expectable" continuity in child rearing and education has, in fact, become a matter of human survival.

The specific kind of preadaptedness of the human infant (namely, the readiness to grow by predetermined steps through institutionalized psychosocial crises) calls not only for one basic environment, but for a whole chain of such successive environments. As the child "adapts" in spurts and stages, he has a claim, at any given stage reached, to the next "average expectable environment." In other words, the human environment must permit and safeguard a series of more or less discontinuous and yet culturally and psychologically consistent steps, each extending further along the radius of expanding life tasks. All of this makes man's so-called biological adaptation a matter of life cycles developing within their community's changing history. Consequently, a psychoanalytic sociology faces the task of conceptualizing man's environment as the persistent endeavor of the older and more adult egos to join in the organizational effort of providing an integrated series of average expectable environments for the young egos.

28. Ernest G. Schachtel: *Metamorphosis*
[1903–]

The theory of attention is crucial for an understanding of both consciousness and repression. In developing a dynamic theory of attention, Freud formulated this insight by saying that "the act of becoming conscious depends upon a definite psychic function—attention—being brought to bear." Not all acts of attention, however, shed the full light of consciousness on the matter attended. For instance, something that strikes one's attention may lead to flight, to a turning away, if it arouses anxiety; and it may lead to an act of *focal attention* if it arouses one's curiosity. By "focal attention," as distinguished from other forms of attention, I designate man's capacity to *center* his attention on an object fully, so that he can perceive or understand it from *many sides,* as clearly as possible. In this presentation, I shall attempt to show (1) that focal attention is the main instrument which, as it gradually develops, enables man to progress from the primitive mental activity of wishing or wanting (primary-process thought) to a grasp of reality (secondary-process thought); and (2) that man's grasp of reality is not merely based on his wish to satisfy primary, biological needs—is not merely, as Freud assumed, a detour on the path to wish fulfillment—but that it also has as a prerequisite an autonomous interest in the environment. Focal attention is the tool of this interest; it appears first in the child's exploratory play and requires relative freedom from need and anxiety. . . .

The most important of the distinguishing characteristics of focal attention are these: (1) Acts of focal attention are *directional;* they do not concern the total field—that is, they are not global, as the most primitive forms of experience are, but focus attention in a particular direction. (2) They are directed at a *particular object,* which may be an external object or an internal object, such as a thought or a feeling. (3) They take hold of the object and aim at its active mental grasp. (4) Each focal act, as a rule, consists of not just *one* sustained approach to the object to which it is directed but *several renewed* approaches. These approaches explore different aspects and relations of the object. Not only are they made from different angles, as it were, but often they are made repeatedly from the same angle and directed at the same facet of the object in an attempt to assimilate it more thoroughly. They also usually—probably always— alternate or oscillate between a more passive, receptive, reactive phase and a more active, taking-hold, structuring, integrating phase. The relation of these two phases to each other and their relative predominance vary considerably both inter- and intraindividually. (5) Acts of focal attention *exclude* the rest of the field (environmental and internal) from that form of consciousness which is designated as focal awareness. . . .

I want to discuss briefly here only one often observed fact: a childs' pleasure in, and insistence on, being read or told the same story over and over again. This discussion will (1) serve as an example for a more detailed description of the exploratory function of focal attention, and (2) show that the child's insistence on repetition is not due primarily to an inertia principle but, on the contrary, is essential for the productive work of exploring and assimilating the objects of the environment—in this case, an object of the cultural environment.

Adult observers have often been struck by the disturbance a child may show at the slightest change—even one word—in a story which has been repeated for the child. This disturbance does not seem to make much sense to the adult mind. What is the difference if a minor episode or a mere word is changed, as long as the main drift of events is retained in the story? This viewpoint overlooks the enormous difference in meaning which the repetition of a story has for the child who listens to it with absorption and for the adult who is bored by it. One tries in vain to encompass the child's experience with categories of the adult mind which are not suitable for grasping the meaning of the situation for the child.

What are the decisive differences between the child's and the adult's experience in listening to the same story over and over again? The age at which such repetition is desired and enjoyed by the child is roughly from two to five years, with considerable individual variation. At the beginning of this period, the child has already learned to perceive distinct and concrete objects, but this learning must necessarily continue, for the object world of the child is constantly and rapidly expanding, and increasingly includes such complicated objects as words and pictures which denote or represent other objects. However, the manner in which discrete objects are perceived by the young child differs a great deal from the manner in which they are perceived by the older child and the adult. The young child perceives objects much more globally and concretely than the older child or adult. This implies that "any phenomenon known in terms of qualities-of-the-whole, rather than in terms of strictly articulated qualities, is apt to be seen by the young child as undergoing a complete change, even if no more than minor details in the situation are altered." From the young child's viewpoint, none of the many elements making up the global situation "need be more essential than any other, since all of them contribute to the characteristic coloration, or tone, of the situational totality."

Since a story contains not only many different objects but also many different relationships among these objects, which unfold in a definite sequence of events, it is much more complex than even the most complex objects in the child's environment. For the young child to grasp and digest a story requires an amount of attention and of effort at understanding which the adult is incapable of imagining, since his grasp of a story rests not only on years of training but also on a quite different, much more abstractive kind of perception and understanding. Only by repeated acts of focal attention, which at one time turn more to one part, at other times to other parts, can the child very gradually come to understand and assimilate a story. A particular part of the story may become something to wonder about even if on some other day it seemed already familiar or not worthy of special attention. To encompass all of it is no small achievement. What if the story should change as the child tries to get hold of it? Any change makes it elusive and frustrates the child's effort to master it. The attempt to assimilate a particular story requires a complex labor of attention and thought; in fact, it usually involves the child's learning the story by heart. This learning-by-heart is a by-product of the child's innumerable acts of focal attention toward the story as a whole and toward its different parts, and of the child's feelings about the story. The fact that this learning-by-heart comes as a by-product—much in contrast to later learning-by-heart in school—indicates the difference in degree and quality of attention between the young child's and the older child's or adult's listening to a story.

The young child who listens to the story not only is engaged in assimilating its complex fabric but, in addition to that, is confronted with the equally or even more difficult problem of finding his way in the puzzling distinctions between reality, representations of reality, possibility, and sheer phantasy. Just as the task of learning that a picture can represent a real object but that it is different from the real object is not an easy one and takes considerable time and effort to master, so it is a difficult task to learn about the various possible relations between a story and reality. Furthermore, it is of great importance to the child that he can *rely* on the story—that it does not suddenly disappear, that it is still there. This is just as important as to be able to rely on the fact that a toy in which the child is interested will not vanish overnight. Before the child can read, the only way to be sure that he can rely on a story is by having it reread or retold to him and making quite sure that it is really the same story.

A change in the story is about as upsetting to the child as it might be to an adult to discover that overnight the table in the living room had changed its shape. The idea that one can *make* a story, hence also *change* it, dawns much later on the child than the earlier implicit conviction that a story is a piece of reality on which one can rely, so that any change of it interferes drastically with the important task of getting thoroughly acquainted with this particular piece of reality. . . .

Moreover, a proper comparison, I believe, of a child's attitude toward a story can be made only with an adult's attitude toward an object of *similar significance*. The story, to the child, is at first strange country which he gradually explores and in which new discoveries are always possible. A comparable relationship exists in our culture between the appreciative adult and a work of art, a piece of music, or a poem. One does not tire easily of looking again and again at a cherished painting, of listening many times over to a beloved piece of music or a poem. Every renewed encounter may reveal new aspects and lead to deeper understanding. Any change in the poem, the painting, the music would destroy it. Because of the quasi-organic, lifelike character of the real work of art, such a change would indeed make it into something very different.

In other words, if the adult matures to a stage where he is capable of meaningful encounter with a significant human creation, then his relationship to this creation is likely to require many contacts with it, just as the child's relationship to the story does. The meaning of such significant encounters is very different from the kind of reading or listening which has the purpose of killing time, of being entertained passively or thrilled and titillated. For inherent in every real encounter with a work of art, a myth, a fairy tale is an active effort of the total personality, which is also inherent—in a somewhat different way—in the child's attempt to gradually assimilate the story. The motive of inertia seems to me considerably stronger in the adult who wants to see a new movie or read a new mystery every night than in the child who wants to hear the same story retold. The former avoids meaningful and enriching experience; the latter seeks it.

Thus the child's insistence on repetition of the same story serves primarily the purpose of assimilating it, of getting fully acquainted with all its aspects by many acts of focal attention, and of making quite sure that it is still there and can be explored and enjoyed with some measure of dependability. . . .

Focal attention to people is slower and longer in developing than focal attention to other objects of the environment. Even after the child has developed the capacity for object-centered focal attention with regard to his peers or to some adults, his own parents still may not be seen focally—that is, from all sides and in all their aspects. The reason for this is, of course, that the parents, especially the mother, are of such overwhelming significance as the need-satisfying and also as the anxiety-arousing "objects" that they are relatively slow in emerging for the child as people with an existence of their own, independent of the child's needs and fears. To this is added another factor: Many parents prevent the child from seeing them in all their different aspects, focally, as they really are. They do this out of their own needs and anxieties, in order to perpetuate the child's dependence on them, or in order to maintain in their own and their children's minds an idealized image of themselves as the good or model parents. To this end they discourage, consciously as well as unconsciously, the childs' focally attentive and explorative approach. The parents must not have any weaknesses or shortcomings; the child must not be critical of them; they must be exempt from the realistic curiosity of the child. Thus the idea that parents are people about whom one may have opinions and whom one may critically judge—that they are people like other people—may come as a shock to the child, or, indeed, may never occur to him. If the parent, by forbidding gestures or other manifestations of the parental tabu on focal attention to the parent as a person, arouses sufficiently severe and pervasive anxiety in the child, such anxiety will interfere effectively with any focal attention toward the parent and, possibly, toward people in general. Thus people will continue to be experienced predominantly as anxiety-arousing and need-satisfying "objects" by the person whose focal attention to the parents has been disrupted and diverted by anxiety. Actually, this is the case, to a greater or lesser extent, in most neurotic and psychotic patients. This same strategy of arousing fear in order to discourage focal attention toward a person, a problem, a situation—to discourage exploring them from all angles, objectively—has always been and continues to be favored as an instrument of *social power;* it is used by all those who have a stake in hindering or preventing man's search for truth and freedom, who thereby maintain their own irrational authority unquestioned.

29. Lawrence Kohlberg: "The Cognitive-Developmental Approach to Moral Education" and "The Claim to Moral Adequacy of a Highest Stage of Moral Judgment"   [1927–]

The cognitive-developmental approach was fully stated for the first time by John Dewey. The approach is called *cognitive* because it recognizes that moral education, like intellectual education, has its basis in stimulating the *active thinking* of the child about moral issues and decisions. It is called developmental because it sees the aims of moral education as movement through moral stages. . . .

The concept of stages (as used by Piaget and myself) implies the following characteristics:

1. Stages are "structured wholes," or organized systems of thought. Individuals are *consistent* in level of moral judgment.

2. Stages form an *invariant sequence*. Under all conditions except extreme trauma, movement is always forward, never backward. Individuals never skip stages; movement is always to the next stage up.

3. Stages are "hierarchical integrations." Thinking at a higher stage includes or comprehends within it lower-stage thinking. There is a tendency to function at or prefer the highest stage available. . . .

Over a period of almost twenty years of empirical research, my colleagues and I have rather firmly established a culturally universal invariant sequence of stages of moral judgment; these stages are grossly summarized in Table 1:

Table 1. Definition of Moral Stages

I. Preconventional level

At this level the child is responsive to cultural rules and labels of good and bad, right or wrong, but interprets these labels either in terms of the physical or the hedonistic consequences of action (punishment, reward, exchange of favors) or in terms of the physical power of those who enunciate the rules and labels. The level is divided into the following two stages:

Stage 1: *The punishment-and-obedience orientation.* The physical consequences of action determine its goodness or badness regardless of the human meaning or value of these consequences. Avoidance of punishment and unquestioning deference to power are valued in their own right, not in terms of respect for an underlying moral order supported by punishment and authority (the latter being stage 4).

Stage 2: *The instrumental-relativist orientation.* Right action consists of that which instrumentally satisfies one's own needs and occasionally the needs of others. Human relations are viewed in terms like those of the market place. Elements of fairness, of reciprocity, and of equal sharing are present, but they are always interpreted in a physical pragmatic way. Reciprocity is a matter of "you scratch my back and I'll scratch yours," not of loyalty, gratitude, or justice.

II. Conventional level

At this level, maintaining the expectations of the individual's family, group, or nation is perceived as valuable in its own right, regardless of immediate and obvious consequences. The attitude is not only one of *conformity* to personal expectations and social order, but of loyalty to it, of actively *maintaining*, supporting, and justifying the order, and of identifying with the persons or group involved in it. At this level, there are the following two stages:

Stage 3: *The interpersonal concordance or "good boy—nice girl" orientation.* Good behavior is that which pleases or helps others and is approved by them. There is much conformity to stereotypical images of what is majority or "natural" behavior. Behavior is frequently judged by intention—"he means well" becomes important for the first time. One earns approval by being "nice."

Stage 4: *The "law and order" orientation.* There is orientation toward authority, fixed rules, and the maintenance of the social order. Right behavior consists of doing one's duty, showing respect for authority, and maintaining the given social order for its own sake.

III. Postconventional, autonomous, or principled level

At this level, there is a clear effort to define moral values and principles that have validity and application apart from the authority of the groups or persons holding these principles and apart from the individual's own identification with these groups. This level again has two stages:

Stage 5: *The social-contract legalistic orientation,* generally with utilitarian overtones. Right action tends to be defined in terms of general individual rights, and standards which have been critically examined and agreed upon by the whole society. There is a clear awareness of the relativism of personal values and opinions and a corresponding emphasis upon procedural rules for reaching consensus. Aside from what is constitutionally and democratically agreed upon, the right is a matter of personal "values" and "opinion." The result is an emphasis upon the "legal point of view," but with an emphasis upon the possibility of changing law in terms of rational considerations of social unity (rather than freezing it in terms of stage 4 "law and order"). Outside the legal realm, free agreement and contract is the binding element of obligation. This is the "official" morality of the American government and constitution.

Stage 6: *The universal-ethical-principle orientation.* Right is defined by the decision of conscience in accord with self-chosen *ethical principles* appealing to logical comprehensiveness, universality, and consistency. These principles are abstract and ethical (the Golden Rule, the categorical imperative); they are not concrete moral rules like the Ten Commandments. At heart, these universal principles of *justice,* of the *reciprocity* and *equality* of human *rights,* and of respect for the dignity of human beings as *individual persons.*

As Table 1 indicates, the last stage, stage 6, has a distinctively Kantian ring, centering moral judgment on concepts of obligation as these are defined by principles of respect for persons and of justice. In part, this corresponds to an initial "formalist" or "structuralist" bias of both our moral and our psychological theory. Our psychological theory of morality derives largely from Piaget, who claims that both logic and morality develop through stages and that each stage is a structure which, formally considered, is in better equilibrium than its predecessor. It assumes, that is, that each new (logical or moral) stage is a new structure which includes elements of earlier structures but transforms them in such a way as to represent a more stable and extensive equilibrium. Our theory assumes that new moral structures presuppose new logical structures, i.e., that a new logical stage (or substage) is a necessary but not sufficient condition for a new moral stage. It assumes, however, that moral judgments (or moral equilibrium) involve two related processes or conditions absent in the logical domain. First, moral judgments involve role-taking, taking the point of view of others conceived as *subjects* and coordinating those points of view, whereas logic involves only coordinating points of view upon objects. Second, equilibrated moral judgments involve principles of justice or fairness. A moral situation in disequilibrium is one in which there are unresolved conflicting claims. A resolution of the situation is one in which each is "given his due" according to some principle of justice that can be recognized as fair by all the conflicting parties involved. . . .

To understand moral stages, it is important to clarify their relations to stage of logic or intelligence, on the one hand, and to moral behavior on the other. Maturity of moral judgment is not highly correlated with IQ or verbal intelligence (correlations are only in the 30s, accounting for 10% of the variance). Cognitive development, in the stage sense, however, is more important for moral development than such correlations suggest. Piaget has found that after the child learns to speak there are three major stages of reasoning: the intuitive, the concrete operational, and the formal operational. At around age 7, the child enters the stage of concrete logical thought: He can make logical inferences, classify, and handle quantitative relations about concrete things. In adolescence individuals usually enter the stage of formal operations. At this stage they can reason abstractly, i.e., consider all possibilities, form hypotheses, deduce implications from hypotheses, and test them against reality.

Since moral reasoning clearly is reasoning, advanced moral reasoning depends upon advanced logical reasoning; a person's logical stage puts a certain ceiling on the moral stage he can attain. . . .

The moral stages are *structures of moral judgment* or *moral reasoning. Structures* of moral judgment must be distinguished from the *content* of moral judgment. As an example, we cite responses to a dilemma used in our various studies to identify moral stage. The dilemma raises the issue of stealing a drug to save a dying woman. The inventor of the drug is selling it for 10 times what it costs him to make it. The woman's husband cannot raise the money, and the seller refuses to lower the price or wait for payment. What should the husband do?

The choice endorsed by a subject (steal, don't steal) is called the *content* of his moral judgment in the situation. His reasoning about the choice defines the structure of his moral judgment. This reasoning centers on the following 10 universal moral values or issues of concern to persons in these moral dilemmas:

1. Punishment
2. Property
3. Roles and concerns of affection
4. Roles and concerns of authority
5. Law
6. Life
7. Liberty
8. Distributive justice
9. Truth
10. Sex

A moral choice involves choosing between two (or more) of these values as they *conflict* in concrete situations of choice.

The stage or structure of a person's moral judgment defines: 1) *what* he finds valuable in each of these moral issues (life, law), i.e., how he defines the value, and 2) *why* he finds it valuable, i.e., the reasons he gives for valuing it. As an example, at Stage 1 life is valued in terms of the power or possessions of the person involved; at Stage 2, for its usefulness in satisfying the needs of the individual in question or others; at Stage 3, in terms of the individual's relations with others and their valuation of him; at Stage 4, in terms of social or religious law. Only at Stages 5 and 6 is each life seen as inherently worthwhile, aside from other considerations. . . .

While moral philosophical criteria of adequacy of moral judgment help define a standard of psychological adequacy or advance, the study of psychological advance feeds back and clarifies these criteria. Our psychological theory as to why individuals move from one stage to the next is grounded on a moral-philosophical theory which specifies that the later stage is morally better or more adequate than the earlier stage. Our psychological theory claims that individuals prefer the highest stage of reasoning they comprehend, a claim supported by research. This claim of our psychological theory derives from a philosophical claim that a later stage is "objectively" preferable or more adequate by certain *moral* criteria. This philosophic claim, however, would for us be thrown into question if the facts of moral advance were inconsistent with its psychological implications. . . .

Assuming for the moment the existence of a natural structure called "stage 6," how can developmental analysis aid in justifying its claim to adequacy? By claiming that stage 6 is more adequate than stage 5 by certain formal criteria which also make stage 5 more adequate than stage 4. Two such criteria are differentiation and integration. In our earlier paper ("From Is to Ought") we elaborated the formal concepts of differentiation and integration that apply to both the psychological and the normative analysis of moral deliberation, and linked the concepts to formalistic concepts of moral judgments as prescriptive and universal. Increased differentiation and integration are anchored in the "is" side by their explanatory power in the study of the development of directed thinking, and on the "ought" side by their necessary inclusion in rational justification and choice. To illustrate how and why this might be the case, we shall consider some usages of the categories of "rights" and "duties" at stages 5 and 6, and the sense in which this suggests that moral theories derived from stage 6 structures are more advanced than moral theories derived from stage 5 structures. Table 2 shows usage of "rights" and "duties" at each stage:

Table 2. Six Stages in the Usage of Categories of Rights and Obligations

Stage 1. *Having a Right:* Means having the power or authority to control something or someone, or it is confused with being right (in accordance with authority).

Obligation: Or "should" is what one "has to do" because of the demands of external authorities, rules, or the external situation.

Stage 2. *Having a Right:* Implies freedom of the self to choose and to control the self and its possessions. One has a right to ignore the positive claims or welfare of another as long as one does not directly violate his freedom, or injure him. (Having a right differentiated from being right, and from being given the power to, by a status one holds.)

Obligation: Obligation or "should" is a hypothetical imperative contingent on choice in terms of an end. In this sense, obligations are limited to oneself and one's ends. ("Should" or obligation differentiated from "has to" from external or authoritative compulsion.)

Stage 3. *Having a Right:* Implies an expectation of control and freedom which a "good" or natural person would claim. A right is based either on a rule or on a legitimate expectation toward others, e.g., you have a right to have your property respected since you worked hard to acquire the property. Rights are earned. (Having a right differentiated from the freedom to control and choose.)

Obligation: "Should" or "duty" equals a role-obligation, what it is incumbent on a member of a social position to do for his role-partners as defined by rules, by the expectation of the role-partner, or by what a good role-occupant (a good husband, a good doctor) would do. (Obligation differentiated from being a means to a desired end.)

Stage 4. *Having a Right:* Rights are: (a) categorical general freedoms and expectations which all members of society have, and (b) rights awarded to particular roles by society. General rights usually take primacy over role-rights. (Having a right differentiated from a particular legitimate expectation).

Obligation: Obligations are responsibilities, i.e., welfare states of others or of society for which one is accountable. These responsibilities arise through: (a) being a member of society, and (b) voluntarily entering into roles which entail these responsibilities. (Obligation or duty as commitment and responsibility differentiated from what is typically expected of a role-occupant.)

Stage 5. *Having a Right:* Has an awareness of human or natural rights or liberties which are prior to society and which society is to protect. It is usually thought by stage 5 that freedoms should be limited by society and law only when they are incompatible with the like freedoms of others. (Natural rights differentiated from societally awarded rights.)

Obligation: Obligations are what one has contracted to fulfill in order to have one's own rights respected and protected. These obligations are defined in terms of a rational concern for the welfare of others. (Obligations as required rational concern for welfare differentiated from fixed responsibilities.)

Stage 6. *Having a Right:* There are universal rights of just treatment which go beyond liberties and which represent universalizable claims of one individual upon another.

Obligation: Any right or just claim by an individual gives use to a corresponding duty to another individual.

Table 2 suggests that each higher stage's usage of the categories of rights and duties is *more differentiated and integrated* than the prior stage. We list, in the parentheses, the differentiation of the concept of "right" and "obligation" made by each stage not made at the prior stages. At stage 2, a right as a freedom is differentiated from a physical or social power; at stage 3 it is differentiated as an expectation to be supported by others from an actual physical or psychological freedom, etc. The sense in which each stage is *better integrated* is seen in the fact that only at stage 6 are rights and duties completely correlative. . . .

Since Kant, formalists have argued that rational moral judgments must be irreversible, consistent, and universalizable, and that this implies the prescriptivity of such judgments. We claim that only the substantive moral judgments made at stage 6 fully meet these conditions, and that each higher stage meets these conditions better than each lower stage. In fully meeting these conditions, stage 6 moral structures are ultimately equilibrated.

For developmental theory, meeting these conditions of moral judgment is parallel with the equilibration of fully logical thought in the realm of physical or logical facts. According to Piaget and others, the keystone of logic is reversibility. A logical train of thought is one in which one can move back and forth between premises and conclusions without distortion. Mathematmaterial thinking is an example; $A + B$ is the same as $B + A$. Or again, the operation $A + B = C$ is reversible by the operation $C - B = A$. In one sense, the elements of reversible moral thought are the moral categories as these apply to the universe of moral actors. To say that rights and duties are correlative is to say that one can move from rights to duties and back without change or distortion. Univeralizability and consistency are fully attained by the reversibility of prescriptions of actions. Reversibility of moral judgment is what is ultimately meant by the criterion of the fairness of a moral decision. Procedurally, fairness as impartiality means reversibility in the sense of a decision on which all interested parties could agree insofar as they can consider their own claims impartially, as the just decider would.

If we have a reversible solution, we have one that could be reached as right starting from anyone's perspective in the situation, given each person's intent to put himself in the shoes of the other.

Reversibility meets a second criterion of formalism: universalizability. As reversibility starts with the slogan, "Put yourself in the other guy's shoes when you decide," universalizability starts with the slogan, "What if everyone did it; what if everyone used this principle of choice?" It is clear that universalizability is implied by reversibility. If something is fair or right to do from the conflicting points of view of all those involved in the situation, it is something we can wish all men to do in all similar situations. Reversibility tells us more than universalizability, then, in resolving dilemmas, but it implies universalizability. . . .

From a psychological side, then, political development is part of moral development. The same is true from the philosophic side. In the *Republic,* Plato sees political education as part of a broader education for moral justice and finds a rationale for such education in terms of universal philosophic principles rather than the demands of a particular society.

PART FOUR

THE PSYCHOLOGY OF POWER: FIVE CLASSIC PROPOSITIONS

The essays in this part advance arguments about the proper or necessary forms of political organization, given the emotional predispositions of people. All these arguments, with the possible exception of Rousseau's, contradict the comfortable platitudes of modern liberal democracy, and all of these arguments make an intellectual and experiential appeal, again with the possible exception of Rousseau, to readers who are at the same time appalled by them. One way to evaluate the political consequences of these propositions is to examine the adequacy of the emotional images which serve as their postulates. For this reason, all selections concentrate on the psychological passages in each work; excerpts of only the most general political consequences that each writer draws from these psychological suppositions are presented. It may be helpful to review briefly how these essays are tied to other works in this volume.

Hobbes's ideas on power flow logically from his views of human imagination; if imagination is our only real means of making sense of a world about which direct experience gives us very insufficient information, then when we fantasize about what we want, what we could have, what we might enjoy, our imaginative powers run wild. Since the boundaries of possible desire are limitless, our sense of needing and using power becomes limitless; we thus derive an insatiable desire for power because of the very cognitive tools we possess for thinking about our lives in society.

Machiavelli's *The Prince* also has its grounding in essays which have already appeared in this volume. Machiavelli is a role-theorist *par excellence*. This role-playing is no matter of social graces or manners, but a pressing necessity for a ruler who would control subjects unable to control themselves. This ruler creates a persona which nicely balances generosity and terror; no matter how a ruler feels at a given moment, he must always act as if these two passions were in equilibrium in his temperament. This interplay of terror and kindness hypnotizes his subjects and cows them into voluntary obedience. Once they are mesmerized, the ruler is free to pursue the interests of his city-state, out of sight and scrutiny of his subjects, who are all wrapped up in the qualities of his personality. Machiavelli thus sees imposture as a political good, whereas both Plato and Rousseau portrayed it in Part Two as an evil. The writings of Machiavelli form as well part of the intellectual tradition which informs Lyman and Scott's work on political theater.

. The essay of La Boétie's presented here is deceptively simple. He is no defender of voluntary servitude. He argues that social conditions of stability have made servitude something men desire out of their desire for comfort; the more anarchic social conditions become, the more the equation of blind obedience and material well-being might be challenged. It was for this reason that anarchists like Kropotkin, in the nineteenth century, and Herbert Read, in the 1930s, claimed La Boétie for their own. And his argument goes even a step further. Unlike Freud, Darwin, or any of the other writers we have encountered who conceived of a "human nature" anterior to society, La Boétie believes that this instinctive, natural creature, if he exists at all, is far weaker and less important than the human being created by social conditions—conditions like the experience of relative stability in legal, economic, and moral institutions. The human being appears in La Boétie's pages as pre-eminently socializable, and it is for this reason that he has also been claimed as the first behavioristic writer—as dubious a distinction as that may be.

Rousseau's ideas about political freedom in *The Social Contract* may seem to contradict his ideas on collective personality, also from *The Social Contract* and presented in Part One of this book. Whereas here we have an argument for a "natural" desire for liberty in society, earlier we had an argument for the transformation of human nature in society, so that to talk about the "natural" man was to talk about an unreal abstraction. Some commentators on Rousseau, like Jean Staroubinski, believe that the contradiction exists and is important, in that no view of the human being in society can avoid positing rights as "natural" and the socialized person as "unnatural"; other commentators, like Judith Shklar and Ben Barber, believe Rousseau is consistent in that the social man can take into society rights which also exist apart from his social experience. This scholarly debate about what Rousseau intends matters because it suggests how any argument about human liberty derived from the psychology of man "in nature" may be necessarily an illogical proposition. This doesn't mean the argument is unreal; rather, that an argument about man's natural "desire" for liberty may never achieve rational consistency of the sort, say, of Hobbes, who is rather skeptical about the value of liberty.

Nietzsche's theory of two different forms of psychological aristocracy is basically a picture of the virtues—rather suspect virtues for Nietzsche—of self-denial versus the virtues of instinctual release. Nietzsche's picture of instinctual release, his "aristocracy of the blond beasts," shares some elements with Le Bon. Instinctual release and consciousness are portrayed by both writers as antagonistic principles; the conscious man is a repressed figure. Nietzsche differs sharply from Le Bon in his moral valuations of instinct. Whereas Nietzsche believes only the instinctually free have transcended the vulgar restraints of normal society, Le Bon believes that instinctual release is a profoundly conservative social force. Perhaps one reason for the different political value Nietzsche and Le Bon put on instinctual release is that for Nietzsche, spontaneous instinctual expression is an experience which has an individualistic effect, so that the instinctually free man withdraws from other people who are not similarly liberated, whereas, for Le

Bon, instinctual release occurs only in crowds, and the man so released has no life of his own but only the life he shares with others as part of the mass. Therefore Nietzsche's blond beast is a challenger of society and Le Bon's chained man needs momentary occasions when he can join with others to discharge his pent-up energies.

There has been a great deal of debate about whether or not Nietzsche's writings prefigure twentieth-century fascist ideology. The most intelligent discussion of this issue occurs in Walter Kaufmann's *Nietzsche*. As to the contemporary impact of the other writers on the psychology of power—a good overall assessment is R. V. Sampson, *The Psychology of Power*. The most distinguished modern commentator on Hobbes is Leo Strauss; see especially his *Political Philosophy of Hobbes* and *Reflections on Tyranny*. Machiavelli has been used as a social-psychological source by writers as diverse as the Italian Communist Gramsci and an analyst of behavior in American corporations; Gramsci's *The Modern Prince* has recently been retranslated into English. An active branch of modern empirical studies in social psychology has been concerned with the questions of obedience raised by La Boétie and Rousseau. A representative sample of this work is: Stanley Milgram, *Obedience to Authority;* Hannah Arendt, *Eichmann in Jerusalem;* Erich Fromm, *Escape from Freedom;* and Nikolaas Tinbergen, *Social Behaviour in Animals.*

30. Thomas Hobbes: *Leviathan*   [1588–1679]

The power of a man, to take it universally, is his present means; to obtain some future apparent good; and is either *original* or *instrumental.*

Natural power, is the eminence of the faculties of body, or mind: as extraordinary strength, form, prudence, arts, eloquence, liberality, nobility. *Instrumental* are those powers, which acquired by these, or by fortune, are means and instruments to acquire more: as riches, reputation, friends, and the secret working of God, which men call good luck. For the nature of power, is in this point, like to fame, increasing as it proceeds; or like the motion of heavy bodies, which the further they go, make still the more haste.

The greatest of human powers, is that which is compounded of the powers of most men, united by consent, in one person, natural, or civil, that has the use of all their powers depending on his will; such as is the power of a commonwealth: or depending on the wills of each particular; such as is the power of a faction or of divers factions leagued. Therefore to have servants, is power; to have friends, is power: for they are strengths united. . . .

Also, what quality soever maketh a man beloved, or feared of many; or the reputation of such quality, is power; because it is a means to have the assistance, and service of many. . . .

The *value,* or WORTH of a man, is as of all other things, his price; that is to say, so much as would be given for the use of his power: and therefore is not absolute; but a thing dependent on the need and judgment of another. An able conductor of soldiers, is of great price in time of war present, or imminent; but in peace not so. A learned and uncorrupt judge, is much worth in time of peace; but not so much in war. And as in other things, so in men, not the seller, but the buyer determines the price. For let a man, as most men do, rate themselves at the highest value they can; yet their true value is no more than it is esteemed by others. . . .

I put for a general inclination of all mankind, a perpetual and restless desire of power after power, that ceaseth only in death. And the cause of this, is not always that a man hopes for a more intensive delight, than he has already attained to; or that he cannot be content with a moderate power: but because he cannot assure the power and means to live well, which he hath present, without the acquisition of more. And from hence it is, that kings, whose power is greatest, turn their endeavours to the assuring it at home by laws, or abroad by wars: and when that is done, there succeedeth a new desire; in some, of fame from new conquest; in others, of ease and sensual pleasure; in others of admiration, or being flattered for excellence in some art, or other ability of the mind.

Competition of riches, honour, command, or other power, inclineth to contention, enmity, and war: because the way of one competitor, to the attaining of his desire is to kill, subdue, supplant, or repel the other. Particularly, competition of praise, inclineth to a reverence of antiquity. For men contend with the living, not with the dead; to these ascribing more than due, that they may obscure the glory of the other.

Desire of ease, and sensual delight, disposeth men to obey a common power: because by such desires, a man doth abandon the protection that might be hoped for from his own industry, and labour. Fear of death, and wounds, disposeth to the same; and for the same reason. On the contrary, needy men, and hardy, not contented with their present condition: as also, all men that are ambitious of military command are inclined to continue the causes of war; and to stir up trouble and sedition: for there is no honour military but by war; nor any such hope to mend an ill game, as by causing a new shuffle.

Desire of knowledge, and arts of peace, inclineth men to obey a common power: for such desire, containeth a desire of leisure; and consequently protection from some other power than their own.

Desire of praise, disposeth to laudable actions, such as please them whose judgment they value; for of those men whom we contemn, we contemn also the praises. Desire of fame after death does the same. And though after death, there be no sense of the praise given us on earth, as being joys, that are either swallowed up in the unspeakable joys of Heaven, or extinguished in the extreme torments of hell: yet is not such fame vain; because men have a present delight therein, from the foresight of it, and of the benefit that may redound thereby to their posterity: which though they now see not, yet they imagine; and anything that is pleasure to the sense, the same also is pleasure in the imagination.

To have received from one, to whom we think ourselves equal, greater benefits than there is hope to require, disposeth to counterfeit love; but really secret hatred; and puts a man into the estate of a desperate debtor, that in declining the sight of his creditor, tacitly wishes him there, where he might never see him more. For benefits oblige, and obligation is thraldom; and unrequitable obligation perpetual thraldom; which is to one's equal, hateful. But to have received benefits from one, whom we acknowledge for superior, inclines to love; because the obligation is no new depression: and cheerful acceptation, which men call *gratitude,* is such an honour done to the obliger, as is taken generally for retribution. Also to receive benefits, though from an equal, or inferior, as long as there is hope of requital, disposeth to love: for in the intention of the receiver, the obligation is of aid and service mutual; from whence proceedeth an emulation of who shall exceed in benefiting; the most noble and profitable contention possible; wherein the victor is pleased with his victory, and the other revenged by confessing it.

To have done more hurt to a man, than he can, or is willing to expiate, inclineth the doer to hate the sufferer. For he must expect revenge, or forgiveness; both which are hateful.

Fear of oppression, disposeth a man to anticipate, or to seek aid by society: for there is no other way by which a man can secure his life and liberty. . . .

Nature hath made men so equal, in the faculties of the body, and mind; as that though there be found one man sometimes manifestly stronger in body, or of quicker mind than another; yet when all is reckoned together, the difference between man, and man, is not so considerable, as that one man can thereupon claim to himself any benefit, to which another may not pretend, as well as he. For as to the strength of body, the weakest has strength enough to kill the strongest, either by secret machination, or by confederacy with others, that are in the same danger with himself.

From this equality of ability, ariseth equality of hope in the attaining of our ends. And therefore if any two men desire the same thing, which nevertheless they cannot both enjoy, they become enemies; and in the way to their end, which is principally their own conservation, and sometimes their delectation only, endeavour to destroy, or subdue one another. And from hence it comes to pass, that where an invader hath no more to fear, than another man's single power; if one plant, sow, build, or possess a convenient seat, others may probably be expected to come prepared with forces united, to dispossess, and deprive him, not only of the fruit of his labour, but also of his life, or liberty. And the invader again is in the like danger of another.

And from this diffidence of one another, there is no way for any man to secure himself, so reasonable, as anticipation; that is, by force, or wiles, to master the persons of all men he can, so long, till he see no other power great enough to endanger him: and this is no more than his own conservation requireth, and is generally allowed. Also because there be some, that taking pleasure in contemplating their own power in the acts of conquest, which they pursue farther than their security requires; if others, that otherwise would be glad to be at ease within modest bounds should not by invasion increase their power, they would not be able, long time, by standing only on their defence, to subsist. And by consequence, such augmentation of dominion over men being necessary to a man's conservation, it ought to be allowed him.

Again, men have no pleasure, but on the contrary a great deal of grief, in keeping company, where there is no power able to over-awe them all. For every man looketh that his companion should value him, at the same rate he sets upon himself: and upon all signs of contempt, or undervaluing, naturally endeavours, as far as he dares, (which amongst them that have no common power to keep them in quiet, is far enough to make them destroy each other), to extort a greater value from his contemners, by damage; and from others, by the example. . . .

Whatsoever therefore is consequent to a time of war, where every man is enemy to every man; the same is consequent to the time, wherein men live without other security, than what their own strength, and their own invention shall furnish them withal. In such condition, there is no place for industry; because the fruit thereof is uncertain: and consequently no culture of the earth; no navigation, nor use of the commodities that may be imported by sea; no commodious building; no instruments of moving, and removing, such things as require much force; no knowledge of the face of the earth; no account of time; no arts; no letters; no society; and which is worst of all, continual fear, and danger of violent death; and the life of man, solitary, poor, nasty, brutish, and short.

31. Niccolò Machiavelli: *The Prince* [1469–1527]

How we live is so far removed from how we ought to live, that he who abandons what is done for what ought to be done, will rather learn to bring about his own ruin than his preservation. A man who wishes to make a profession of goodness in everything must necessarily come to grief among so many who are not good. Therefore it is necessary for a prince, who wishes to maintain himself, to learn how not to be good, and to use this knowledge and not use it, according to the necessity of the case.

Leaving on one side, then, those things which concern only an imaginary prince, and speaking of those that are real, I state that all men, and especially princes, who are placed at a greater height, are reputed for certain qualities which bring them either praise or blame. Thus one is considered liberal, another *misero* or miserly (using a Tuscan term, seeing that *avaro* with us still means one who is rapaciously acquisitive and *misero* one who makes grudging use of his own); one a free giver, another rapacious; one cruel, another merciful; one a breaker of his word, another trustworthy; one effeminate and pusillanimous, another fierce and highspirited; one humane, another haughty; one lascivious, another chaste; one frank, another astute; one hard, another easy; one serious, another frivolous; one religious, another an unbeliever, and so on. I know that every one will admit that it would be highly praiseworthy in a prince to possess all the above-named qualities that are reputed good, but as they cannot all be possessed or observed, human conditions not permitting of it, it is necessary that he should be prudent enough to avoid the scandal of those vices which would lose him the state, and guard himself if possible against those which will not lose it him, but if not able to, he can indulge them with less scruple. And yet he must not mind incurring the scandal of those vices, without which it would be difficult to save the state, for if one considers well, it will be found that some things which seem virtues would, if followed, lead to one's ruin, and some others which appear vices result in one's greater security and wellbeing. . . .

Beginning now with the first qualities above named, I say that it would be well to be considered liberal; nevertheless liberality such as the world understands it will injure you, because if used virtuously and in the proper way, it will not be known, and you will incur the disgrace of the contrary vice. But one who wishes to obtain the reputation of liberality among men, must not omit every kind of sumptuous display, and to such an extent that a prince of this character will consume by such means all his resources, and will be at last compelled, if he wishes to maintain his name for liberality, to impose heavy taxes on his people, become extortionate, and do everything possible to obtain money. This will make his subjects begin to hate him, and he will be little esteemed being poor, so that having by this liberality injured many and benefited but few, he will feel the first little disturbance and be endangered by every peril. If he recognises this and wishes to change his system, he incurs at once the charge of niggardliness.

A prince, therefore, not being able to exercise this virtue of liberality without risk if it be known, must not, if he be prudent, object to be called miserly. In course of time he will be thought more liberal, when it is seen that by his parsimony his revenue is sufficient, that he can defend himself against those who make war on him, and undertake enterprises without burdening his people, so that he is really liberal to all those from whom he does not take, who are infinite in number, and niggardly to all to whom he does not give, who are few. . . . For these reasons a prince must care little for the reputation of being a miser, if he wishes to avoid robbing his subjects, if he wishes to be able to defend himself, to avoid becoming poor and contemptible, and not to be forced to become rapacious; this niggardliness is one of those vices which enable him to reign. . . . There is nothing which destroys itself so much as liberality, for by using it you lose the power of using it, and become either poor and despicable, or, to escape poverty, rapacious and hated. And of all things that a prince must guard against, the most important are being despicable or hated, and liberality will lead you to one or the other of these conditions. It is, therefore, wiser to have the name of a miser, which produces disgrace without hatred, than to incur of necessity the name of being rapacious, which produces both disgrace and hatred.

From this arises the question whether it is better to be loved more than feared, or feared more than loved. The reply is, that one ought to be both feared and loved, but as it is difficult for the two to go together, it is much safer to be feared than loved, if one of the two has to be wanting. For it may be said of men in general that they are ungrateful, voluble, dissemblers, anxious to avoid danger, and covetous of gain; as long as you benefit them, they are entirely yours; they offer you their blood, their goods, their life, and their children, as I have before said, when the necessity is remote; but when it approaches, they revolt. And the prince who has relied solely on their words, without making other preparations, is ruined; for the friendship which is gained by purchase and not through grandeur and nobility of spirit is bought but not secured, and at a pinch is not to be expended in your service. And men have less scruple in offending one who makes himself loved than one who makes himself feared; for love is held by a chain of obligation which, men being selfish, is broken whenever it serves their purpose; but fear is maintained by a dread of punishment which never fails.

Still, a prince should make himself feared in such a way

that if he does not gain love, he at any rate avoids hatred; for fear and the absence of hatred may well go together, and will be always attained by one who abstains from interfering with the property of his citizens and subjects or with their women. And when he is obliged to take the life of any one, let him do so when there is a proper justification and manifest reason for it; but above all he must abstain from taking the property of others, for men forget more easily the death of their father than the loss of their patrimony. Then also pretexts for seizing property are never wanting, and one who begins to live by rapine will always find some reason for taking the goods of others, whereas causes for taking life are rarer and more fleeting. . . .

I conclude, therefore, with regard to being feared and loved, that men love at their own free will, but fear at the will of the prince, and that a wise prince must rely on what is in his power and not on what is in the power of others, and he must only contrive to avoid incurring hatred, as has been explained.

How laudable it is for a prince to keep good faith and live with integrity, and not with astuteness, every one knows. Still the experience of our times shows those princes to have done great things who have had little regard for good faith, and have been able by astuteness to confuse men's brains, and who have ultimately overcome those who have made loyalty their foundation.

You must know, then, that there are two methods of fighting, the one by law, the other by force: the first method is that of men, the second of beasts; but as the first method is often insufficient, one must have recourse to the second. It is therefore necessary for a prince to know well how to use both the beast and the man. This was covertly taught to rulers by ancient writers, who relate how Achilles and many others of those ancient princes were given to Chiron the centaur to be brought up and educated under his discipline. The parable of this semi-animal, semi-human teacher is meant to indicate that a prince must know how to use both natures, and that the one without the other is not durable.

A prince being thus obliged to know well how to act as a

beast must imitate the fox and the lion, for the lion cannot protect himself from traps, and the fox cannot defend himself from wolves. One must therefore be a fox to recognise traps, and a lion to frighten wolves. Those that wish to be only lions do not understand this. Therefore, a prudent ruler ought not to keep faith when by so doing it would be against his interest, and when the reasons which made him bind himself no longer exist. If men were all good, this precept would not be a good one; but as they are bad, and would not observe their faith with you, so you are not bound to keep faith with them. Nor have legitimate grounds ever failed a prince who wished to show colourable excuse for the non-fulfilment of his promise. Of this one could furnish an infinite number of modern examples, and show how many times peace has been broken, and how many promises rendered worthless, by the faithlessness of princes, and those that have been best able to imitate the fox have succeeded best. But it is necessary to be able to disguise this character well, and to be a great feigner and dissembler; and men are so simple and so ready to obey present necessities, that one who deceives will always find those who allow themselves to be deceived.

It is not, therefore, necessary for a prince to have all the above-named qualities, but it is very necessary to seem to have them. I would even be bold to say that to possess them and always to observe them is dangerous, but to appear to possess them is useful. Thus it is well to seem merciful, faithful, humane, sincere, religious, and also to be so; but you must have the mind so disposed that when it is needful to be otherwise you may be able to change to the opposite qualities. And it must be understood that a prince, and especially a new prince, cannot observe all those things which are considered good in men, being often obliged, in order to maintain the state, to act against faith, against charity, against humanity, and against religion. And, therefore, he must have a mind disposed to adapt itself according to the wind, and as the variations of fortune dictate, and, as I said before, not deviate from what is good, if possible, but be able to do evil if constrained.

A prince must take great care that nothing goes out of his mouth which is not full of the above-named five qualities, and, to see and hear him, he should seem to be all mercy, faith, integrity, humanity, and religion. And nothing is more necessary than to seem to have this last quality, for men in general judge more by the eyes than by the hands, for every one can see, but very few have to feel. Everybody sees what you appear to be, few feel what you are, and those few will not dare to oppose themselves to the many, who have the majesty of the state to defend them; and in the actions of men, and especially of princes, from which there is no appeal, the end justifies the means. Let a prince therefore aim at conquering and maintaining the state, and the means will always be judged honourable and praised by every one, for the vulgar is always taken by appearances and the issue of the event; and the world consists only of the vulgar, and the few who are not vulgar are isolated when the many have a rallying point in the prince. A certain prince of the present time, whom it is well not to name, never does anything but preach peace and good faith, but he is really a great enemy to both, and either of them, had he observed them, would have lost him state or reputation on many occasions.

32. Étienne de La Boétie:
The Discourse of Voluntary Servitude
(The Politics of Obedience)   [1530–1563]

For the present I should like merely to understand how it happens that so many men, so many villages, so many cities, so many nations, sometimes suffer under a single tyrant who has no other power than the power they give him; who is able to harm them only to the extent to which they have the willingness to bear with him; who could do them absolutely no injury unless they preferred to put up with him rather than contradict him. Surely a striking situation! Yet it is so common that one must grieve the more and wonder the less at the spectacle of a million men serving in wretchedness, their necks under the yoke, not constrained by a greater multitude than they, but simply, it would seem, delighted and charmed by the name of one man alone whose power they need not fear, for he is evidently the one person whose qualities they cannot admire because of his inhumanity and brutality toward them. A weakness characteristic of human kind is that we often have to obey force; we have to make concessions; we ourselves cannot always be the stronger. . . .

But O good Lord! What strange phenomenon is this? What name shall we give it? What is the nature of this misfortune? What vice is it, or, rather, what degradation? To see an endless multitude of people not merely obeying, but driven to servility? Not ruled, but tyrannized over? These wretches have no wealth, no kin, nor wife nor children, not even life itself that they can call their own. They suffer plundering, wantonness, cruelty, not from an army, not from a barbarian horde, on account of whom they must shed their blood and sacrifice their lives, but from a single man; not from a Hercules nor from a Samson, but from a single little man. Too frequently this same little man is the most cowardly and effeminate in the nation, a stranger to the powder of battle and hesitant on the sands of the tournament; not only without energy to direct men by force, but with hardly enough virility to bed with a common woman! Shall we call subjection to such a leader cowardice? Shall we say that those who serve him are cowardly and faint-hearted? If two, if three, if four, do not defend themselves from the one, we might call that circumstance surprising but nevertheless conceivable. In such a case one might be justified in suspecting a lack of courage. But if a hundred, if a thousand endure the caprice of a single man, should we not rather say that they lack not the courage but the desire to rise against him, and that such an attitude indicates indifference rather than cowardice? When not a hundred, not a thousand men, but a hundred provinces, a thousand cities, a million men, refuse to assail a single man from whom the kindest treatment received is the infliction of serfdom and slavery, what shall we call that? Is it cowardice? Of course there is in every vice inevitably some limit beyond which one cannot go. Two, possibly ten, may fear one; but when a thousand, a million men, a thousand cities, fail to protect themselves against the domination of one man, this cannot be called cowardly, for cowardice does not sink to such a depth, any more than valor can be termed the effort of one individual to scale a fortress, to attack an army, or to conquer a kingdom. What monstrous vice, then, is this which does not even deserve to be called cowardice, a vice for which no term can be found vile enough, which nature herself disavows and our tongues refuse to name? . . .

It is therefore the inhabitants themselves who permit, or, rather, bring about, their own subjection, since by ceasing to submit they would put an end to their servitude. A people enslaves itself, cuts its own throat, when, having a choice between being vassals and being free men, it deserts its liberties and takes on the yoke, gives consent to its own misery, or, rather, apparently welcomes it. . . .

I do not know how it happens that nature fails to place within the hearts of men a burning desire for liberty, a blessing so great and so desirable that when it is lost all evils follow thereafter, and even the blessings that remain lose taste and savor because of their corruption by servitude. Liberty is the only joy upon which men do not seem to insist; for surely if they really wanted it they would receive it. Apparently they refuse this wonderful privilege because it is so easily acquired. . . .

In the first place, all would agree that, if we led our lives according to the ways intended by nature and the lessons taught by her, we should be intuitively obedient to our parents; later we should adopt reason as our guide and become slaves to nobody. Concerning the obedience given instinctively to one's father and mother, we are in agreement, each one admitting himself to be a model. . . . Surely if there is anything in this world clear and obvious, to which one cannot close one's eyes, it is the fact that nature, handmaiden of God, governess of men, has cast us all in the same mold in order that we may behold in one another companions, or rather brothers. . . . Since she has revealed in every possible manner her intention, not so much to associate us as to make us one organic whole, there can be no further doubt that we are all naturally free, inasmuch as we are all comrades. Accordingly it should not enter the mind of anyone that nature has placed some of us in slavery, since she has actually created us all in one likeness.

Therefore it is fruitless to argue whether or not liberty is natural, since none can be held in slavery without being wronged, and in a world governed by a nature, which is reasonable, there is nothing so contrary as an injustice. . . .

It cannot be denied that nature is influential in shaping us to her will and making us reveal our rich or meager endowment; yet it must be admitted that she has less power over us than custom, for the reason that native endowment, no matter how good, is dissipated unless encouraged, whereas environment always shapes us in its own way, whatever that may be, in spite of nature's gifts. The good seed that nature plants in us is so slight and so slippery that it cannot withstand the least harm from wrong nourishment; it flourishes less easily, becomes spoiled, withers, and comes to nothing. . . . This is why men born under the yoke and then nourished and reared in slavery are content, without further effort, to live in their native circumstance, unaware of any other state or right, and considering as quite natural the condition into which they were born. . . .

In connection with this, let us imagine some newborn individuals, neither acquainted with slavery nor desirous of liberty, ignorant indeed of the very words. If they were permitted to choose between being slaves and free men, to which would they give their vote? There can be no doubt that they would much prefer to be guided by reason itself than to be ordered about by the whims of a single man. . . . But certainly all men, as long as they remain men, before letting themselves become enslaved must either be driven by force or led into it by deception; conquered by foreign armies, as were Sparta and Athens by the forces of Alexander or by political factions, as when at an earlier period the control of Athens had passed into the hands of Pisistrates. When they lose their liberty through deceit they are not so often betrayed by others as misled by themselves. . . . It is truly the nature of man to be free and to wish to be so, yet his character is such that he instinctively follows the tendencies that his training gives him.

Let us therefore admit that all those things to which he is trained and accustomed seem natural to man and that only that is truly native to him which he receives with his primitive, untrained individuality. Thus custom becomes the first reason for voluntary servitude. Men are like handsome race horses who first bite the bit and later like it, and rearing under the saddle a while soon learn to enjoy displaying their harness and prance proudly beneath their trappings. Similarly men will grow accustomed to the idea that they have always been in subjection, that their fathers lived in the same way; they will think they are obliged to suffer this evil, and will persuade themselves by example and imitation of others, finally investing those who order them around with proprietary rights, based on the idea that it has always been that way.

I come now to a point which is, in my opinion, the mainspring and the secret of domination, the support and foundation of tyranny. Whoever thinks that halberds, sentries, the placing of the watch, serve to protect and shield tyrants is, in my judgment, completely mistaken. These are used, it seems to me, more for ceremony and a show of force than for any reliance placed in them. The archers forbid the entrance to the palace to the poorly dressed who have no weapons, not to the well armed who can carry out some plot. Certainly it is easy to say of the Roman emperors that fewer escaped from danger by aid of their guards than were killed by their own archers. It is not the troops on horseback, it is not the companies afoot, it is not arms that defend the tyrant. This does not seem credible on first thought, but it is nevertheless true that there are only four or five who maintain the dictator, four or five who keep the country in bondage to him. Five or six have always had access to his ear, and have either gone to him of their own accord, or else have been summoned by him, to be accomplices in his cruelties, companions in his pleasures, panders to his lusts, and sharers in his plunders. These six manage their chief so successfully that he comes to be held accountable not only for his own misdeeds but even for theirs. The six have six hundred who profit under them, and with the six hundred they do what they have accomplished with their tyrant. The six hundred maintain under them six thousand, whom they promote in rank, upon whom they confer the government of provinces or the direction of finances, in order that they may serve as instruments of avarice and cruelty, executing orders at the proper time and working such havoc all around that they could not last except under the shadow of the six hundred, nor be exempt from law and punishment except through their influence.

The consequence of all this is fatal indeed. And whoever is pleased to unwind the skein will observe that not the six thousand but a hundred thousand, and even millions, cling to the tyrant by this cord to which they are tied . . . men accept servility in order to acquire wealth; as if they could acquire anything of their own when they cannot even assert that they belong to themselves, or as if anyone could possess under a tyrant a single thing in his own name. Yet they act as if their wealth really belonged to them, and forget that it is they themselves who give the ruler the power to deprive everybody of everything, leaving nothing that anyone can identify as belonging to somebody.

33. Jean-Jacques Rousseau: *The Social Contract*   [1712–1778]

The oldest of all societies, and the only natural one, is that of the family; yet children remain tied to their father by nature only so long as they need him for their preservation. As soon as this need ends, the natural bond is dissolved. Once the children are freed from the obedience they owe their father, and the father is freed from his responsibilities towards them, both parties equally regain their independence. If they continue to remain united, it is no longer nature, but their own choice, which unites them; and the family as such is kept in being only by agreement.

This common liberty is a consequence of man's nature. Man's first law is to watch over his own preservation; his first care he owes to himself; and as soon as he reaches the age of reason, he becomes the only judge of the best means to preserve himself; he becomes his own master.

The family may therefore perhaps be seen as the first model of political societies: the head of the state bears the image of the father, the people the image of his children, and all, being born free and equal, surrender their freedom only when they see advantage in doing so. The only difference is that in the family, a father's love for his children repays him for the care he bestows on them, while in the state, where the ruler can have no such feeling for his people, the pleasure of commanding must take the place of love.

Grotius denies that all human government is established for the benefit of the governed, and he cites the example of slavery. His characteristic method of reasoning is always to offer fact as a proof of right. It is possible to imagine a more logical method, but not one more favourable to tyrants.

According to Grotius, therefore, it is doubtful whether humanity belongs to a hundred men, or whether these hundred men belong to humanity, though he seems throughout his book to lean to the first of these views, which is also that of Hobbes. These authors show us the human race divided into herds of cattle, each with a master who preserves it only in order to devour its members.

Just as a shepherd possesses a nature superior to that of his flock, so do those shepherds of men, their rulers, have a nature superior to that of their people. Or so, we are told by Philo, the Emperor Caligula argued, concluding, reasonably enough on this same analogy, that kings were gods or alternatively that the people were animals.

The reasoning of Caligula coincides with that of Hobbes

and Grotius. Indeed Aristotle, before any of them, said that men were not at all equal by nature, since some were born for slavery and others born to be masters.

Aristotle was right; but he mistook the effect for the cause. Anyone born in slavery is born for slavery—nothing is more certain. Slaves, in their bondage, lose everything, even the desire to be free. They love their servitude even as the companions of Ulysses loved their life as brutes. But if there are slaves by nature, it is only because there has been slavery against nature. Force made the first slaves; and their cowardice perpetuates their slavery.

I have said nothing of the King Adam or of the Emperor Noah, father of the three great monarchs who shared out the universe among them, like the children of Saturn, with whom some authors have identified them. I hope my readers will be grateful for this moderation, for since I am directly descended from one of those princes, and perhaps in the eldest line, how do I know that if the deeds were checked, I might not find myself the legitimate king of the human race? However that may be, there is no gainsaying that Adam was the king of the world, as was Robinson Crusoe of his island, precisely because he was the sole inhabitant; and the great advantage of such an empire was that the monarch, secure upon his throne, had no occasion to fear rebellions, wars or conspirators.

The strongest man is never strong enough to be master all the time, unless he transforms force into right and obedience into duty. Hence 'the right of the strongest'—a 'right' that sounds like something intended ironically, but is actually laid down as a principle. But shall we never have this phrase explained? Force is a physical power; I do not see how its effects could produce morality. To yield to force is an act of necessity, not of will; it is at best an act of prudence. In what sense can it be a moral duty?

Let us grant, for a moment, that this so-called right exists. I suggest it can only produce a tissue of bewildering nonsense; for once might is made to be right, cause and effect are reversed, and every force which overcomes another force inherits the right which belonged to the vanquished. As soon as man can disobey with impunity, his disobedience becomes legitimate; and as the strongest is always right, the only problem is how to become the strongest. But what can be the validity of a right which perishes with the force on which it rests? If force compels obedience, there is no need to invoke a duty to obey, and if force ceases to compel obedience, there is no longer any obligation. Thus the word 'right' adds nothing to what is said by 'force'; it is meaningless.

'Obey those in power.' If this means 'yield to force' the precept is sound, but superfluous; it has never, I suggest, been violated. All power comes from God, I agree; but so does every disease, and no one forbids us to summon a physician. If I am held up by a robber at the edge of a wood, force compels me to hand over my purse. But if I could somehow contrive to keep the purse from him, would I still be obliged in conscience to surrender it? After all, the pistol in the robber's hand is undoubtedly a *power*.

Surely it must be admitted, then, that might does not make right, and that the duty of obedience is owed only to legitimate powers. Thus we are constantly led back to my original question.

Since no man has any natural authority over his fellows, and since force alone bestows no right, all legitimate authority among men must be based on covenants.

Grotius says: 'If an individual can alienate his freedom and become the slave of a master, why may not a whole people alienate its freedom and become the subject of a king?' In this remark there are several ambiguous words which call for explanation; but let us confine ourselves to one—to 'alienate'. To alienate is to give or sell. A man who becomes the slave of another does not give himself, he sells himself in return for at least a subsistence. But in return for what could a whole people be said to sell itself? A king, far from nourishing his subjects, draws his nourishment from them; and kings, according to Rabelais, need more than a little nourishment. Do subjects, then, give their persons to the king on condition that he will accept their property as well? If so, I fail to see what they have left to preserve.

It will be said that a despot gives his subjects the assurance of civil tranquillity. Very well, but what does it profit them, if those wars against other powers which result from a despot's ambition, if his insatiable greed, and the oppressive demands of his administration, cause more desolation than civil strife would cause? What do the people gain if their very condition of civil tranquillity is one of their hardships? There is peace in dungeons, but is that enough to make dungeons desirable? The Greeks lived in peace in the cave of Cyclops awaiting their turn to be devoured.

To speak of a man giving himself in return for nothing is to speak of what is absurd, unthinkable; such an action would be illegitimate, void, if only because no one who did it could be in his right mind. To say the same of a whole people is to conjure up a nation of lunatics; and right cannot rest on madness.

Even if each individual could alienate himself, he cannot alienate his children. For they are born men; they are born free; their liberty belongs to them; no one but they themselves has the right to dispose of it. Before they reach the years of discretion, their father may, in their name, make certain rules for their protection and their welfare, but he cannot give away their liberty irrevocably and unconditionally, for such a gift would be contrary to the natural order and an abuse of paternal right. Hence, an arbitrary government would be legitimate only if every new generation were free to accept or reject it, and in that case the government would cease to be arbitrary.

To renounce freedom is to renounce one's humanity, one's rights as a man and equally one's duties. There is no possible *quid pro quo* for one who renounces everything; indeed such renunciation is contrary to man's very nature; for if you take away all freedom of the will, you strip a man's actions of all moral significance. Finally, any covenant which stipulated absolute dominion for one party and absolute obedience for the other would be illogical and nugatory. Is it not evident that he who is entitled to demand everything owes nothing? And does not the single fact of there being no reciprocity, no mutual obligation, nullify the act? For what right can my slave have against me? If everything he has belongs to me, his right is *my* right, and it would be nonsense to speak of my having a right *against* myself.

34. Friedrich Nietzsche: *The Genealogy of Morals* [1844–1900]

What is the true etymological significance of the various symbols for the idea "good" which have been coined in the various languages? I then found that they all led back to *the same evolution of the same idea*—that everywhere "aristocrat," "noble" (in the social sense), is the root idea, out of which have necessarily developed "good" in the sense of "with aristocratic soul," "noble," in the sense of "with a soul of high calibre," "with a privileged soul"—a development which invariably runs parallel with that other evolution by which "vulgar," "plebeian," "low," are made to change finally into "bad." From the standpoint of the Genealogy of Morals this discovery seems to be substantial: the lateness of it is to be attributed to the retarding influence exercised in the modern world by democratic prejudice in the sphere of all questions of origin. . . .

The idea of political superiority always resolves itself into the idea of psychological superiority, in those cases where the highest caste is at the same time the *priestly* caste, and in accordance with its general characteristics confers on itself the privilege of a title which alludes specifically to its priestly function. It is in these cases, for instances, that "clean" and "unclean" confront each other for the first time as badges of class distinction; here again there develops a "good" and a "bad," in a sense which has ceased to be merely social. . . . The "clean man" is originally only a man who washes himself, who abstains from certain foods which are conducive to skin diseases, who does not sleep with the unclean women of the lower classes, who has a horror of blood—not more, not much more!

On the other hand, the very nature of a priestly aristocracy shows the reason why just at such an early juncture there should ensure a really dangerous sharpening and intensification of opposed values: it is, in fact, through these opposed values that gulfs are cleft in the social plane, which a veritable Achilles of free thought would shudder to cross. There is from the outset a certain *diseased taint* in such sacerdotal aristocracies, and in the habits which prevail in such societies—habits which, *averse* as they are to action, constitute a compound of introspection and explosive emotionalism, as a result of which there appears that introspective morbidity and neurasthenia, which adheres almost inevitably to all priests at all times. . . .

The priestly mode of valuation can branch off from the knightly aristocratic mode, and then develop into the very antithesis of the latter: special impetus is given to this opposition, by every occasion when the castes of the priests and warriors confront each other with mutual jealousy and cannot agree over the prize. The knightly-aristocratic "values" are based on a careful cult of the physical, on a flowering, rich, and even effervescing healthiness, that goes considerably beyond what is necessary for maintaining life, on war, adventure, the chase, the dance, the tourney—on everything, in fact, which is contained in strong, free, and joyous action. The priestly-aristocratic mode of valuation is—we have seen—based on other hypotheses: it is bad enough for this class when it is a question of war! Yet the priests are, as is notorious, *the worst enemies*—why? Because they are the weakest. Their weakness causes their hate to expand into a monstrous and sinister shape, a shape which is most crafty and most poisonous. The really great haters in the history of the world have always been priests, who are also the cleverest haters—in comparison with the cleverness of priestly revenge, every other piece of cleverness is practically negligible. Human history would be too fatuous for anything were it not for the cleverness imported into it by the weak—take at once the most important instance. All the world's efforts against the "aristocrats," the "mighty," the "masters," the "holders of power," are negligible by comparison with what has been accomplished against those classes by *the Jews*—the Jews, that priestly nation which eventually realised that the one method of effecting satisfaction on its enemies and tyrants was by means of a radical transvaluation of values, which was at the same time an act of the *cleverest revenge*. Yet the method was only appropriate to a nation of priests, to a nation of the most jealously nursed priestly revengefulness. It was the Jews who, in opposition to the aristocratic equation (good = aristocratic = beautiful = happy = loved by the gods), dared with a terrifying logic to suggest the contrary equation, and indeed to maintain with the teeth of the most profound hatred (the hatred of weakness) this contrary equation, namely, "the wretched are alone the good; the poor, the weak, the lowly, are alone the good; the suffering, the needy, the sick, the loathsome, are the only ones who are pious, the only ones who are blessed, for them alone is salvation—but you, on the other hand, you aristocrats, you men of power, you are to all eternity the evil, the horrible, the covetous, the insatiate, the godless: eternally also shall you be the unblessed, the cursed, the damned!" . . .

[The aristocrats] enjoy there freedom from all social control, they feel that in the wilderness they can give vent with impunity to that tension which is produced by enclosure and imprisonment in the peace of society, they *revert* to the innocence of the beast-of-prey conscience, like jubilant monsters, who perhaps come from a ghostly bout of murder, arson, rape, and torture with bravado and a moral equanimity, as though merely some wild student's prank had been played, perfectly convinced that the poets have now an ample theme to sing and celebrate. It is impossible not to recognise at the core of all these aristocratic races the beast of prey; the magnificent *blond brute,* avidly rampant for spoil and victory. . . .

Entertaining, as I do, these thoughts, I am, let me say in parenthesis, fundamentally opposed to helping our pessimists to new water for the discordant and groaning mills of their disgust with life; on the contrary, it should be shown specifically that, at the time when mankind was not yet ashamed of its cruelty, life in the world was brighter than it is nowadays when there are pessimists. The darkening of the heavens over man has always increased in proportion to the growth of man's shame *before man*. The tired pessimistic outlook, the mistrust of the riddle of life, the icy negation of disgusted ennui, all those are not the signs of the *most evil* age of the human race: much rather do they come first to the light of day, as the swamp-flowers, which they are, when the swamp to which they belong, comes into existence—I mean the diseased refinement and moralisation, thanks to which the "animal man" has at last learned to be ashamed of all his instincts. On the road to angel-hood (not to use in this context a harder word) man has developed that dyspeptic stomach and coated tongue, which have made not only the joy and innocence of the animal repulsive to him, but also life itself:—so that sometimes he stands with stopped nostrils before his own self. . . . Nowadays, when suffering is always trotted out as the first argument *against* existence, as its most sinister query, it is well to remember the times when men judged on converse principles because they could not dispense with the *infliction* of suffering, and saw therein a magic of the first order, a veritable bait of seduction to life.

We may perhaps be allowed to admit the possiblity of the craving for cruelty not necessarily having become really extinct: it only requires, in view of the fact that pain hurts more nowadays, a certain sublimation and subtilisation, it must especially be translated to the imaginative and psychic plane, and be adorned with such smug euphemisms, that even the most fastidious and hypocritical conscience could never grow suspicious of their real nature ("Tragic pity" is one of these euphemisms: another is *"les nostalgies de la croix"*). What really raises one's indignation against suffering is not suffering intrinsically, but the senselessness of suffering; such a *senselessness,* however, existed neither in Christianity, which interpreted suffering into a whole mysterious salvation-apparatus, nor in the beliefs of the naïve ancient man, who only knew how to find a meaning in suffering from the standpoint of the spectator, or the inflictor of the suffering. In order to get the secret, undiscovered, and unwitnessed suffering out of the world it was almost compulsory to invent gods and a hierarchy of intermediate beings, in short, something which wanders even among secret places, sees even in the dark, and makes a point of never missing an interesting and painful spectacle. It was with the help of such inventions that life got to learn the *tour de force,* which has become part of its stock-in-trade, the *tour de force* of self-justification. . . .

As it grows more powerful, the community tends to take the offences of the individual less seriously, because they are now regarded as being much less revolutionary and dangerous to the corporate existence: the evil-doer is no more outlawed and put outside the pale, the common wrath can no longer vent itself upon him with its old licence,—on the contrary, from this very time it is against this wrath, and particularly against the wrath of those directly injured, that the evil-doer is carefully shielded and protected by the community. As, in fact, the penal law develops, the following characteristics become more and more clearly marked: compromise with the wrath of those directly affected by the misdeed; a consequent endeavour to localise the matter and to prevent a further, or indeed a general spread of the disturbance; attempts to find equivalents and to settle the whole matter (*compositio*); above all, the will, which manifests itself with increasing definiteness, to treat every offence as in a certain degree capable of *being paid off,* and consequently, at any rate up to a certain point, to *isolate* the offender from his act. As the power and the self-consciousness of a community increases, so proportionately does the penal law become mitigated; conversely every weakening and jeopardising of the community revives the harshest forms of that law. The creditor has always grown more humane proportionately as he has grown more rich; finally the amount of injury he can endure without really suffering becomes the criterion of his wealth. It is possible to conceive of a society blessed with so great a *consciousness of its own power* as to indulge in the most aristocratic luxury of letting its wrong-doers go *scot-free.*—"What do my parasites matter to me?" might society say. "Let them live and flourish! I am strong enough for it."—The justice which began with the maxim, "Everything can be paid off, everything must be paid off," ends with connivance at the escape of those who cannot pay to escape—it ends, like every good thing on earth, by *destroying itself.*—The self-destruction of Justice! we know the pretty name it calls itself—*Grace!* it remains, as is obvious, the privilege of the strongest, better still, their superlaw.

PART FIVE

MARXIAN PSYCHOLOGY: WHAT IT CAN AND CANNOT BE

One measure of the strength of any intellectual movement is the amount of controversy it can inspire. Just as ideas which are not debatable are seldom interesting, interpretations of experience which do not lead to conflicting points of view are seldom realistic. The great strength of Marxian theory, especially the humanistic dimension of Marx's thought, is that it systematically encourages conflicting points of view. It does so because, as a dialectical mode of thought, it focuses on contradictions which successive moments of history create cumulatively in a society; as we have seen in Marx's own interpretations of class consciousness in 1848, these phenomena of contradiction are the proper Marxian study of society, and contradictions are never subject to a single interpretative resolution.

For this reason, the Marxian tradition of analysis properly includes those who begin with the tenets of Marx himself and then rebel against him in contradiction. These writers who have needed Marx to fight against him have kept his thought alive—they have certainly kept him much more alive than those writers of a slavish cast of mind who want to show that Marx was an oracle about everything that occurred during and since his lifetime. And no subject has aroused this healthy debate more than Marx's psychological ideas.

In this part, we examine some of the central issues in the controversy over whether the Marxian position can, or should, have a psychological dimension. We begin with the argument of the distinguished East European writer István Mészáros that an intellectually complete and emotionally persuasive picture of the phenomenon of alienation can be derived from Marx's basic principles. Mézáros draws especially on Marx's early writings such as the *Grundrisse*. These writings have attracted other writers who believe that a valid set of psychological assumptions about human desire and human need governs Marx's writings. The reader may wish to consult the work of another East European, Leszek Kolokowski, especially his group of essays collected together under the title *Toward a Marxist Humanism*. Of more narrowly social-science appeal but also valuable is the collection of essays edited by Robin Blackburn called *Ideology in Social Science*.

Two kinds of rebellions against the psychological assumptions of Marx's writings are presented here. In one, Marxian assumptions are taken as inadequate by themselves to explain the forces of domination and repression in society; in the other, the image of man as emotionally expressive through work—an image which governs Marx's thought—is attacked.

The argument that Marx is an inadequate guide to mass psychology has been most forcefully advanced in our time by Wilhelm Reich. Because of Reich's peculiar notions about sexual freedom and his invention of such physically therapeutic devices as the orgone box, his writings have been dismissed *in toto* (and Reich was incarcerated in a mental hospital for them), or he has been converted into a cult figure. Whatever the worth of such ideas as "orgasm anxiety" or "vegeto-therapy," Reich was an acute social observer, and his portrayal of the mass psychology of fascism, from which our section is drawn, is not only a sharp historical portrait but a basic challenge to Marx's notions of repression. Or more exactly, it is a challenge to what Reich perceives as a vulgarization of Marx's ideas by followers who made his exploratory insights into a fixed system. Reich's own ideas are not entirely novel; we have encountered different antecedents for them in both

Freud and Le Bon. But Reich has focused the discussion of mass psychology not on masses or crowds in general, but on masses and crowds faced with specific economic and political dilemmas; these they attempt to solve by means of mass passion when all else has failed.

In the work of the contemporary French writer Jean Baudrillard, Marx is challenged in altogether another way. Here it is not the ideas of repression and alienation which are criticized, but Marx's own ideals, ideals in which the human being realizes himself through productive work. This image is of *homo faber,* man as maker; against it, Baudrillard sets *homo ludens,* man at play. Baudrillard argues that people are free only when they cut loose from feeling they must always produce, always create; only when they interact with one another without an end in sight, only when they engage in those acts of play which he calls "pure symbolic interchange" are they free. Baudrillard therefore believes the Marxian ideal is insufficiently radical in that it is still tied to the Protestant, capitalist ethos of work. Baudrillard no less than Reich has become the object of a cult; he is credited as one of the ideologists of revolution-as-play and revolution-as-theater which ruled the May events in France in 1968. This cult worship obscures something of the seriousness of his work. He echoes the value set on free play which first appears in Plato's *Laws,* and his theory compliments the historical researches on the importance of the play element in culture conducted by Johann Huizinga in the latter's *Homo Ludens.* Baudrillard's thought is also the product of such classic historical studies as Jane Harrison's *Ancient Art in Ritual.*

If the critical and utopian aspects of Marx can be attacked on psychological grounds, the Marxian tradition can also be defended against psychology. This is the intention of Georg Lukács, in his *History and Class Consciousness.* Lukács' work is convoluted and no single selection can represent it adequately. The passages presented here show only the grounds on which Lukács believes consciousness, of a politically meaningful kind, has little to do with states of feeling and mostly to do with rational knowledge. For Lukács, rational objectivity and political mobilization go together; he avoids a psychological critique of society because he fears this will always slip back into an absorption in subjective, individual self-consciousness. Psychological awareness, Lukács believes, may make people highly sensitized to their sufferings, but also passive about erasing them. Lukács is more generally representative of a segment of Marxian analysis which rejects psychological inquiry as the ultimate form of bourgeois ideology, for an account of subjective feeling appears in this view as antithetical to the collective, impersonal pursuit of objective class interests. It is not that Lukács himself denies the importance of consciousness; class consciousness is for him the critical element in revolutionary action, so that people, instead of being forced to act, realize they have to act. But the consciousness he has in mind is a form of collective knowledge. It is collective "nous," to use the Aristotelian term with which we began, and this collective mind becomes potent at the moment it stops reflecting upon its sufferings and moves to the level of purposive, nonsubjective behavior.

Thus we end in Lukács with more than a defense of Marxism against the supposed dangers of psychological subjectivity; his is an attack on the very idea that an inquiry into states of feeling has a role to play in active political change.

35. István Mészáros:
Marx's Theory of Alienation   [1930–]

One cannot take for granted anything more than the fact that man is a part of nature, and only on this basis may one ask the question: what is *specific* about man as part of nature. In this context two important questions have to be asked:

1. What are the *general* characteristics of a *natural being*?
2. What are the *specific* characteristics of a *human* natural being?

"Man"—writes Marx—"is directly a natural being". "As a natural being and as a living natural being he is on the one hand furnished with natural powers of life—he is an active natural being. These forces exist in him as tendencies and abilities—as impulses. On the other hand, as a natural, corporeal, sensuous, objective being he is a suffering, conditioned and limited creature, like animals and plants. That is to say, the objects of his impulses exist outside him, as objects independent of him; yet these objects are objects of his need—essential objects, indispensable to the manifestation and confirmation of his essential powers". Marx goes on to say that the concept of an *objective being* necessarily implies *another being* which is the *object* of that objective being. This relation is, however, by no means one-sided: the *object* in its turn has the objective being for *its object*. "As soon as I have an object, this object has me for an object". That is to say, I am affected by this object, or in other words, I am in some specific way subjected to it. Considered at this level, my relation to my objects is the same as that between nonhuman natural objects. "The sun is the object of the plant—an indispensable object to it, confirming its life—just as the plant is an object of the sun, of the sun's objective essential power".

But Marx carries this line of thought even further and emphasizes that *every* natural being has its nature *outside itself:* "A being which does not have its nature outside itself is not a natural being and plays no part in the system of nature. A being which has no object outside itself is not an objective being. A being which is not itself an object for some third being has no being for its object; i.e. it is not objectively related. Its be-ing is not objective. *An unobjective being is a nullity—an un-being".* From this two important conclusions follow:

(1) that the "nature" of *any* objective being is not some mysteriously hidden "essence", but something that naturally defines itself as the necessary relation of the objective being to its objects, i.e. it is a specific objective relation; (only "un-

beings" or "nullities" need be "defined" in mystifying references to mysterious essences);

(2) that "having one's nature outside oneself" is the necessary mode of existence of *every* natural being, and is by no means specific about *man*. Thus if someone wants to identify *externalization* with *human alienation* (as Hegel did, for instance), he can only do this by confounding the whole with one specific *part* of it. Consequently "objectification" and "externalization" are relevant to alienation only insofar as they take place in an *inhuman* form. (As if the sun's "life-awakening power" turned *against* the sun under conditions when the sun could in principle prevent this from happening.)

As regards man's status as a *specific* part of nature, Marx writes: "But man is not merely a natural being, he is a human natural being. That is to say, he is a *being for himself*. Therefore he is a *species being,* and has to confirm and manifest himself as such both in his being and in his knowing. Therefore, human objects are not natural objects as they *immediately* present themselves, and neither is human sense as it immediately is as it is objectively—human sensibility, human objectivity. Neither nature objectively nor nature subjectively is directly given in a form adequate to the human being. And as everything natural has to have its beginning, man too has his act of coming-to-be—history—which, however, is for him a known history, and hence as an act of coming-to-be it is a *conscious self-transcending act of coming-to-be*. History is the true natural history of man".

To render clearer this passage let us contrast the views expressed in it with Hume's assertion according to which "An affectation betwixt the sexes is a passion evidently implanted in human nature". This assertion, even if it claims to have the truth-value of self-evidence, is nothing more than an unhistorical *assumption* that, on closer inspection, turns out to be false on two counts:

(1) insofar as this passion is "implanted in nature", it is not confined to human beings, i.e. it is not a *human* passion;

(2) insofar as it is a specifically human passion, it is not at all *"implanted* in human nature", but it is a *human achievement*. The essential characteristic of this passion as a *human*

passion is that it is inseparable from the consciousness of the "other sex" being a particular *human being* and at the same time it is also inseparable from the consciousness of the self as that of a *humanly* passionate being. This human achievement is what Marx calls, rather obscurely, "a conscious self-transcending act of coming-to-be" in which *nature transcends itself* (or "mediates itself with itself") and becomes *man*, remaining in this "self-transcendence", of course, a natural being.

Nothing is therefore "implanted in *human* nature". Human nature is not something *fixed by nature*, but, on the contrary, a 'nature" which is *made by man* in his acts of "self-transcendence" as a natural being. It goes without saying that human beings—due to their natural-biological constitution—have *appetites* and various natural propensities. But in the "conscious self-transcending act of coming-to-be" they must become *human* appetites and propensities, fundamentally changing their character by being transformed into something *inherently historical*. (Without this transformation both art and morality would be unknown to man: they are only possible because man is the creator of his *human* appetites. And both art and morality—both inherently historical—are concerned with the properly human appetites and propensities of man, and not with the direct, unalterable determinations of the natural being. Where there is no—inherently historical—alternative, there is no room for either art or morality.) Therefore in only one sense may one speak of "human nature": in the sense whose centre of reference is historical change and its foundation, human society. In Marx's words: "The nature which comes to be in human history—the genesis of human society—is man's real nature; hence nature as it comes to be through industry, even though in an estranged form, is true *anthropological* nature".

Putting into relief the specifically human about all the natural needs of man, does not, of course, mean arguing for a new kind of "higher self" to sit in judgment over these natural needs. There is nothing wrong with man's natural appetites, provided they are stilled in a *human way*. This human way for satisfying one's natural appetites—which, as needs and appetites, are transformed in the process of "self-transcendence" and "self-mediation"—will depend on the actual degree of civilization, and the social practice that corresponds to it, to which one belongs. And when one says that the primitive natural needs and appetites have become human, this is only to stress that they are now *specifically natural*.

This is why human fulfilment cannot be conceived in abstraction from, or in opposition to, nature. To divorce oneself from "anthropological nature" in order to find fulfilment in the realm of abstract ideas and ideals is just as inhuman as living one's life in blind submission to crude natural needs. It is by no means accidental that so many of the worst immoralities throughout the history of mankind were committed in the name of high-sounding moral ideals utterly divorced from the reality of man.

In the same way, the fact that "self-consciousness" is an essential feature of human gratification cannot mean that self-consciousness alone may be opposed to the "world of estrangement", which happens to be the world of objects. "Self-consciousness" that divorces itself from the world of objects (i.e. a consciousness whose centre of reference is the object-less abstract self) does not *oppose* alienation but, on the contrary, *confirms* it. This is why Marx scorns the abstract philosopher who "sets up himself (that is, one who is himself *an abstract form of estranged man*) as the measuring-rod for the estranged world". The objectivity of this philosopher is false objectivity, because he deprives himself of all real objects.

We are not free to choose our self-consciousness. Human self-consciousness—the consciousness of a specific natural being—must be "sensuous consciousness", because it is the consciousness of a sensuous (sensible) natural being. However, "sensuous consciousness is not the abstractly sensuous consciousness but a *humanly sensuous consciousness*". And since the activities of this specific natural being are necessarily displayed in a *social* framework, true self-consciousness of this being must be his consciousness of being a *social* being. Any abstraction from these basic characteristics could only result in an *alienated* self-consciousness.

Here we can see, why Marx had to correct the Hegelian ideas he incorporated in his picture of man the way he did:

(1) Starting from the fact that man is a specific part of nature, he could not confine *labour*—in his attempt to account for human *genesis*—to "abstractly mental labour". What is abstractly mental cannot generate on its own something inherently natural, whereas on the natural basis of reality one can account for the genesis of "abstractly mental labour".

(2) For the same reason he could not accept the identification of "objectifying" with "alienation". In relation to an *objective natural being* what is called "objectification" cannot be simply declared "alienation" (or "estrangement"), because this objectification is its *natural* and necessary mode of existence. On the other hand if we conceive an "abstractly spiritual being" whose adequate mode of existence would be of course merely spiritual, in relation to this being "objectification" and "estrangement" become identical. However, apart from this case—in which both "natural" and "objective" are excluded from the definition of this merely spiritual being—only two possibilities are open to the philosopher:

(*a*) to give up the *objectivity* of the *natural* being (in order to accept the necessity of alienation) and thus to end up with a contradiction in terms;

(*b*) to insist that *objectification* is the only possible mode of existence for a natural being (as we have seen, the sun too "objectifies itself" in the living plant; of course the sun cannot think of itself, but this is no reason for depriving it of its objective self—"lifegiving power", etc.—and for denying its objectification), but *some forms* of objectification are *inadequate* to the "essence" = "nature outside it" = "social mode of existence" of the human being.

(3) Consequently: if it is the *inadequacy* of some forms of objectification that may properly be called alienation, it is not true that objectivity equals "estranged human relations", although it may be true that the objectivity of civilized society as we have known it *so far* carried with it estranged human relations. By contrast, an adequate form of human objectification would produce social objectivity as *objectified* but *non-alienated* human relations.

(4) From the previous points it must follow that the

"supersession" of alienation has to be envisaged in terms of the actual *social reality,* i.e. as a transcendence of alienation in social practice as opposed to mere imagination.

THE ALIENATION OF HUMAN POWERS

The foregoing considerations are essential to decide "what is human" and what should be rejected as alienation. They not only turn down the "measuring-rod" provided by the abstract philosopher, characterizing it as a particular embodiment of alienated activity, but also offer a new measure by saying that there can be no other *measure of humanness* than *man himself.*

It would be no use to try and answer the question that arises at this point, namely: "which man", by saying: "non-alienated man." Such an answer would amount to reasoning in a circle. What we are after is, precisely, to find out what is "non-alienated". The facts that one may refer to, as elements and stages of a possible definition, are:

(1) man is a *natural* being;

(2) as a natural being he has natural *needs* and natural *powers* for their gratification;

(3) he is a being who lives in a *society* and *produces* the conditions necessary for his existence in an inherently *social* way;

(4) as a productive social being he acquires *new needs* ("needs created through social partnership") and *new powers* for their gratification;

(5) as a productive social being, he transforms the world around him in a specific way, leaving *his* mark on it; nature thus becomes *"anthropological nature"* in this man-nature relationship; everything now becomes at least potentially, a part of human relations; (nature in these relations appears in a great variety of forms ranging from material elements of utility to objects of scientific hypothesis and of aesthetic pleasure);

(6) by establishing on a natural basis his own conditions of life in the form of social-economic institutions and their products, man "duplicates himself" *practically,* thus laying the foundations of "contemplating himself in a world that he has created";

(7) by means of his new powers which are, just as his new needs, "created through social partnership" and interaction, and on the basis of the "practical duplication" just referred to, he also *"duplicates himself intellectually"*.

Considering these characteristics not in isolation, but in their manifold interrelatedness, it will be seen that the gratification of human needs takes place in an alienated form if this means either a submission to the *crude* natural appetites, or the *cult of the self*—whether this self is described as a creature who is by nature selfish or as an abstract self-consciousness.

The abstract philosopher's approach to the problem of alienation is itself an alienated one. Not only because it confines itself to man's ability to "duplicate himself intellectually", ignoring that only the conditions enumerated in points 1 to 6 make this duplication possible. And not only because he does not distinguish between *alienated* and *true* intellectual self-duplication, but also because he opposes an alienated intellectual self-duplication as true self-confirmation to those conditions (i.e. the objectified social reality) without which no self-confirmation is conceivable for a human (social) natural being.

On the other hand, the submission to the crude naturalness of a given appetite is alienation because it opposes itself, even if unconsciously, to *human* development. It negates (practically or theoretically) the social changes by virtue of which the originally merely natural needs too are now *mediated* in a complex way, so that they have lost their primitive character. It is by no means a mere historical coincidence that the century that has achieved the highest degree of *sophistication* in every sphere has also produced the most remarkable *cult of the primitive,* from philosophical and psychological theories to social and artistic practices.

When we come to consider "privatization" in the light of the formerly enumerated characteristics, its alienated nature becomes transparent, because "privatization" means abstracting (in practice) from the *social side* of human activity. If, however, the social activity of production is an elementary condition for the *human* existence of the individual (with his increasingly complex and socially embedded needs), this act of abstracting—whatever form it might take—is necessarily alienation, because it confines the individual to his "crude solitariness". Society is man's "second nature", in the sense in which the original natural needs are transformed by it, and at the same time integrated into an enormously more extensive network of needs which are all together the product of socially active man. To abstract therefore from this aspect of man in the *cult of the self* as opposed to social man amounts to the cult of an over-simplified alienated self, because the true self of the human being is necessarily a *social self,* whose "nature is outside itself", i.e. it defines itself in terms of specific and immensely complex interpersonal, social relations. Even the *potentialities* of the individual can only be defined in terms of relations of which the individual is but a part. For someone to be a "potentially great piano player" not only the existence of a—socially produced—musical instrument is necessary, but even more so the highly complex social activity of discriminative musical enjoyment.

In all these cases alienation appears as *divorcing* the individual from the social, the natural from the self-conscious. By contraposition it follows that in a non-alienated human relation individual and social, natural and self-conscious must belong together—and form a *complex unity.* And this brings us to another important question: what is the connection between alienation and those needs and powers which are the outcome of social intercourse, i.e. the product of society?

Here we have first to distinguish between two senses of both *natural* and *artificial* as used by Marx. In sense one, natural means simply "that which is a direct product of nature"; and in opposition to it artificial means "man-made". In sense two, however, what is not a direct product of nature but is generated through a *social intermediary* is "natural" insofar as it is identical with man's "second nature", i.e. his nature as created through the functioning of sociality. (It is important to distinguish between "sociality" and "society". The latter, as contrasted with the "sensuous" (sensible) immediateness of the particular individuals, is an abstraction: to grasp it one must transcend this immediateness of the individuals. "Sociality", however, is actually inherent in every single individual. This is why a society may never be justifiably called "natural", whereas sociality is rightly defined as man's second nature.) The opposite to this second sense of natural is clearly not "man-made"—it *is* man-made—but "that which opposes itself to human nature as sociality". Only this second sense of "artificial" is morally relevant. Man-made needs and appetites are not artificial in the second sense provided they are in *harmony* with the functioning of man as a *social* natural being. If, however, they are in disharmony with it, or may even carry it to a point of break-down, they must be rejected as *artificial needs*.

It is worth comparing the Marxian view with Hume's classification of human needs and powers: "There are three different species of goods which we are possessed of; the *internal* satisfaction of our minds; the *external* advantages of our body; and the enjoyment of such *possessions* as we have acquired by our industry and good fortune. We are perfectly secure in the enjoyment of the first. The second may be ravished from us, but can be of no advantage to him who deprives us of them. The last only are both exposed to the violence of others, and may be transferred without suffering any loss or alteration; while at the same time there is not a *sufficient quantity* of them to supply every one's *desires* and *necessities*. As the improvement, therefore, of these goods is the chief advantage of society, so the instability of their possession, along with their *scarcity,* is the chief impediment".

One should notice first of all that while Hume attaches the adjectives *internal* to class one, and *external* to class two, he is unable to attach any qualifying adjective to class three. And no wonder: beyond the "internal" and "external" there is only the realm of abstraction. To "abstract enjoyment" only an *abstract need* can correspond, e.g. the need of abstracting from the fact that what is for me only an abstract need of possession, in no connection with my actual human needs, to other people may well be essentials ("necessities") to the gratification of their actual human needs. (This consideration presents, if nothing else, a *prima facie* case for tackling the problem of justice and injustice on lines opposed to those of Hume.)

Furthermore, the question of necessary *scarcity* here arises only in relation to my abstract need of possession. Actual human needs and appetites, whether internal or external, can, in fact, be stilled, whereas there is nothing to limit an *abstract* need—e.g. if the objects of my appetite are not food or poetry, but the multiplication of my money—except the scarcity of the objects to which it is related. However, abstract appetites are *inherently* insatiable—i.e. there is nothing in their nature to limit them "from the inside", in contrast to my mental and bodily appetites—therefore their objects are just as "scarce" in relation to *one* person as to *any number* of them. In other words scarcity is no argument in favour of excluding other people from possession, let alone for establishing "natural justice" on the grounds of such an exclusion. All the less so, because in the only sense in which one may properly speak of a problem of scarcity, it is simply a correlation between the existing actual human needs and the available powers, goods, etc., for their gratification. But this is, of course, a historically changing *contingent* relation, and not a matter of some *apriori necessity* on whose ground one may erect a Humean or even Kantian structure of morality.

As we see Hume, paradoxically, helps to confirm Marx's contention that the "need of possession" is an *abstract* and *artificial* need. Every abstract need—since it abstracts from man—is, by implication, artificial. And thus "abstract", "artificial" and "alienated" become equivalent, in relation to both *needs* and *powers*. The reason why this is so is because abstract (artificial) needs cannot generate powers that correspond to the essential (social) nature of man. They can only generate *abstract powers* which are divorced from the human being and even set up against him. Or the other way round: abstract powers can only generate abstract, artificial needs.

36. Wilhelm Reich:
The Mass Psychology of Fascism   [1897–1957]

The German freedom movement prior to Hitler was inspired by Karl Marx's economic and social theory. Hence, an understanding of German fascism must proceed from an understanding of Marxism.

In the months following National Socialism's seizure of power in Germany, even those individuals whose revolutionary firmness and readiness to be of service had been proven again and again, expressed doubts about the correctness of Marx's basic conception of social processes. These doubts were generated by a fact that, though irrefutable, was at first incomprehensible: Fascism, the most extreme representative of political and economic reaction in both its goals and its nature, had become an international reality and in many countries had visibly and undeniably outstripped the socialist revolutionary movement. That this reality found its strongest expression in the highly industrialized countries only heightened the problem. The rise of nationalism in all parts of the world offset the failure of the workers' movement in a phase of modern history in which, as the Marxists contended, "the capitalist mode of production had become economically ripe for explosion." Added to this was the deeply ingrained remembrance of the failure of the Workers' International at the outbreak of World War I and of the crushing of the revolutionary uprisings outside of Russia between 1918 and 1923. They were doubts, in short, which were generated by grave facts; if they were justified, then the basic Marxist conception was false and the workers' movement was in need of a decisive reorientation, provided one still wanted to achieve its goals. If, however, the doubts were not justified, and Marx's *basic* conception of sociology was correct, then not only was a thorough and extensive analysis of the reasons for the continual failure of the workers' movement called for, but also—and this above all—a complete elucidation of the unprecedented mass movement of fascism was also needed. Only from this could a new revolutionary practice result.

A change in the situation was out of the question unless it could be proven that either the one or the other was the case. It was clear that neither an appeal to the "revolutionary class consciousness" of the working class nor the practice *à la Coué* —the camouflaging of defeats and the covering of important facts with illusions—a practice that was in vogue at that time, could lead to the goal. One could not content oneself with the fact that the workers' movement was also "progressing," that here and there resistance was being offered and strikes were being called. . . .

Exponents of Marxism had no answer. It became more and more clear that their political mass propaganda, dealing as it did solely with the discussion of *objective* socio-economic processes at a time of crisis (capitalist modes of production, economic anarchy, etc.), did not appeal to anyone other than the minority already enrolled in the Left front. The playing up of material needs and of hunger was not enough, for *every* political party did that much, even the church; so that in the end it was the mysticism of the National Socialists that triumphed over the economic theory of socialism, and at a time when the economic crisis and misery were at their worst. Hence, one had to admit that there was a glaring omission in the propaganda and in the overall conception of socialism and that, moveover, this omission was the source of its "political errors." It was an error in the Marxian comprehension of political reality, and yet all the prerequisites for its correction were contained in the methods of dialectical materialism. They had simply never been turned to use. In their political practice, to state it briefly at the outset, the Marxists *had failed to take into account the character structure of the masses and the social effect of mysticism.* . . .

Those who followed, and were practically involved in the revolutionary Left's application of Marxism between 1917 and

1933, had to notice that it was restricted to the sphere of *objective* economic processes and governmental policies, but that it neither kept a close eye on nor comprehended the development and contradictions of the so-called "subjective factor" of history, i.e., the ideology of the masses. The revolutionary Left failed, above all, to make fresh use of its own method of dialectical materialism, to keep it alive, to comprehend every *new* social reality from a new perspective with this method.

The use of dialectical materialism to comprehend *new* historical realities was not cultivated, and fascism was a reality that neither Marx nor Engels was familiar with, and was caught sight of by Lenin only in its beginnings. The reactionary conception of reality shuts its eyes to fascism's contradictions and actual conditions. Reactionary politics automatically makes use of those social forces that oppose progress; it can do this successfully only as long as science neglects to unearth *those* revolutionary forces that must of necessity overpower the reactionary forces. As we shall see later, not only regressive but also very energetic progressive social forces emerged in the rebelliousness of the lower middle classes, which later constituted the *mass basis* of fascism. This contradiction was overlooked; indeed, the role of the lower middle classes was altogether in eclipse until shortly before Hitler's seizure of power. . . . In fact, it was not only the middle class that turned to the Right, but broad and not always the worst elements of the proletariat. . . . One also failed to see that, at the outset and during the initial stages of its development to a mass movement, fascism was directed against the upper middle class and hence could not be disposed of *"merely* as a bulwark of big finance," if only because it was a mass movement.

According to Marx's theory the *economic* preconditions for a social revolution were given: capital was concentrated in the hands of the few, the growth of national economy to a world economy was completely at variance with the custom and tariff system of the national states; capitalist economy had achieved hardly half of its production capacity, and there could no longer be any doubt about its basic anarchy. The majority of the population of the highly industrialized countries was living in misery; some fifty million people were unemployed in Europe; hundreds of millions of workers scraped along on next to nothing. But the expropriation of the expropriators failed to take place and, contrary to expectations, at the crossroads between "socialism and barbarism," it was in the direction of barbarism that society first proceeded. . . .

Rationally considered, one would expect economically wretched masses of workers to develop a keen consciousness of their social situation; one would further expect this consciousness to harden into a determination to rid themselves of their social misery. In short, one would expect the socially wretched working man to revolt against the abuses to which he is subjected and to say: "After all, I perform responsible social work. It is upon me and those like me that the weal and ill of society rests. I myself assume the responsibility for the work that must be done." In such a case, the thinking ("consciousness") of the worker would be in keeping with his social situation. The Marxist called it "class consciousness." We want to call it "consciousness of one's skills," or "consciousness of one's social responsibility." The cleavage between the social situation of the working masses and their consciousness of this situation implies that, instead of improving their social position, the working masses worsen it. It was precisely the wretched masses who helped to put fascism, extreme political reaction, into power.

It is a question of the role of ideology and the emotional attitude of these masses seen as a historical factor, a question of the *repercussion of the ideology on the economic basis*. If the material wretchedness of the broad masses did not lead to a social revolution; if, objectively considered, contrary revolutionary ideologies resulted from the crisis, then the development of the ideology of the masses in the critical years thwarted the "efflorescence of the forces of production," prevented, to use Marxist concepts, the "revolutionary resolution of the contradictions between the forces of production of monopolistic capitalism and its methods of production." . . .

Thus, the basic problem is this: What causes this cleavage, or to put it another way, what prevents the economic situation from coinciding with the psychic structure of the masses? It is a problem, in short, of comprehending the nature of the psychological structure of the masses and its relation to the economic basis from which it derives. . . .

The ideology of every social formation has the function not only of reflecting the economic process of this society, but also and more significantly of embedding his economic process in the *psychic structures of the people who make up the society.* Man is subject to the conditions of his existence in a twofold way: directly through the immediate influence of his economic and social position, and indirectly by means of the ideologic structure of the society. His psychic structure, in other words, is forced to develop a contradiction corresponding to the contradiction between the influence exercised by his material position and the influence exercised by the ideological structure of society. The worker, for instance, is subject to the situation of his work as well as to the general ideology of the society. Since man, however, regardless of class, is not only the object of these influences but also reproduces them in his *activities,* his thinking and acting must be just as contradictory as the society from which they derive. But, inasmuch *as a social ideology changes man's psychic structure, it has not only reproduced itself in man but, what is more significant, has become an active force, a material power in man, who in turn has become concretely changed, and, as a consequence thereof, acts in a different and contradictory fashion.* It is in this way and *only* in this way that the repercussions of a society's ideology on the economic basis from which it derives is possible. The "repercussion" loses its apparent metaphysical and psychologistic character when it can be comprehended as the functioning of the character structure of socially active man. As such, it is the object of natural scientific investigations of the character. Thus, the statement that the "ideology" changes at a slower pace than the economic basis is invested with a definite cogency. The basic traits of the character structures corresponding to a definite historical situation are formed in early childhood, and are far more conservative than the forces of technical production. It results from this that, as time goes on, *the psychic structures lag behind the rapid changes of the social conditions from which they derived, and later come into conflict with new forms of life.* This is the basic trait of the nature of so-called tradition, i.e., of the contradiction between the old and the new social situation. . . .

Even Lenin noted a peculiar, irrational behavior on the part of the masses before and in the process of a revolt. On the soldiers' revolt in Russia in 1905, he wrote:

> The soldier had a great deal of sympathy for the cause of the peasant; at the mere mention of land, his eyes blazed with passion. Several times military power passed into the hands of the soldiers, but this power was hardly ever used resolutely. The soldiers wavered. A few hours after they had disposed of a hated superior, they released the others, entered into negotiations with the authorities, and then had themselves shot, submitted to the rod, had themselves yoked again.

To help clarify our approach to the investigation of such irrational *mass* psychological phenomena, it is necessary to take a cursory glance at the line of questioning of *sex-economy*. *Sex-economy* is a field of research that grew out of the sociology of human sexual life many years ago, through the application of functionalism in this sphere, and has acquired a number of new insights. . . .

Psychoanalysis discloses the effects and mechanisms of sexual suppression and repression and of their pathological consequences in the individual. Sex-economic sociology goes further and asks: *For what sociological reasons is sexuality suppressed by the society and repressed by the individual?* The church says it is for the sake of salvation beyond the grave; mystical moral philosophy says that it is a direct result of man's eternal ethical and moral nature; the Freudian philosophy of civilization contends that this takes place in the interest of "culture." One becomes a bit skeptical and asks how is it possible for the masturbation of small children and the sexual intercourse of adolescents to disrupt the building of gas stations and the manufacturing of airplanes. It becomes apparent that it is not cultural activity itself which demands suppression and repression of sexuality, but only the present *forms* of this activity, and so one is willing to sacrifice these forms if by so doing the terrible wretchedness of children and adolescents could be eliminated. The question, then, is no longer one relating to culture, but one relating to social order. If one studies the history of sexual suppression and the etiology of sexual repression, one finds that it cannot be traced back to the beginnings of cultural development; suppression and repression, in other words, are not the presuppositions of cultural development. It was not until relatively late, with the establishment of an authoritarian patriarchy and the beginning of the division of the classes, that suppression of sexuality begins to make its appearance. It is at this stage that sexual interests in general begin to enter the service of a minority's interest in material profit; in the patriarchal marriage and family this state of affairs assumes a solid organizational form. With the restriction and suppression of sexuality, the nature of human feeling changes; a sex-negating religion comes into being and gradually develops its own sex-political organization, the church with all its predecessors, the aim of which is nothing other than the eradication of man's sexual desires and consequently of what little happiness there is on earth. There is good reason for all this when seen from the perspective of the now-thriving exploitation of human labor.

To comprehend the relation between sexual suppression and human exploitation, it is necessary to get an insight into the basic social institution in which the economic and sex-economic situation of patriarchal authoritarian society are interwoven. Without the inclusion of this institution, it is not possible to understand the sexual economy and the ideological process of a patriarchal society. The psychoanalysis of men and women of all ages, all countries, and every social class shows that: *The interlacing of the socio-economic structure with the sexual structure of society and the structural reproduction of society take place in the first four or five years and in the authoritarian family.* The church only continues this function later. Thus, the authoritarian state gains an enormous interest in the authoritarian family: *It becomes the factory in which the state's structure and ideology are molded.*

We have found the social institution in which the sexual and the economic interests of the authoritarian system converge. Now we have to ask *how* this convergence takes place and *how* it operates. Needless to say, the analysis of the typical character structure of reactionary man (the worker included) can yield an answer only if one is at all conscious of the necessity of posing such a question. The moral inhibition of the child's natural sexuality, the last stage of which is the severe impairment of the child's *genital* sexuality, makes the child afraid, shy, fearful of authority, obedient, "good," and "docile" in the authoritarian sense of the words. It has a crippling effect on man's rebellious forces because every vital life-impulse is now burdened with severe fear; and since sex is a forbidden subject, thought in general and man's critical faculty also become inhibited. In short, morality's aim is to produce acquiescent subjects who, despite distress and humiliation, are adjusted to the authoritarian order. Thus, the family is the authoritarian state in miniature, to which the child must learn to adapt himself as a preparation for the general social adjustment required of him later. *Man's authoritarian structure*—this must be clearly established—*is basically produced by the embedding of sexual inhibitions and fear in the living substance of sexual impuls*es.

We will readily grasp why sex-economy views the family as the most important source for the reproduction of the authoritarian social system when we consider the situation of the average conservative worker's wife. Economically she is just as distressed as a liberated working woman, is subject to the same economic situation, but *she* votes for the Fascist party; if we further clarify the actual difference between the sexual ideology of the average liberated woman and that of the average reactionary woman, then we recognize the decisive importance of sexual structure. Her anit-sexual moral inhibitions prevent the conservative woman from gaining a consciousness of her social situation and bind her just as firmly to the church as they make her fear "sexual Bolshevism." Theoretically, the state of affairs is as follows: The vulgar Marxist who thinks in mechanistic terms assumes that discernment of the social situation would have to be especially keen when sexual distress is added to economic distress. If this assumption were true, the majority of adolescents and the majority of women would have to be far more rebellious than the majority of men. Reality reveals an entirely different picture, and the economist is at a complete loss to know how to deal with it. He will find it incomprehensible that the reactionary woman is not even interested in hearing his economic program. The explanation is: The suppression of one's primitive material needs compasses a different result than the suppression of one's sexual needs. The former incites to rebellion, whereas the latter—inasmuch as it causes sexual needs to be repressed, withdraws them from consciousness and anchors itself as a moral defense—prevents rebellion against *both* forms of suppression. Indeed, the inhibition of rebellion itself is unconscious. In the consciousness of the average nonpolitical man there is not even a trace of it.

The result is conservatism, fear of freedom, in a word, reactionary thinking.

It is not only by means of this process that sexual repression strengthens political reaction and makes the individual in the masses passive and nonpolitical; it creates a secondary force in man's structure—an artificial interest, which actively supports the authoritarian order. When sexuality is prevented from attaining natural gratification, owing to the process of sexual repression, what happens is that it seeks various kinds of substitute gratifications. Thus, for instance, natural aggression is distorted into brutal sadism, which constitutes an essential part of the mass-psychological basis of those imperialistic wars that are instigated by a few. . . .

The sexual morality that inhibits the will to freedom, as well as those forces that comply with authoritarian interests, derive their energy from repressed sexuality. Now we have a better comprehension of an essential part of the process of the "repercussion of ideology on the economic basis": *sexual inhibition changes the structure of economically suppressed man in such a way that he acts, feels, and thinks contrary to his own material interests.*

Thus, mass psychology enables us to substantiate and interpret Lenin's observation. In their officers the soldiers of 1905 unconsciously perceived their childhood fathers (condensed in the conception of God), who denied sexuality and whom one could neither kill nor want to kill, though they shattered one's joy of life. Both their repentance and their irresolution subsequent to the seizure of power were an expression of its opposite, hate transformed into pity, which as such could not be translated into action.

Thus, the practical problem of mass psychology is to actuate the passive majority of the population, which always helps political reaction to achieve victory, and to eliminate those inhibitions that run counter to the development of the will to freedom born of the socio-economic situation.

37. Jean Baudrillard:
The Mirror of Production

A specter haunts the revolutionary imagination: the phantom of production. Everywhere it sustains an unbridled romanticism of productivity. . . . In order to achieve a radical critique of political economy, it is not enough to unmask what is hidden behind the concept of consumption: the anthropology of needs and of use value. We must also unmask everything hidden behind the concepts of production, mode of production, productive forces, relations of production, etc. All the fundamental concepts of Marxist analysis must be questioned. . . . The liberation of productive forces is confused with the liberation of man. . . .

Marxist analysis unmasked the myth of the People and revealed what it ideally hides: wage earners and the class struggle. On the other hand, Marxism only partially dislocated the myth of Nature and the idealist anthropology it supports. . . . Starting with the 18th century, the idea of Man divides into a naturally good man (a projection of man sublimated as a productive force) and an instinctively evil man endowed with evil powers. The entire philosophical debate is organized around these sham alternatives, which result simply from the elevation of man to an economic abstraction. Marxism and all revolutionary perspectives are aligned on the optimist vision. They preserve the idea of an innate human rationality, a positive potentiality that must be liberated, even in the latest Freudo-Marxist version in which the unconscious itself is reinterpreted as "natural" wealth, a hidden positivity that will burst forth in the revolutionary act. . . .

Marxism has not disencumbered itself of the moral philosophy of the Enlightenment. It has rejected its naive and sentimental side (Rousseau and Bernardin de Saint-Pierre), its cloying and fantastic religiosity (from the noble savage and the Age of Gold to the sorcerer's apprentice), but it holds onto the religion: the moralizing phantasm of a Nature to be conquered. . . .

Marx says, "Just as the savage must wrestle with Nature to satisfy his wants, to maintain and reproduce life, so must civilized man, and he must do so in all social formations and under all possible modes of production. With his development this realm of physical necessity expands as a result of his wants: but, at the same time, the forces in production which satisfy these wants also increase." What is not recognized here—and what allies Marx with the foundations of political economy—is that in his symbolic exchanges primitive man *does not gauge himself in relation to Nature.* He is not aware of Necessity, a Law that takes effect only with the objectification of Nature. The Law takes its definitive form in capitalist political economy; moreover, it is only the philosophical expression of Scarcity. Scarcity, which itself arises in the market economy, is not a *given* dimension of the economy. Rather, it is what *produces and reproduces* economic exchange. . . .

Parallel to the concepts of Necessity, Scarcity, and Need in the (vulgar or dialectical) materialist code, the psychoanalytic concepts of Law, Prohibition, and Repression are also rooted in the objectification of Nature.

Vernant cites the story of Lycurgus. Lycurgus kills his son Dryas or, in other versions, cuts off his foot believing he is trimming a vine. In another story, Phylacus makes his son impotent while trimming a tree or butchering livestock. Hence the violence against nature (the rupture of exchange with a symbolic obligation toward it) is immediately expiated. All the myths of a vengeful, bad, *castrating* nature take root here. And this is no mere metaphor, as the story clearly indicates. The rupture is immediately the foundation of *castration,* of the Oedipus complex (in this case parental, since the father emasculates the son), and of Law. For only then does Nature appear as an implacable necessity, "the alienation of man's own body." Marx adopted this Law of Necessity along with the Promethean and Faustian vision of its perpetual transcendence, just as psychoanalysis adopted the principle of castration and repression, prohibition and law. . . . But in no sense is it a fundamental structure. Neither Law nor Necessity exist at the level of reciprocity and symbolic exchange. . . . In this sense law, which is called the foundation of the symbolic order and of exchange, results instead from the rupture of exchange and the loss of the symbolic.

Under the sign of Necessity and Law, the same fate—sublimation—awaits Marxism and psychoanalysis. We have seen how materialism's reference to "objective" Necessity led it to fantasize in its revolutionary perspectives the reverse schemes of Freedom and Abundance (the universality of needs and capacities) which are only the sublimated counterparts of Law and Necessity. Similarly, the analytic reference to the Unconscious, product of repression and prohibition, leads to the same step (today psychoanalysis is being short-circuited on a very large scale, and this turning away cannot be called accidental): an ideal reference to a "liberation" of the Unconscious and to its universalization by removing repression. In this case as well, an ideal-revolutionary sublimation of a *content* results from accepting an essential *form* given as irreducible. . . .

At all levels, the system is sick from desublimation, from liberalization, from tolerance, while seeking to transcend itself in order to survive. Consumption, satisfaction of needs, sexual liberation, women's rights, etc., etc.—it is prepared to grant anything in order to reduce social abstraction so that people will play the game. . . . Sexuality, which was once repressed, is liberated as a game of signs. It objectifies sexuality as the functionality of the body and the profitability of the pleasure principle. Information is liberated, but only in order to be better managed and stylized by the media. Everywhere the pressure of the system of political economy is heightened. The final avatars are anti-pollution and job enrichment. Here also the system seems to slacken its limits and restore nature and work in their dignity: a desublimation of productive forces in relation to traditional exploitation. But we know very well that a symbolic relation of man to nature or to his work will not reemerge here. There will only be a more flexible and reinforced operationality of the system. . . . In short, what haunts the system is symbolic demand. . . . Let us say that the system is structurally incapable of liberating human potentials except as *productive* forces, that is, according to an operational finality that leaves no room for the reversion of the loss, the gift, the sacrifice and hence for the possibility of symbolic exchange.

The example of consumption is significant. The feudal system died because it could not find the path to rational productivity. The bourgeoisie knew how to make the people work, but it also narrowly escaped destruction in 1929 because it did not know how to make them consume. It was content, until then, to socialize people by force and exploit them through labor. But the crisis in 1929 marked the point of asphyxiation: the problem was no longer one of production but one of circulation. Consumption became the strategic element; the people were henceforth mobilized as consumers; their "needs" became as essential as their labor power. By this operation, the system assured its economic survival at a fantastically expanded level. But something else is at play in the strategy of consumption. By allowing for the possibility of expanding and consuming, by organizing social redistribution (social security, allotments, salaries that are no longer defined as the strict economic reproduction of labor power) by launching advertising, human relations, etc., the system created the illusion of a symbolic participation (the illusion that something that is taken and won is also redistributed, given, and sacrificed). In fact, this entire symbolic simulation is uncovered as leading to super-profits and super-power. In spite of all its good will (at least among those capitalists who are aware of the necessity of tempering the logic of the system in order to avoid an explosion in the near future), it cannot make consumption a true *consummation,* a festival, a waste. . . .

Proudhon had envisaged "the polyvalence by which the worker, accomplishing the whole cycle of production, would become once again the master of the complete process." Whether this demand today is individual (it gets stranded in the potter or the neo-artisan), communal or collective, it is always the ideal of a reappropriation of labor and this ideal depends on sublimation. It perpetuates, under the autonomy of the laborer, the principle of the sublimation of labor. It is contemporaneous, in the shadow of the industrial system and its constraints, with the manipulated resurrection of the body and sexuality in which each becomes again the master of his body and the free agent of his pleasure, at once interiorizing the sexual *function* and reinvesting the body as the *instrument of the production* of pleasure. Once again there is outlined a Golden Age of functional and productive Eros. . . . But such mastery is absurd since its definition encloses itself in terms of labor and use value. The individual who "controls" his labor is an idealization of this basic constraint. It is simply the slave who has become *his own master,* since the master-slave couple is interiorized in the same individual without ceasing to function as an alienated structure. He "disposes" of himself; he is his own usufruct.

38. Georg Lukács:
History and Class Consciousness   [1885–1971]

Marx's chief work breaks off just as he is about to embark on the definition of class. This omission was to have serious consequences both for the theory and the practice of the proletariat. For on this vital point the later movement was forced to base itself on interpretations, on the collation of occasional utterances by Marx and Engels and on the independent extrapolation and application of their method. In Marxism the division of society into classes is determined by position within the process of production. But what, then, is the meaning of class consciousness? The question at once branches out into a series of closely interrelated problems. First of all, how are we to understand class consciousness (in theory)? Second, what is the (practical) function of class consciousness, so understood, in the context of the class struggle? This leads to the further question: is the problem of class consciousness a 'general' sociological problem or does it mean one thing for the proletariat and another for every other class to have emerged hitherto? And lastly, is class consciousness homogeneous in nature and function or can we discern different gradations and levels in it? And if so, what are their practical implications for the class struggle of the proletariat? . . .

By relating consciousness to the whole of society it becomes possible to infer the thoughts and feelings which men would have in a particular situation if they were *able* to assess both it and the interests arising from it in their impact on immediate action and on the whole structure of society. That is to say, it would be possible to infer the thoughts and feelings appropriate to their objective situation. The number of such situations is not unlimited in any society. However much detailed researches are able to refine social typologies there will always be a number of clearly distinguished basic types whose characteristics are determined by the types of position available in the process of production. Now class consciousness consists in fact of the appropriate and rational reactions 'imputed' [zugerechnet] to a particular typical position in the process of production. This consciousness is, therefore, neither the sum nor the average of what is thought or felt by the single individuals who make up the class. And yet the historically significant actions of the class as a whole are determined in the last resort by this consciousness and not by the thought of the individual—and these actions can be understood only by reference to this consciousness.

This analysis establishes right from the start the distance

that separates class consciousness from the empirically given, and from the psychofogically describable and explicable ideas which men form about their situation in life. . . .

Regarded abstractly and formally, then, class consciousness implies a class-conditioned *unconsciousness* of one's own socio-historical and economic condition. . . . For if from the vantage point of a particular class the totality of existing society is not visible; if a class thinks the thoughts imputable to it and which bear upon its interests right through to their logical conclusion and yet fails to strike at the heart of that totality, then such a class is doomed to play only a subordinate role. It can never influence the course of history in either a conservative or progressive direction. Such classes are normally condemned to passivity, to an unstable oscillation between the ruling and the revolutionary classes, and if perchance they do erupt then such explosions are purely elemental and aimless. They may win a few battles but they are doomed to ultimate defeat.

For a class to be ripe for hegemony means that its interests and consciousness enable it to organise the whole of society in accordance with those interests. The crucial question in every class struggle is this: which class possesses this capacity and this consciousness at the decisive moment? This does not preclude the use of force. It does not mean that the class-interests destined to prevail and thus to uphold the interests of society as a whole can be guaranteed an automatic victory. On the contrary, such a transfer of power can often only be brought about by the most ruthless use of force (as e.g. the primitive accumulation of capital). But it often turns out that questions of class consciousness prove to be decisive in just those situations where force is unavoidable and where classes are locked in a life-and-death-struggle. . . .

It must not be thought, however, that all classes ripe for hegemony have a class consciousness with the same inner structure. Everything hinges on the extent to which they can become conscious of the actions they need to perform in order to obtain and organise power. The question then becomes: how far does the class concerned perform the actions history has imposed on it 'consciously' or 'unconsciously'? And is that consciousness 'true' or 'false'. These distinctions are by no means academic. Quite apart from problems of culture where such fissures and dissonances are crucial, in all practical matters too the fate of a class depends on its ability to elucidate and solve the problems with which history confronts it. And here it becomes transparently obvious that class consciousness is concerned neither with the thoughts of individuals, however advanced, nor with the state of scientific knowledge. For example, it is quite clear that ancient society was broken economically by the limitations of a system built on slavery. But it is equally clear that neither the ruling classes nor the classes that rebelled against them in the name of revolution or reform could perceive this. In consequence the practical emergence of these problems meant that the society was necessarily and irremediably doomed. . . .

Class consciousness is identical with neither the psychological consciousness of individual members of the proletariat, nor with the (mass-psychological) consciousness of the proletariat as a whole; but it is on the contrary, *the sense, become conscious, of the historical role of the class.* . . .

To say that class consciousness has no psychological reality does not imply that [consciousness] is a mere fiction. Its reality is vouched for by its ability to explain the infinitely painful path of the proletarian revolution.

PART SIX

PSYCHOANALYTIC SOCIOLOGY: FOUR DIRECTIONS

In this final part, we examine some of the contemporary ideas about society which have developed out of the work of Freud. Like the prior part on the psychology of Marx, the question here is how far a body of theory can be expanded. The parallels between the two parts go one step further. Just as Marxism as a living critical tradition suffers when it becomes the official ideology of government bureaucrats, psychoanalysis has become intellectually arid as it has been adopted as an official ideology of medical bureaucrats. In both cases, the theory is taught as an established science, one whose premises are never doubted and whose "application" only remains to be worked out. The embalming of both Marx and Freud as official sciences means that their ideas are kept alive from decade to decade by "unsound," "non-professional," or otherwise deviant writers. Thus none of the writers in this section are psychoanalysts with medical degrees, just as none of the writers in the last were considered, at least for long, "reliable" Communist Party members.

The reader who would like to examine relatively intelligent statements of psychoanalytic orthodoxy is referred to Charles Brenner, M.D., *An Elementary Textbook of Psychoanalysis,* for the theory itself, and Weinstein and Platt, *Psychoanalytic Sociology,* for the theory applied to social conditions. The most distinguished criticism of the psychoanalytic movement is probably Philip Rieff's *The Uses of Faith after Freud*. Two extensions of psychoanalytic work which the reader of this book might also find interesting are the relationship of psychoanalysis and art, for which Ernst Kris's *Psychoanalytic Explorations in Art* and William Phillips' *Art and Psychoanalysis* are particularly good, and the development of ego psychology, a branch of psychoanalytic inquiry focused on the human being's mechanisms for copying with the world, rather than his instinctual drives. In addition to Erikson, whose developmental psychology belongs in this school, see volumes of collected papers by, respectively, Heinz Hartmann, George Klein, and Robert Holt. Finally, reasons of space preclude presentation here of the various groups of English writers on the infant and his social world; among these writers are Melanie Klein and Joan Riviere (see their *Love, Hate, and Reparation*) and D. W. Winnicott (*The Child, the Family, and the Outside World*).

One of the enduring themes in work on psychoanalysis and society is the effort to connect Freud with Marx. The Frankfurt School, referred to in Part Three and represented there by Max Horkheimer's essay on the family, has been a leader in this effort. Herbert Marcuse, a younger member of the original Frankfurt group, addresses this problem in the passages from *Eros and Civilization* presented here. Marcuse focuses on a particular problem: can we conceive of a surplus of psychic repression in society similar in form to the creation of economic surplus-value? (The analysis of surplus-value revealed to Marx the grounds on which economic oppression was created.) Marcuse answers this question in the affirmative; he describes this union of psychological and economic surplus-value as the "performance principle" in society. His work shares much with the writing of Baudrillard, presented in Part Five.

Beyond this fusion of theories, the relations of psychoanalysis and society can be worked out in two counterposed directions. In one, psychoanalytic ideas are adapted to serve as tools for analysis of social problems; after the analyst has confronted a particular problem, he then in retrospect tries to define what was adequate and what inadequate in the psychoanalytic presuppositions with which he began. This effort is represented here by Philip E. Slater's "On Social Regression." Writers working in another direction take psychoanalysis as itself a symptom of modern culture, and try to understand the conditions of the culture—its beliefs, its practices, its taboos—by understanding their appearance as psychoanalytic concepts. This form of inquiry is in general called "the sociology of knowledge." Obviously, the danger of this approach is reductionism; a writer expresses only what the values of the culture dictate be expressed. This is a danger analogous to, and was condemned by Marx as, a form of vulgar Marxism. A sensitive and intelligent example of interpreting psychoanalysis in cultural terms is offered, by contrast, in Juliet Mitchell's *Psychoanalysis and Feminism*. Here the biological base of psychoanalysis is denied. Freud's struggle to complete a theory are seen as both symptomatic of, and guides to, the effort to construct a theory of cultural evolution, one using psychoanalytic concepts as historically descriptive.

Finally, Freud's moral outlook on society has remained a vital and disturbing force. In its pessimistic grandeur, Freud's thought has influenced a wide spectrum of writers, from the Spanish anarchist Xavier Rubert de Ventos to the historian Christopher Lasch to the sociologist Philip Rieff. For these writers Freud provides an image of the limits of human happiness in society, and the problems which arise when human beings attempt to transcend those limits. For the Left, Freud's morality serves as a critique of the bourgeois ideal of self-fulfillment; for the Right, as an explanation for the necessary restrictions upon government in satisfying the needs of its citizens. Freud's moral vision is rendered here in a passage from Rieff's *The Triumph of the Therapeutic;* Rieff wants to understand the moral position Freud occupied in refusing to be a moralist.

39. Herbert Marcuse: "The Dialectic of Civilization" in *Eros and Civilization*   [1898–]

Freud attributes to the sense of guilt a decisive role in the development of civilization; moreover, he establishes a correlation between progress and *increasing* guilt feeling. He states his intention "to represent the sense of guilt as the most important problem in the evolution of culture, and to convey that the price of progress in civilization is paid in forfeiting happiness through the heightening of the sense of guilt."[1] Recurrently Freud emphasizes that, as civilization progresses, guilt feeling is "further reinforced," "intensified," is "ever-increasing."[2] The evidence adduced by Frued is twofold: first, he derives it analytically from the theory of instincts, and, second, he finds the theoretical analysis corroborated by the great diseases and discontents of contemporary civilization: an enlarged cycle of wars, ubiquitous persecution, anti-Semitism, genocide, bigotry, and the enforcement of "illusions," toil, sickness, and misery in the midst of growing wealth and knowledge.

We have briefly reviewed the prehistory of the sense of guilt; it has "its origin in the Oedipus complex and was acquired when the father was killed by the association of the brothers."[3] They satisfied their aggressive instinct; but the love which they had for the father caused remorse, created the superego by identification, and thus created the "restrictions which should prevent a repetition of the deed."[4] Subsequently, man abstains

[1] *Civilization and Its Discontents* (London: Hogarth Press, 1949), p. 123.

[2] *Ibid.*, pp. 120–122.

[3] *Ibid.*, p. 118.

[4] *Ibid.*, p. 120.

from the deed; but from generation to generation the aggressive impulse revives, directed against the father and his successors, and from generation to generation aggression has to be inhibited anew:

> Every renunciation then becomes a dynamic fount of conscience; every fresh abandonment of gratification increases its severity and intolerance . . . every impulse of aggression which we omit to gratify is taken over by the super-ego and goes to heighten its aggressiveness (against the ego).[5]

The excessive severity of the superego, which takes the wish for the deed and punishes even suppressed aggression, is now explained in terms of the eternal struggle between Eros and the death instinct: the aggressive impulse against the father (and his social successors) is a derivative of the death instinct; in "separating" the child from the mother, the father also inhibits the death instinct, the Nirvana impulse. He thus does the work of Eros; love, too, operates in the formation of the superego. The severe father, who as the forbidding representative of Eros subdues the death instinct in the Oedipus conflict, enforces the first "communal" (social) relations: his prohibitions create identification among the sons, aim-inhibited love (affection), exogamy, sublimation. On the basis of renunciation, Eros begins its cultural work of combining life into ever larger units. And as the father is multiplied, supplemented, and replaced by the authorities of society, as prohibitions and inhibitions spread, so do the aggressive impulse and its objects. And with it grows, on the part of society, the need for strengthening the defenses—the need for reinforcing the sense of guilt:

> Since culture obeys an inner erotic impulse which bids it bind mankind into a closely knit mass, it can achieve this aim only by means of its vigilance in fomenting an ever-increasing sense of guilt. That which began in relation to the father ends in relation to the community. If civilization is an inevitable course of development from the group of the family to the group of humanity as a whole, then an intensification of the sense of guilt—resulting from the innate conflict of ambivalence, from the eternal struggle between the love and the

[5] *Ibid.*, p. 114.

death trends—will be inextricably bound up with it, until perhaps the sense of guilt may swell to a magnitude that individuals can hardly support.[6]

In this quantitative analysis of the growth of the sense of guilt, the change in the *quality* of guiltiness, its growing irrationality, seems to disappear. Indeed, Freud's central sociological position prevented him from following this avenue. To him, there was no higher rationality against which the prevailing one could be measured. If the irrationality of guilt feeling is that of civilization itself, then it is rational; and if the abolition of domination destroys culture itself, then it remains the supreme crime, and no effective means for its prevention are irrational. However, Freud's own theory of instincts impelled him to go further and to unfold the entire fatality and futility of this dynamic. Strengthened defense against aggression is necessary; but in order to be effective the defense against enlarged aggression would have to strengthen the sex instincts, for only a strong Eros can effectively "bind" the destructive instincts. And this is precisely what the *developed civilization is incapable of doing* because it depends for its very existence on extended and intensified regimentation and control. The chain of inhibitions and deflections of instinctual aims cannot be broken. "Our civilization is, generally speaking, founded on the suppression of instincts."[7]

Civilization is first of all progress in *work*—that is, work for the procurement and augmentation of the necessities of life. This work is normally without satisfaction in itself; to Freud it is unpleasurable, painful. In Freud's metapsychology there is no room for an original "instinct of workmanship," "mastery instinct," etc.[8] The notion of the conservative nature of the instincts under the rule of the pleasure and Nirvana principles strictly precludes such assumptions. When Freud incidentally

[6] *Ibid.*, pp. 121–122.
[7] " 'Civilized' Sexual Morality and Modern Nervousness," in *Collected Papers* (London: Hogarth Press, 1950), II, p. 82.
[8] Ives Hendrick, "Work and the Pleasure Principle," in *Psychoanalytic Quarterly,* XII (1943), p. 314. For a further discussion of this paper, see Chapter 10 below.

mentions the "natural human aversion to work,"[9] he only draws the inference from his basic theoretical conception. The instinctual syndrome "unhappiness and work" recurs throughout Freud's writings,[10] and his interpretation of the Prometheus myth is centered on the connection between curbing of sexual passion and civilized work.[11] The basic work in civilization is non-libidinal, is labor; labor is "unpleasantness," and such unpleasantness has to be enforced. "For what motive would induce man to put his sexual energy to other uses if by any disposal of it he could obtain fully satisfying pleasure? He would never let go of this pleasure and would make no further progress."[12] If there is no original "work instinct," then the energy required for (unpleasurable) work must be "withdrawn" from the primary instincts—from the sexual and from the destructive instincts. Since civilization is mainly the work of Eros, it is first of all withdrawal of libido: culture "obtains a great part of the mental energy it needs by subtracting it from sexuality."[13]

But not only the work impulses are thus fed by aim-inhibited sexuality. The specifically "social instincts" (such as the "affectionate relations between parents and children, . . . feelings of friendship, and the emotional ties in marriage") contain impulses which are "held back by internal resistance" from attaining their aims;[14] only by virtue of such renunciation do they become sociable. Each individual contributes his renunciations (first under the impact of external compulsion, then internally), and from "these sources the common stock of the material and ideal wealth of civilization has been accumu-

[9] *Civilization and Its Discontents,* p. 34 note.
[10] In a letter of April 16, 1896, he speaks of the "moderate misery necessary for intensive work." Ernest Jones, *The Life and Work of Sigmund Freud,* Vol. I (New York: Basic Books, 1953), p. 305.
[11] *Civilization and Its Discontents,* pp. 50–51 note; *Collected Papers,* V, 288ff. For Freud's apparently contradictory statement on the libidinal satisfaction provided by work (*Civilization and Its Discontents,* p. 34 note), see page 212 below.
[12] "The Most Prevalent Form of Degradation in Erotic Life," in *Collected Papers,* IV, p. 216.
[13] *Civilization and Its Discontents,* p. 74.
[14] "The Libido Theory," in *Collected Papers,* V, p. 134.

lated."[15] Although Freud remarks that these social instincts "need not be described as sublimated" (because they have not abandoned their sexual aims but rest content with "certain approximations to satisfaction"), he calls them "closely related" to sublimation.[16] Thus the main sphere of civilization appears as a sphere of *sublimation*. But sublimation involves *desexualization*. Even if and where it draws on a reservoir of "neutral displaceable energy" in the ego and in the id, this neutral energy "proceeds from the narcissistic reservoir of libido," i.e., it is desexualized Eros.[17] The process of sublimation alters the balance in the instinctual structure. Life is the fusion of Eros and death instinct; in this fusion, Eros has subdued its hostile partner. However:

> After sublimation the erotic component no longer has the power to bind the whole of the destructive elements that were previously combined with it, and these are released in the form of inclinations to aggression and destruction.[18]

Culture demands continuous sublimation; it thereby weakens Eros, the builder of culture. And desexualization, by weakening Eros, unbinds the destructive impulses. Civilization is thus threatened by an instinctual de-fusion, in which the death instinct strives to gain ascendancy over the life instincts. Originating in renunciation and developing under progressive renunciation, civilization tends toward self-destruction.

This argument runs too smooth to be true. A number of objections arise. In the first place, not all work involves desexualization, and not all work is unpleasurable, is renunciation. Secondly, the inhibitions enforced by culture also affect—and perhaps even chiefly affect—the derivatives of the death instinct, aggressiveness and the destruction impulses. In this respect at least, cultural inhibition would accrue to the strength of Eros. Moreover, work in civilization is itself to a great extent *social utilization* of aggressive impulses and is thus work in the

[15] " 'Civilized' Sexual Morality . . .," p. 82.
[16] "The Libido Theory," p. 134.
[17] *The Ego and the Id* (London: Hogarth Press, 1950), pp. 38, 61–63. See Edward Glover, "Sublimation, Substitution, and Social Anxiety," in *International Journal of Psychoanalysis,* Vol. XII, No. 3 (1931), p. 264.
[18] *The Ego and the Id,* p. 80.

service of Eros. An adequate discussion of these problems presupposes that the theory of the instincts is freed from its exclusive orientation on the performance principle, that the image of a non-repressive civilization (which the very achievements of the performance principle suggest) is examined as to its substance. Such an attempt will be made in the last part of this study; here, some tentative clarifications must suffice.

The psychical sources and resources of work, and its relation to sublimation, constitute one of the most neglected areas of psychoanalytic theory. Perhaps nowhere else has psychoanalysis so consistently succumbed to the official ideology of the blessings of "productivity."[19] Small wonder then, that in the Neo-Freudian schools, where (as we shall see in the Epilogue) the ideological trends in psychoanalysis triumph over its theory, the tenor of work morality is all-pervasive. The "orthodox" discussion is almost in its entirety focused on "creative" work, especially art, while work in the realm of necessity—labor—is relegated to the background.

To be sure, there is a mode of work which offers a high degree of libidinal satisfaction, which is pleasurable in its execution. And artistic work, where it is genuine, seems to grow out of a non-repressive instinctual constellation and to envisage non-repressive aims—so much so that the term *sublimation* seems to require considerable modification if applied to this kind of work. But the bulk of the work relations on which civilization rests is of a very different kind. Freud notes that the "daily work of·earning a livelihood affords particular satisfaction when it has been selected by free choice."[20] However, if "free choice" means more than a small selection between pre-established necessities, and if the inclinations and impulses used in work are other than those preshaped by a repressive reality principle, then satisfaction in daily work is only a rare privilege. The work that created and enlarged the material basis of civilization was chiefly labor, alienated labor, painful and miserable—and still is. The performance of such work hardly gratifies *individual* needs and inclinations. It was imposed upon man by brute

19 Ives Hendrick's article cited above is a striking example.
20 *Civilization and Its Discontents,* p. 34 note.

necessity and brute force; if alienated labor has anything to do with Eros, it must be very indirectly, and with a considerably sublimated and weakened Eros.

But does not the civilized inhibition of *aggressive* impulses in work offset the weakening of Eros? Aggressive as well as libidinal impulses are supposed to be satisfied in work "by way of sublimation," and the culturally beneficial "sadistic character" of work has often been emphasized.[21] The development of technics and technological rationality absorbs to a great extent the "modified" destructive instincts:

> The instinct of destruction, when tempered and harnessed (as it were, inhibited in its aim) and directed towards objects, is compelled to provide the ego with satisfaction of its needs and with power over nature.[22]

Technics provide the very basis for progress; technological rationality sets the mental and behaviorist pattern for productive performance, and "power over nature" has become practically identical with civilization. Is the destructiveness sublimated in these activities sufficiently subdued and diverted to assure the work of Eros? It seems that socially useful destructiveness is less sublimated than socially useful libido. To be sure, the diversion of destructiveness from the ego to the external world secured the growth of civilization. However, extroverted destruction remains destruction: its objects are in most cases actually and violently assailed, deprived of their form, and reconstructed only after partial destruction; units are forcibly divided, and the component parts forcibly rearranged. Nature is literally "violated." Only in certain categories of sublimated aggressiveness (as in surgical practice) does such violation directly strengthen the life of its object. Destructiveness, in extent and intent, seems to be more directly satisfied in civilization than the libido.

However, while the destructive impulses are thus being satisfied, such satisfaction cannot stabilize their energy in the service of Eros. Their destructive force must drive them beyond

[21] See Alfred Winterstein, "Zur Psychologie der Arbeit," in *Imago*, XVIII (1932), 141.
[22] *Civilization and Its Discontents*, p. 101.

this servitude and sublimation, for their aim is, not matter, not nature, not any object, but life itself. If they are the derivatives of the death instinct, then they cannot accept as final any "substitutes." Then, through constructive technological destruction, through the constructive violation of nature, the instincts would still operate toward the annihilation of life. The radical hypothesis of *Beyond the Pleasure Principle* would stand: the instincts of self-preservation, self-assertion, and mastery, in so far as they have absorbed this destructiveness, would have the function of assuring the organism's "own path to death." Freud retracted this hypothesis as soon as he had advanced it, but his formulations in *Civilization and Its Discontents* seem to restore its essential content. And the fact that the destruction of life (human and animal) has progressed with the progress of civilization, that cruelty and hatred and the scientific extermination of men have increased in relation to the real possibility of the elimination of oppression—this feature of late industrial civilization would have instinctual roots which perpetuate destructiveness beyond all rationality. The growing mastery of nature then would, with the growing productivity of labor, develop and fulfill the human needs *only as a by-product:* increasing cultural wealth and knowledge would provide the material for progressive destruction and the need for increasing instinctual repression.

This thesis implies the existence of objective criteria for gauging the degree of instinctual repression at a given stage of civilization. However, repression is largely unconscious and automatic, while its degree is measurable only in the light of consciousness. The differential between (phylogenetically necessary) repression and surplus-repression[23] may provide the criteria. Within the total structure of the repressed personality, surplus-repression is that portion which is the result of specific societal conditions sustained in the specific interest of domination. The extent of this surplus-repression provides the standard of measurement: the smaller it is, the less repressive is the stage of civilization. The distinction is equivalent to that between the

[23] See page 34 [in *Eros and Civilization*].

biological and the historical sources of human suffering. Of the three "sources of human suffering" which Freud enumerates—namely, "the superior force of nature, the disposition to decay of our bodies, and the inadequacy of our methods of regulating human relations in the family, the community and the state"[24] —at least the first and the last are in a strict sense *historical* sources: the superiority of nature and the organization of societal relations have essentially changed in the development of civilization. Consequently, the necessity of repression, and of the suffering derived from it, varies with the maturity of civilization, with the extent of the achieved rational mastery of nature and of society. Objectively, the need for instinctual inhibition and restraint depends on the need for toil and delayed satisfaction. The same and even a reduced scope of instinctual regimentation would constitute a higher degree of repression at a mature stage of civilization, when the need for renunciation and toil is greatly reduced by material and intellectual progress—when civilization could actually afford a considerable release of instinctual energy expended for domination and toil. Scope and intensity of instinctual repression obtain their full significance only in relation to the historically possible extent of freedom. For Freud, is progress in civilization progress in freedom?

We have seen that Freud's theory is focused on the recurrent cycle "domination-rebellion-domination." But the second domination is not simply a repetition of the first one; the cyclical movement is *progress* in domination. From the primal father via the brother clan to the system of institutional authority characteristic of mature civilization, domination becomes increasingly impersonal, objective, universal, and also increasingly rational, effective, productive. At the end, under the rule of the fully developed performance principle, subordination appears as implemented through the social division of labor itself (although physical and personal force remains an indispensable instrumentality). Society emerges as a lasting and expanding system of useful performances; the hierarchy of functions and relations assumes the form of objective reason: law

[24] *Civilization and Its Discontents,* p. 43.

and order are identical with the life of society itself. In the same process, repression too is depersonalized: constraint and regimentation of pleasure now become a function (and "natural" result) of the social division of labor. To be sure, the father, as *paterfamilias,* still performs the basic regimentation of the instincts which prepares the child for the surplus-repression on the part of society during his adult life. But the father performs this function as the representative of the family's position in the social division of labor rather than as the "possessor" of the mother. Subsequently, the individual's instincts are controlled through the social utilization of his labor power. He has to work in order to live, and this work rquires not only eight, ten, twelve daily hours of his time and therefore a corresponding diversion of energy, but also during these hours and the remaining ones a behavior in conformity with the standards and morals of the performance principle. Historically, the reduction of Eros to procreative-monogamic sexuality (which completes the subjection of the pleasure principle to the reality principle) is consummated only when the individual has become a subject-object of labor in the apparatus of his society; whereas, ontogenetically, the primary suppression of infantile sexuality remains the precondition for this accomplishment.

The development of a hierarchical system of social labor not only rationalizes domination but also "contains" the rebellion against domination. At the individual level, the primal revolt is contained within the framework of the normal Oedipus conflict. At the societal level, recurrent rebellions and revolutions have been followed by counter-revolutions and restorations. From the slave revolts in the ancient world to the socialist revolution, the struggle of the oppressed has ended in establishing a new, "better" system of domination; progress has taken place through an improving chain of control. Each revolution has been the conscious effort to replace one ruling group by another; but each revolution has also released forces that have "overshot the goal," that have striven for the abolition of domination and exploitation. The ease with which they have been defeated demands explanations. Neither the prevailing constellation of power, nor immaturity of the productive forces, nor absence of class consciousness provides an adequate answer. In every revolution, there seems to have been a historical moment when the struggle against domination might have been victorious—but the moment passed. An element of *self-defeat* seems to be involved in this dynamic (regardless of the validity of such reasons as the prematurity and inequality of forces). In this sense, every revolution has also been a betrayed revolution.

Freud's hypothesis on the origin and the perpetuation of guilt feeling elucidates, in psychological terms, this sociological dynamic: it explains the "identification" of those who revolt with the power against which they revolt. The economic and political incorporation of the individuals into the hierarchical system of labor is accompanied by an instinctual process in which the human objects of domination reproduce their own repression. And the increasing rationalization of power seems to be reflected in an increasing rationalization of repression. In retaining the individuals as instruments of labor, forcing them into renunciation and toil, domination no longer merely or primarily sustains specific privileges but also sustains society as a whole on an expanding scale. The guilt of rebellion is thereby greatly intensified. The revolt against the primal father eliminated an individual person who could be (and was) replaced by other persons; but when the dominion of the father has expanded into the dominion of society, no such replacement seems possible, and the guilt becomes fatal. Rationalization of guilt feeling has been completed. The father, restrained in the family and in his individual biological authority, is resurrected, far more powerful, in the administration which preserves the life of society, and in the laws which preserve the administration. These final and most sublime incarnations of the father cannot be overcome "symbolically," by emancipation: there is no freedom from administration and its laws because they appear as the ultimate guarantors of liberty. The revolt against them would be the supreme crime again—this time not against the despot-animal who forbids gratification but against the wise order which secures the goods and services for the progressive satisfaction of human needs. Rebellion now appears as the crime against the whole of human society and therefore as beyond reward and beyond redemption.

However, the very progress of civilization tends to make this rationality a spurious one. The existing liberties and the existing gratifications are tied to the requirements of domination; they themselves become instruments of repression. The excuse of scarcity, which has justified institutionalized repression since its inception, weakens as man's knowledge and control over nature enhances the means for fulfilling human needs with a minimum of toil. The still prevailing impoverishment of vast areas of the world is no longer due chiefly to the poverty of human and natural resources but to the manner in which they are distributed and utilized. This difference may be irrelevant to politics and to politicians but it is of decisive importance to a theory of civilization which derives the need for repression from the "natural" and perpetual disproportion between human desires and the environment in which they must be satisfied. If such a "natural" condition, and not certain political and social institutions, provides the rationale for repression, then it has become irrational. The culture of industrial civilization has turned the human organism into an ever more sensitive, differentiated, exchangeable instrument, and has created a social wealth sufficiently great to transform this instrument into an end in itself. The available resources make for a *qualitative* change in the human needs. Rationalization and mechanization of labor tend to reduce the quantum of instinctual energy channeled into toil (alienated labor), thus freeing energy for the attainment of objectives set by the free play of individual faculties. Technology operates against the repressive utilization of energy in so far as it minimizes the time necessary for the production of the necessities of life, thus saving time for the development of needs *beyond* the realm of necessity and of necessary waste.

But the closer the real possibility of liberating the individual from the constraints once justified by scarcity and immaturity, the greater the need for maintaining and streamlining these constraints lest the established order of domination dissolve. Civilization has to defend itself against the specter of a world which could be free. If society cannot use its growing productivity for reducing repression (because such usage would upset the hierarchy of the *status quo*), productivity must be turned *against* the individuals; it becomes itself an instrument of universal control. Totalitarianism spreads over late industrial civilization wherever the interests of domination prevail upon productivity, arresting and diverting its potentialities. The people have to be kept in a state of permanent, mobilization, internal and external. The rationality of domination has progressed to the point where it threatens to invalidate its foundations; therefore it must be reaffirmed more effectively than ever before. This time there shall be no killing of the father, not even a "symbolic" killing—because he may not find a successor.

The "automatization" of the superego[25] indicates the defense mechanisms by which society meets the threat. The defense consists chiefly in a strengthening of controls not so much over the instincts as over consciousness, which, if left free, might recognize the work of repression in the bigger and better satisfaction of needs. The manipulation of consciousness which has occurred throughout the orbit of contemporary industrial civilization has been described in the various interpretations of totalitarian and "popular cultures": co-ordination of the private and public existence of spontaneous and required reactions. The promotion of thoughtless leisure activities, the triumph of anti-intellectual ideologies, exemplify the trend. This extension of controls to formerly free regions of consciousness and leisure permits a relaxation of sexual taboos (previously more important because the over-all controls were less effective). Today compared with the Puritan and Victorian periods, sexual freedom has unquestionably increased (although a reaction against the 1920s is clearly noticeable). At the same time, however, the sexual relations themselves have become much more closely assimilated with social relations; sexual liberty is harmonized with profitable conformity. The fundamental antagonism between sex and social utility—itself the reflex of the conflict between pleasure principle and reality principle—is blurred by the progressive encroachment of the reality principle on the pleasure principle. In a world of alienation, the liberation of Eros would necessarily operate as a destructive, fatal force—as the total negation of the principle which governs the repressive reality. It is not an accident that the great literature of Western

[25] See pages 29–30 [in *Eros and Civilization*].

civilization celebrates only the "unhappy love," that the Tristan myth has become its representative expression. The morbid romanticism of the myth is in a strict sense "realistic." In contrast to the destructiveness of the liberated Eros, the relaxed sexual morality within the firmly entrenched system of monopolistic controls itself serves the system. The negation is co-ordinated with "the positive": the night with the day, the dream world with the work world, phantasy with frustration. Then, the individuals who relax in this uniformly controlled reality recall, not the dream but the day, not the fairy tale but its denunciation. In their erotic relations, they "keep their appointments"—with charm, with romance, with their favorite commercials.

But, within the system of unified and intensified controls, decisive changes are taking place. They affect the structure of the supergo and the content and manifestation of guilt feeling. Moreover, they tend toward a state in which the completely alienated world, expending its full power, seems to prepare the stuff and material for a new reality principle.

The superego is loosened from its origin, and the traumatic experience of the father is superseded by more exogenous images. As the family becomes less decisive in directing the adjustment of the individual to society, the father-son conflict no longer remains the model-conflict. This change derives from the fundamental economic processes which have characterized, since the beginning of the century, the transformation of "free" into "organized" capitalism. The independent family enterprise and, subsequently, the independent personal enterprise cease to be the units of the social system; they are being absorbed into large-scale impersonal groupings and associations. At the same time, the social value of the individual is measured primarily in terms of standardized skills and qualities of adjustment rather than autonomous judgment and personal responsibility.

The technological abolition of the individual is reflected in the decline of the social function of the family.[26] It was

---

[26] For the analysis of these processes, see *Studien über Autorität und Familie,* ed. Max Horkheimer (Paris: Felix Alcan, 1936); Max Horkheimer, *Eclipse of Reason* (New York: Oxford University Press, 1946).

formerly the family which, for good or bad, reared and educated the individual, and the dominant rules and values were transmitted personally and transformed through personal fate. To be sure, in the Oedipus situation, not individuals but "generations" (units of the genus) faced each other; but in the passing and inheritance of the Oedipus conflict they became individuals, and the conflict continued into an individual life history. Through the struggle with father and mother as personal targets of love and aggression, the younger generation entered societal life with impulses, ideas, and needs which were largely *their own*. Consequently, the formation of their superego, the repressive modification of their impulses, their renunciation and sublimation were very personal experiences. Precisely because of this, their adjustment left painful scars, and life under the performance principle still retained a sphere of private non-conformity.

Now, however, under the rule of economic, political, and cultural monopolies, the formation of the mature superego seems to skip the stage of individualization: the generic atom becomes directly a social atom. The repressive organization of the instincts seems to be *collective*, and the ego seems to be prematurely socialized by a whole system of extra-familial agents and agencies. As early as the preschool level, gangs, radio, and television set the pattern for conformity and rebellion; deviations from the pattern are punished not so much within the family as outside and against the family. The experts of the mass media transmit the required values; they offer the perfect training in efficiency, toughness, personality, dream, and romance. With this education, the family can no longer compete. In the struggle between the generations, the sides seem to have shifted: the son knows better; he represents the mature reality principle against its obsolescent paternal forms. The father, the first object of aggression in the Oedipus situation, later appears as a rather inappropriate target of aggression. His authority as transmitter of wealth, skills, experiences is greatly reduced; he has less to offer, and therefore less to prohibit. The progressive father is a most unsuitable enemy and a most unsuitable "ideal"—but so is any father who no longer shapes the child's economic, emotional, and intellectual future. Still, the prohibitions continue to prevail, the repressive control of the instincts persists, and so does the aggressive impulse. Who are the father-substitutes against which it is primarily directed?

As domination congeals into a system of objective administration, the images that guide the development of the superego become depersonalized. Formerly the superego was "fed" by the master, the chief, the principal. These represented the reality principle in their tangible personality: harsh and benevolent, cruel and rewarding, they provoked and punished the desire to revolt; the enforcement of conformity was their personal function and responsibility. Respect and fear could therefore be accompanied by hate of what they were and did as persons; they presented a living object for the impulses and for the conscious efforts to satisfy them. But these personal father-images have gradually disappeared behind the institutions. With the rationalization of the productive apparatus, with the multiplication of functions, all domination assumes the form of administration. At its peak, the concentration of economic power seems to turn into anonymity: everyone, even at the very top, appears to be powerless before the movements and laws of the apparatus itself. Control is normally administered by offices in which the controlled are the employers and the employed. The masters no longer perform an individual function. The sadistic principals, the capitalist exploiters, have been transformed into salaried members of a bureaucracy, whom their subjects meet as members of another bureaucracy. The pain, frustration, impotence of the individual derive from a highly productive and efficiently functioning system in which he makes a better living than ever before. Responsibility for the organization of his life lies with the whole, the "system," the sum total of the institutions that determine, satisfy, and control his needs. The aggressive impulse plunges into a void—or rather the hate encounters smiling colleagues, busy competitors, obedient officials, helpful social workers who are all doing their duty and who are all innocent victims.

Thus repulsed, aggression is again introjected: not suppression but the suppressed is guilty. Guilt of what? Material and intellectual progress has weakened the force of religion below the point where it can sufficiently explain the sense of guilt. The aggressiveness turned against the ego threatens to become senseless: with his consciousness co-ordinated, his privacy abolished, his emotions integrated into conformity, the individual has no longer enough "mental space" for developing himself *against* his sense of guilt, for living with a conscience of his own. His ego has shrunk to such a degree that the multiform antagonistic processes between id, ego, and superego cannot unfold themselves in their classic form.

Still, the guilt is there; it seems to be a quality of the whole rather than of the individuals—collective guilt, the affliction of an institutional system which wastes and arrests the material and human resources at its disposal. The extent of these resources can be defined by the level of fulfilled human freedom attainable through truly rational use of the productive capacity. If this standard is applied, it appears that, in the centers of industrial civilization, man is kept in a state of impoverishment, both cultural and physical. Most of the clichés with which sociology describes the process of dehumanization in present-day mass culture are correct; but they seem to be slanted in the wrong direction. What is retrogressive is not mechanization and standardization but their containment, not the universal co-ordination but its concealment under spurious liberties, choices, and individualities. The high standard of living in the domain of the great corporations is *restrictive* in a concrete sociological sense: the goods and services that the individuals buy control their needs and petrify their faculties. In exchange for the commodities that enrich their life, the individuals sell not only their labor but also their free time. The better living is offset by the all-pervasive control over living. People dwell in apartment concentrations—and have private automobiles with which they can no longer escape into a different world. They have huge refrigerators filled with frozen foods. They have dozens of newspapers and magazines that espouse the same ideals. They have innumerable choices, innumerable gadgets which are all of the same sort and keep them occupied and divert their attention from the real issue—which is the awareness that they could both work less and determine their own needs and satisfactions.

The ideology of today lies in that production and consumption reproduce and justify domination. But their ideological character does not change the fact that their benefits are real. The repressiveness of the whole lies to a high degree in its efficacy: it enhances the scope of material culture, facilitates the procurement of the necessities of life, makes comfort and luxury cheaper, draws ever-larger areas into the orbit of industry—while at the same time sustaining toil and destruction. The individual pays by sacrificing his time, his consciousness, his dreams; civilization pays by sacrificing its own promises of liberty, justice, and peace for all.

The discrepancy between potential liberation and actual repression has come to maturity: it permeates all spheres of life the world over. The rationality of progress heightens the irrationality of its organization and direction. Social cohesion and administrative power are sufficiently strong to protect the whole from direct aggression, but not strong enough to eliminate the accumulated aggressiveness. It turns against those who do not belong to the whole, whose existence is its denial. This foe appears as the archenemy and Anti-christ himself: he is everywhere at all times; he represents hidden and sinister forces, and his omnipresence requires total mobilization. The difference between war and peace, between civilian and military populations, between truth and propaganda, is blotted out. There is regression to historical stages that had been passed long ago, and this regression reactivates the sado-masochistic phase on a national and international scale. But the impulses of this phase are reactivated in a new, "civilized" manner: practically without sublimation, they become socially "useful" activities in concentration and labor camps, colonial and civil wars, in punitive expeditions, and so on.

Under these circumstances, the question whether the present stage of civilization is demonstrably more destructive than the preceding ones does not seem to be very relevant. In any case, the question cannot be avoided by pointing to the destructiveness prevalent throughout history. The destructiveness of the present stage reveals its full significance only if the present is measured, not in terms of past stages, but in terms of its own potentialities. There is more than a quantitative difference in whether wars are waged by professional armies in confined spaces, or against entire populations on a global scale; whether technical inventions that could make the world free from misery are used for the conquest or for the creation of suffering; whether thousands are slain in combat or millions scientifically exterminated with the help of doctors and engineers; whether exiles can find refuge across the frontiers or are chased around the earth; whether people are naturally ignorant or are being *made* ignorant by their daily intake of information and entertainment. It is with a new ease that terror is assimilated with normality, and destructiveness with construction. Still, progress continues, and continues to narrow the basis of repression. At the height of its progressive achievements, domination not only undermines its own foundations, but also corrupts and liquidates the opposition against domination. What remains is the negativity of reason, which impels wealth and power and generates a climate in which the instinctual roots of the performance principle are drying up.

The alienation of labor is almost complete. The mechanics of the assembly line, the routine of the office, the ritual of buying and selling are freed from any connection with human potentialities. Work relations have become to a great extent relations between persons as exchangeable objects of scientific management and efficiency experts. To be sure, the still prevailing competitiveness requires a certain degree of individuality and spontaneity; but these features have become just as superficial and illusory as the competitiveness to which they belong. Individuality is literally in name only in the specific representation of types[27] (such as vamp, housewife, Ondine, he-man, career woman, struggling young couple), just as competition tends to be reduced to prearranged varieties in the production of gadgets, wrappings, flavors, colors, and so on. Beneath this

[27] See Leo Lowenthal, "International Who's Who 1937," in *Studies in Philosophy and Social Science* (formerly *Zeitschrift für Sozialforschung*), VIII (1939), 262ff.; and "Historical Perspectives of Popular Culture," in *American Journal of Sociology*, LV (1950), 323ff.

illusory surface, the whole work-world and its recreation have become a system of animate and inanimate things—all equally subject to administration. The human existence in this world is mere stuff, matter, material, which does not have the principle of its movement in itself. This state of ossification also affects the instincts, their inhibitions and modifications. Their original dynamic becomes static: the interactions between ego, superego, and id congeal into automatic reactions. Corporealization of the superego is accompanied by corporealization of the ego, manifest in the frozen traits and gestures, produced at the appropriate occasions and hours. Consciousness, increasingly less burdened by autonomy, tends to be reduced to the task of regulating the co-ordination of the individual with the whole.

This co-ordination is effective to such a degree that the general unhappiness has decreased rather than increased. We have suggested[28] that the individual's awareness of the prevailing repression is blunted by the manipulated restriction of his consciousness. This process alters the contents of happiness. The concept denotes a more-than-private, more-than-subjective condition;[29] happiness is not in the mere feeling of satisfaction but in the reality of freedom and satisfaction. Happiness involves knowledge: it is the prerogative of the *animal rationale*. With the decline in consciousness, with the control of information, with the absorption of individual into mass communication, knowledge is administered and confined. The individual does not really know what is going on; the overpowering machine of education and entertainment unites him with all the others in a state of anaesthesia from which all detrimental ideas tend to be excluded. And since knowledge of the whole truth is hardly conducive to happiness, such general anaesthesia makes individuals happy. If anxiety is more than a general malaise, if it is an existential condition, then this so-called "age of anxiety" is distinguished by the extent to which anxiety has disappeared from expression.

These trends seem to suggest that the expenditure of

---

[28] See page 85 [in *Eros and Civilization*].
[29] See Herbert Marcuse, "Zur Kritik des Hedonismus," in *Zeitschrift für Sozialforschung,* VII (1938), 55ff.

energy and effort for developing one's own inhibitions is greatly diminished. *The living links between the individual and his culture are loosened*. This culture was, in and for the individual, the system of inhibitions that generated and regenerated the predominant values and institutions. Now, the repressive force of the reality principle seems no longer renewed and rejuvenated by the repressed individuals. The less they function as the agents and victims of their own life, the less is the reality principle strengthened through "creative" identifications and sublimations, which enrich and at the same time protect the household of culture. The groups and group ideals, the philosophies, the works of art and literature that still express without compromise the fears and hopes of humanity stand against the prevailing reality principle: they are its absolute denunciation.

The positive aspects of progressive alienation show forth. The human energies which sustained the performance principle are becoming increasingly dispensable. The automatization of necessity and waste, of labor and entertainment, precludes the realization of individual potentialities in this realm. It repels libidinal cathexis. The ideology of scarcity, of the productivity of toil, domination, and renunciation, is dislodged from its instinctual as well as rational ground. The theory of alienation demonstrated the fact that man does not realize himself in his labor, that his life has become an instrument of labor, that his work and its products have assumed a form and power independent of him as an individual. But the liberation from this state seems to require, not the arrest of alienation, but its consummation, not the reactivation of the repressed and productive personality but its abolition. The elimination of human potentialities from the world of (alienated) labor creates the preconditions for the elimination of labor from the world of human potentialities.

40. Philip E. Slater: "On Social Regression" [1927–]

Freud's later instinct theory has tended on the whole to arouse puzzlement rather than stimulate theory, and with few exceptions has been treated with contempt by his detractors and embarrassment by his supporters. To some extent this is due to the limitations of his own presentation, but much confusion has also arisen from the tendency to translate the "life" and "death" instincts into psychological rather than biological constructs, into human "motives" instead of panspecific impulses. . . .

Although Freud clearly intended the two instincts to be viewed as opposites, he did not describe them in precisely complementary terms. The death instinct is most often defined in terms of an ultimate goal, with very little being said about the process through which it pushes toward that goal. In the case of "Eros" quite the reverse is true: it is always defined in terms of an endless process, with no ultimate goal being apparent.

This latter approach seems more fruitful, from a scientific viewpoint, since it is less teleological. If we operate consistently within this framework, the two instincts can be defined simply as the associative and dissociative propensities of living matter, from the molecular to the societal level, from cell colonies to the social groups of animals and humans. If "Eros" is an expanding, complicating tendency, and the "death instinct" a contracting, simplifying one, then it would be most appropriate to view the two instincts merely as opposing forces acting upon the same inert material, i.e., sexual energy or libido. We would then apply the term "Eros" to the expanding tendencies of the libido, i.e., to those forces driving it toward more and more remote objects, along more and more circuitous paths to gratification, toward involvement in larger and larger collectivities.

The term "death instinct" would refer to the contracting tendencies of the libido, i.e., to those forces driving it toward more and more proximate and intimate objects, along more simple and direct paths to more immediate and complete gratification, toward involvement in smaller and smaller collectivities. Since the terms "libidinal diffusion" and "libidinal contraction" are somewhat more immediately descriptive of the processes to be discussed than are "Eros" and "death instinct," and since their conceptual identity is problematic, I shall use the former pair in the ensuing discussion. . . .

If libidinal diffusion involves not only an increase in the number of objects cathected by the individual, but also an increase in the extent to which gratification is "sublimated," circuitous, delayed, and incomplete, one might well ask, why does it occur at all? What prompts the organism to make these "ever more complicated detours"?

Without getting too deeply into this rather abstruse issue we might simply point out the competitive advantage in natural selection enjoyed by those organisms which participate in collectivities, and the still further advantage held by collectivities which are highly organized and integrated. Libidinal diffusion is the social cement which binds living entities together. The more objects an individual can cathect at once, the larger the number of individuals who can co-operate in a joint endeavor. Furthermore, as libido becomes further diffused, and gratification becomes less complete, the individual experiences a constant tension and restless energy which can be harnessed to serve socially useful ends. . . .

Yet is should be abundantly clear from clinical analysis of dreams and projective materials collected from normal individuals, not to mention the universality of incestuous longings in mythology and folklore, that these earlier libidinal cathexes are never entirely uprooted. Indeed, so long as there is sufficient libido left over for completely free choice of objects, it is not important that they should be. But let us consider the consequences of this fact: "healthy" human growth in all existing societies *requires* that libidinal gratification must always be partial and incomplete. For no matter how perfectly gratifying the individual's mature erotic relationships may be, they cannot discharge those fragments of libidinal tension which have been "left behind," attached to their original incestuous objects.

This is, of course, of little practical psychological significance. Such residual libidinal tensions can be discharged in dreams or humor, or sublimated into filial devotion or artistic creativity. But it is important for social theory, since it means that *so long as an individual cathects more than one object he will be unable to achieve a complete absence of libidinal tension,* and hence remains always available for collectivization. . . .

At this point, however, we find ourselves in another dilemma. Whereas at first we were puzzled to discern the basis for the prevalence of an inferior mode of gratification, we now seem to be in the antipodal difficulty of wondering why there should be any limit to libidinal diffusion. For while one can assume that the superior gratificatory attraction inhering in libidinal contraction would always exert a kind of gravitational drag on this trend, the advantages in terms of natural selection would seem to push inevitably toward endless increases in the diffusional direction.

Even from a societal viewpoint, however, unlimited libidinal diffusion would be a doubtful blessing. The most obvious limitation is the necessity for motivation of procreation. Those few attempts, by totalitarian religious communities of a utopian nature, to sublimate and diffuse all sexual tendencies, illustrate this point rather dramatically. Ultimate diffusion led to ultimate extinction. . . .

THREE THREATS TO AGGREGATE MAINTENANCE

Although violation of the incest prohibition constitutes the nearest danger to suprafamilial collectivities, there are other and more extreme forms of libidinal contraction than that against which the taboo most specifically militates. If libidinal cathexis can be withdrawn from larger collectivities and centered in the nuclear family, it can also be withdrawn from the family and centered in any single dyadic relationship, and finally, it can be withdrawn from all object relationships and centered in the ego, as in the classical psychoanalytic discussions of narcissism. All three are simply positions on a continuous dimension of social regression. . . .

The normal response of others to signs of libidinal contraction in an individual with whom these others participate in some collectivity, is what we shall call "social anxiety." They may also display anger, moral indignation, ridicule, or scorn, but the anxiety is clearly the primary response from which the others are derived. Since it is a rather common and familiar sensation to all of us, experienced whenever someone deserts, either physically or psychically, a group in which we are emotionally involved, little need be said about it. The latent danger with which it is concerned is the collapse of the group. It does not spring, however, from any rational consideration of the advantages of societal existence, but is emotional and automatic, and appears concurrently with awareness of group membership, whether in the family of orientation or elsewhere. Presumably its universality is a result of natural selection.

Social anxiety generally elicits, in those who experience it, behavior designed to reform this deviant member who has "regressed," i.e., transferred his libido from a more inclusive to a less inclusive object. But social control is never entirely *post hoc,* and in all surviving societies we find an elaboration of anticipatory institutions which serve to hinder such cathectic withdrawal. It is primarily with these institutions that the remainder of this paper will deal, although post hoc sanctions will also be discussed.

We have said that there exist three principal forms of libidinal contraction or cathectic withdrawal. Each of these forms has a primary anticipatory institution which tends to preclude its emergence:

(1) The most immediate form—withdrawal of cathexis from larger aggregates to within the confines of the nuclear family—we will call "familial withdrawal." Its principal anticipatory institution is the incest taboo.

(2) Withdrawal of cathexis from larger aggregates to a single intimate dyad we will call "dyadic withdrawal." Its principal anticipatory institution is marriage.

(3) The most extreme form—withdrawal of cathexis from all objects to the self—we will call "narcissistic withdrawal." Its principal anticipatory institution is socialization.

These institutions are for the most part so successful in counteracting libidinal contraction that we are usually unaware of the conflict taking place; it is only at certain rough spots in the social fabric that it becomes visible. . . .

I. Narcissistic withdrawal

Narcissistic withdrawal takes many forms, the most familiar of which are psychosis and somatic illness. In these instances, the internal emotional process is given some kind of concrete physical or behavioral manifestation, but this need not always occur. Furthermore, there are types of behavioral social withdrawal, such as reclusiveness or anchoritism, which may not involve a corresponding degree of withdrawal of libidinal cathexis. . . .

The logical extreme of both of these types of narcissistic withdrawal—in fact of all libidinal contraction for the human organism—is death. Death naturally arouses more social anxiety than illness, however, because it is total, permanent, and irreparable. Furthermore, the dead man does not even decently take himself off, but leaves a putrefying corpse as a material reminder that he has "laid his burden down" and that others may do the same if they wish. For this corpse is impervious to social pressures and sanctions—no matter how others plead, nurture, threaten, and cajole, it is obstinately, defiantly asocial. Death is thus a desertion without the saving grace of absence. Nor is there any threat of punishment involved, for the corpse is clearly immune, insensible, and beyond retribution.

All of this serves to make funeral rituals an urgent necessity. First of all, the social fabric must be repaired, the ranks closed, and the virtue and unity of the collectivity dramatized in such a way as to bolster the waverers who might be seduced into following in the footsteps of the departed. . . . Second, the corpse must be incarcerated in the ground or in some other way isolated so as to remove the "bad influence" from sight and awareness. Third, the "independence" of the corpse must be symbolically denied in some way through ritual interaction between mourners and mourned. The corpse is thus almost always bathed, cosmetically treated in some way, and decorated or dressed—in some societies even held in the arms, rocked and kissed—as if, by treating it like an infant, to make one last effort at re-socialization through gratification of the now extinguished dependency needs. Furthermore, by performing these various operations on the corpse, and particularly by disposing of it, the group recaptures the initiative from the prodigal. Instead of being abandoned by him, they have now expelled him, and often do not consider him officially dead before doing so. . . .

Suicide is the most disapproved mode of dying. This disapproval, it must be emphasized, is a response to the suicide's shocking individualistic conclusion that his life is his own affair. In the absence of a theory of libidinal contraction or its equivalent the societal attitude toward suicide becomes incomprehensible.

Durkheim seems to have had this in mind when he stated that both egoistic and anomic suicide "result from the fact that society is not sufficiently in the individual's consciousness," and when he refers to individuals "evading their duties through death." Durkheim's law that suicide rates vary inversely with the totalitarianism of the collectivity (in the sense of the depth, breadth, and intensity of its impingement upon individual activities) is also worthy of note here. We shall see that this law holds for all forms of libidinal contraction.

The Withdrawal in Strength. The forms of narcissistic withdrawal thus far considered have been those associated with a weak and beleaguered ego. This corresponds to the implicit psychoanalytic assumption that in "healthy" states the libido flows out onto objects, while only a weak ego draws it back upon itself in the manner of a wound. But although as a recognition of the statistical correlation between "narcissism" and "ego-weakness" such an assumption is quite useful, it should not mislead us into ignoring the fact that more robust forms of narcissistic withdrawal do exist in reality, and play an even more important role in fantasy.

Of greatest interest in the present context is the combination of strong cathectic withdrawal with a complete absence of behavioral withdrawal—in other words, an individual actively engaged in collectivities with no emotional commitment to them. Insofar as others are aware of his total self-interestedness, he will be viewed as an ambitious and unscrupulous manipulator, and the term "psychopath" may even (rather loosely) be applied. . . .

There is no lever by which such an individual can be persuaded to serve social ends. He is the complete "economic man," motivated solely by rational self-interest. He will conform when it is dangerous not to, but will never scruple to violate any social norm or betray any individual or group if it will further his ends. He thus operates exclusively on the reality principle, which, as Freud notes, "indeed pursues the same ends [as the pleasure principle] but *takes into account* the conditions imposed by the outer world." Such conscious weighing of alternatives is not the kind of conformity which will bring peace of mind to those who are emotionally identified with their society, for social order now exists only when conformity is automatic, unconscious and nonrational.

All of this may seem rather obvious, but it bears some emphasizing in view of the rather widespread tendency to regard the role of society in the internecine struggles of id, ego, and superego merely as one of helping the ego control instinctual demands and pressures. In some respects, however, this allegiance is reversed. Freud notes, for example, that the primary opposition of religion is to the "egoistic instincts" rather than the sexual ones. What is insufficiently recognized is that the socialization process almost invariably guarantees that impulse control is *not* based entirely on the reality principle, but is firmly grounded in a socially manipulable, nonrational basis. Some of the ego's controlling functions must atrophy in order to permit the essentially competitive social institutions—whether in the ancient version of external authorities or the more sophisticated form of an internalized superego—to operate. For social control is more homogeneous, more consistent from person to person than individual, rational control. It permits a smooth predictability in the affairs of men.

This relationship becomes quite clear when we consider

the nature of those figures considered to be the great villains of literature and mythology. It is only here that we find that lack of enmity between ego and id which Freud considered to be healthy and natural. These characters are not in the least impulse-ridden, nor do they suffer from superego anxiety. As a result they are courageous, ambitious and proud, but also heartless, calculating, and unscrupulous. They achieve their goals without "going through channels." The epitome of this type is Milton's Satan, who is egregiously individualistic and hostile to any social organization he cannot dominate. His self-sufficiency and sturdy ego defenses enable him to withstand extreme tortures:

> The mind is its own place, and in itself
> Can make a Heaven of Hell, a Hell of Heaven,
> What matter where, if I be still the same?

The fact that "pride" is the cardinal sin in most religious systems should suffice to make it clear that the strong ego is seen as a greater menace to societal existence than the rampant id. The grossly impulsive individual is too ineffectual to menace anyone for very long and quickly destroys himself by stupid blunders. In our own legal system his inability to control his impulses is regarded as an extenuating circumstance. It is not the crime of passion but the premeditated crime that is most severely punished, which is equivalent to saying that the stronger the ego the greater the crime.

We must of course make clear here what viewpoint we are taking. As a member of a collectivity, social anxiety is aroused in the individual by narcissistic withdrawal—by "Satanic pride." But as a boundary-maintaining organism, instinctual anxiety is aroused in him when he observes a crime of passion or other manifestation of uncontrolled impulses. For the personality system, evil resides in the id, while for the social system, it resides in the ego.

This is the reason why great villains are so ambivalently regarded. Freud says that narcissistic types impress people as "personalities," and it cannot be denied that they invariably steal the show from the "good" characters. They are villains to society, but as representations of the ego they are heroes to the individual. Their deaths are doubly satisfying, for while social control is thus reestablished and evil punished, the villain achieves a secret victory, having established his narcissistic withdrawal on a permanent and invulnerable basis.

In sum, the "strong-ego" narcissist arouses most social anxiety because he appears to have overcome the dependency and guilt which are used as levers to resocialize the less healthy narcissist, and because his is an organization which can more effectively compete with the collectivity in which he is embedded. The most important anticipatory institutions which have arisen to meet this threat are the subversion of the reality principle in the socialization process, and the tendency of the family and peer group to punish narcissistic behavior with deprivation of love before the ego is hardy enough to tolerate such deprivation. These mechanisms are on the whole so effective that we have been forced to cull our major examples from fiction, wherein their existence serves further to ensure their absence from real life. . . .

Strongly narcissistic individuals have a certain seductive fascination for most people, particularly for those with intense dependency needs. This fascination is non-normative and in no way incompatible with a considered appraisal (at a distance) of the narcissistic leader as totally villainous. Its prototype may be seen in the experiment of von Holst, who removed the forebrain (and hence the schooling response) of a fish, which thereupon became the leader of the swarm. At the human level great leaders are similarly sought among those who are deficient in the need to depend on others—i.e., people who are willing to sacrifice security to vanity.

But there are conditions under which this tendency becomes normative. Narcissistic withdrawal is usually tolerated in individuals who are expected to confer some great benefit upon society: leaders, prophets, shamans, inventors, artists, scientists, innovators of all kinds. This expectation allays social anxiety and social control mechanisms are waived—there is no harm if the prophet temporarily leaves the group and goes into the desert because he will return in time, replete with marvelous visions. Similarly, if the leader is selfish, unfeeling, unscrupulous, and vain, this is acceptable because he will take upon himself the group's burdens and lead them to the promised land.

The basis of this tolerance is perhaps some vague awareness that great enterprises require an abundance of libidinal energy, which must hence be withdrawn from the usual social objects. The more robust varieties of narcissist have this libido available for creative innovation, and to the extent that the social value of such innovation is perceived, the price will be paid with commensurate willingness.

In the case, however, of the charismatic leader, the relationship is simpler and more primitive. The individual who has stored up narcissistic libido will attract the libido of others to him, after the physical principle that the greater the mass the greater the attraction. Libido thus has a social significance akin to that of *mana,* and an individual of this kind can be a focus for group loyalty. This is usually achieved by seducing the potential centripetal agent with narcissistic rewards and power.

We might then summarize these observations by saying that a group will not apply negative sanctions to narcissistic withdrawal if such withdrawal seems to increase the libidinal diffusion of other group members. We shall see that the same principle applies to other forms of cathectic withdrawal.

II. DYADIC WITHDRAWAL

Our discussion of narcissistic withdrawal would suggest that the social danger it raises is almost entirely hypothetical. Where it is combined with a weak ego it is impotent as a social force, while where it appears in conjunction with ego-strength, mechanisms have evolved which tend to channel it into what are often socially constructive paths. What diminishes the threat of both forms, then, is the fact that all human beings have needs which can best be satisfied through other human beings. Where the ego is weak the individual is compelled to depend upon others. Where it is strong he will seek out others because they will maximize his gratification. He will expend very little love on them, will in fact try to use and exploit them, ruthlessly, but in order to do so successfully he will in most cases be forced to bargain and compromise (which his inherent pragmatism finds quite natural and easy).

But what if most of the physiological and psychological needs of the individual could be satisfied without immediate recourse to the larger collectivity? Suppose that the libido of the individual were concentrated upon only one other person, who served to gratify all of these needs, and that a reciprocal concentration were made by that other person. A lower level of ego-strength would then be required to make an effective cathectic withdrawal from larger collectivities, and the anticipatory institutions described in the previous section would no longer be adequate.

This is the situation which obtains with dyadic withdrawal. An intimate dyadic relationship always threatens to short-circuit the libidinal network of the community and drain off its source of sustenance. The needs binding the individual to collectivities and reinforcing his allegiance thereto are now satisfied in the dyadic relationship, and the libido attached to these collectivities and diffused through their component members is drawn back and invested in the dyad.

There are several reasons why the dyad lends itself so well to this kind of short-circuiting. One is that, as Simmel pointed out, "the secession of either would destroy the whole. The dyad, therefore, does not attain that superpersonal life which the individual feels to be independent of himself." Another is that all other groups consist of multiple relationships which influence one another, while the dyad consists of only one relationship, influenced by none. In triads and larger groups the libidinal cathexis of the individual is divided and distributed, and there are many points of "leverage" at which he may be influenced or controlled. Furthermore, if part of the attachment of two persons is based upon a common attachment to a third party it may also be based upon attachment to a superindividual concept, to collective ideals.

One may, of course, exaggerate the special qualities of the dyad. In part it is merely the extreme case of a general law

338 THE PSYCHOLOGY OF SOCIETY

which says that intimate involvement of an individual with a group is an inverse function of its size. It is possible, however, to make a sharp separation of the dyad from other forms by virtue of its low combinatorial potential. The intimate dyadic relationship thus forms a nodal point for libidinal contraction. Libidinal cathexis which is withdrawn from larger collectivities can "stick" to the dyad, in a manner analogous to the stopping-places in Freud's parable of fixation.

The Dyad and the Community. If we assume a finite quantity of libido in every individual, then it follows that the greater the emotional involvement in the dyad, the greater will be the cathectic withdrawal from other objects. This accords well with the popular concept of the oblivious lovers, who are "all wrapped up in each other," and somewhat careless of their social obligations. All of the great lovers of history and litera-ture were guilty of striking disloyalties of one kind or another— disregard for the norms governing family and peer group ties, in the story of Romeo and Juliet, becomes, in the affair of Antony and Cleopatra, a disregard for societal responsibilities which embrace most of the civilized world. In Shakespeare's drama, a war of global significance is treated by the lovers as a courtly tournament, and their armies are manipulated as if the outcome were related only to the complexities of the internal dyadic relationship. This is epitomized in a remark by Cleopatra, who expresses her satisfaction with a day of military victory by saying to Antony, "Comest thou smiling from the world's great snare uncaught?"

Given this inverse relationship between dyadic cathexis and societal cathexis, another correlation suggests itself. We may hypothesize that the more totalitarian the collectivity, in terms of making demands upon the individual to involve every area of his life in collective activity, the stronger will be the prohibition against dyadic intimacy. We have already seen that a similar relation holds for suicide, and it may equally be applied to other forms of narcissistic withdrawal.

Strong opposition to dyadic intimacy is often found in youth groups which are formed on the basis of common inter-ests, such as music, camping, travel, or mountain-climbing.

Solidarity in such groups often runs high, and avoidance of even momentary pairing is usually a firmly upheld norm. Extreme prohibitions are also characteristic of utopian communistic communities, religious and otherwise, such as the Oneida experiment. In some instances the dyadic intimacy prohibition is enforced at the same time that sexual promiscuity is encouraged, thus clearly revealing that the basis of the proscription is not fear of sexuality but fear of libidinal contraction—fear lest the functions which the state performs for the individual could be performed for each other by the members of the dyad. Soviet Russia and Nazi Germany also made abortive experiments in this direction, before realizing that as a device for providing societal control over dyadic intimacy, the institution of marriage could scarcely be improved upon.

In some nonliterate societies, the prevention of privacy is managed through such devices as barracks-type living arrangements. I stress this fact because of the widespread notion that "romantic love" is simply an idiosyncrasy of Western civilization, and has no relevance for primitive societies. This view has been challenged by Goode, who argues that it is less rare than supposed, and seems to associate its infrequency, as we have done here, with the notion that "love must be controlled." . . .

One principal issue, then, in this conflict between dyadic intimacy and collective life, is whether the relationship shall be an end in itself (as in "romantic love") or a means to a socially desired end. In this connection let us consider Alexander's remark that *the erotic value of an action is inversely related to the degree to which it loses the freedom of choice and becomes coordinated* and subordinated to other functions and becomes a part of an organized system, of a goal structure." On the individual level he points to the fact that the growing child "first practices most of his biological functions playfully for the mere pleasure he derives from them," but that later they are directed toward utilitarian goals, integrated into a larger system of action, and lose their erotic value. Similarly he sees society as "losing its playful hedonistic qualities as it becomes more and more organized and thus restricts the freedom of the activities of its members. . . . Play requires utmost freedom of choice, which is lost when the activities of man become closely knit into a social fabric." He contrasts the individualistic and playful cat to the collectivistic, organized and unplayful ant, and goes on to note that in the insect states "organization progressed so far that the majority of the members became asexual and what erotic expression remains for them consists in an occasional communal ritualistic performance consisting in to and fro rhythmic movements collectively performed."

This discussion pinpoints the source of the antagonism of "totalitarian" collectivities toward dyadic intimacy. The intimate, exclusive dyadic relationship is essentially "playful" and non-utilitarian. Some kind of organized societal intrusion, as in the institution of marriage, is required to convert it into a socially useful relationship, and insofar as this intrusion is successful the playful aspect of the relationship will tend to disappear. As Alexander points out, "the process toward increased organization or less freedom of choice takes place at the cost of erotic gratification of the individual members of a system, be these organic functions of the body or members of a social organization." . . . We may thus directly equate libidinal diffusion with the de-eroticizing of the sexual life of the individual—the transformation of hedonistic activity into utilitarian activity as Alexander describes it. . . .

Let us now look at examples of dyadic withdrawal in our own society. Although it first appears much earlier, as we shall see, its most familiar manifestations are those occurring in adolescence, when experiments in enduring heterosexual intimacy are first essayed, and soon encounter various kinds of resistance and control from parents, other authorities, and the peer group. The arena of the struggle is often the issue of "going steady," which is generally opposed by adults whether it involves a cathectic withdrawal or not, but which is handled by the peer group with the ardent inconsistency characteristic of fledgling social enterprises. In some group zealous opposition is the rule, while in others there is an equally enthusiastic group endorsement of the practice, transformed in such a way, however, by group regulation, as no longer to constitute dyadic withdrawal. Criteria of sexual desirability are established with fanatical specificity by group norms, so as virtually to eliminate the importance of personal psychological characteristics. The partners are expected to spend the bulk of their time in group activities and to have a relationship of short duration (often measured in weeks). Such institutionalization of the "going steady" relationship is clearly a far more effective instrument against libidinal contraction than adult opposition.

A special example of this type of peer group control is found in the "rating-and-dating complex" described by Waller. Here the most desirable dyadic partner becomes the one who best lives up to group norms, which tend to replace sexual strivings with status and prestige needs. Under these conditions personal intimacy is rarely achieved. If by some accident compatible partners should come together, the rules regulating behavior in the situation would tend to prevent the existence of this compatibility from becoming known to either person.

Norms in many such groups also emphasize sexual antagonism and exploitation. The male often achieves prestige within the male group by maximizing physical contact and minimizing expenditure of money on a date. The female achieves prestige within her group by maximizing expenditure and minimizing sexual contact. The date becomes, in the ideal case, a contest between adversaries. Each has much to win or lose in the way of prestige, depending upon how effectively control of tender and sexual feelings can be maintained. It is not difficult to see how dyadic intimacy is minimized in this situation. If each partner, even in the midst of sexual caresses, is "keeping score" in terms of the peer group norms, little emotional involvement can take place. The boy, for example, knows that his friends will later ask him if he "made out," and his sexual behavior may be determined more by this than by any qualities inherent in his partner. It is of no little significance that the beginning of dyadic intimacy and withdrawal is always signalled by the boy's sudden reluctance to talk about the relationship, a reluctance which invariably arouses social anxiety and ridicule. . . .

Institutions such as marriage or peer group regulation of dyadic relationships block dyadic withdrawal through social intrusion upon the dyad—ritualizing and regulating it, and drawing its members back into their other relationships. For the most part these forms of control are so effective that it is only in large, "loose," pluralistic societies such as our own that dyadic withdrawal occurs with sufficient frequency and intensity to permit easy observation of the forces opposing it. In many primitive societies dyadic relationships are so highly institutionalized and diluted by group bonds that withdrawal has little opportunity to emerge.

In more mutable societies, however, sudden outbreaks of dyadic intimacy in unexpected areas are always occurring, due to the obsolescence of old mechanisms (e.g. chaperonage) or the emergence of new and unregulated areas of contact (e.g. earlier dating). Sporadic accelerations in the process of collectivization (such as occur in utopian religious communities) may also generate a demand for more extreme action. In such circumstances prohibition becomes more common.

The "going steady" controversy in our society is a good example of this phenomenon, in that it revolves around an extension of heterosexual dyadic intimacy into a younger and younger age group in an era in which teen-age marriage is felt to be socially undesirable. In the colonial period, when an unmarried girl of twenty was considered an old maid, the threat of dyadic withdrawal in adolescence was dissipated by marriage, but this is less feasible today, when the educational process is so prolonged and so valued. Furthermore, we have entered an age in which, through geographical mobility and mass communication, libidinal diffusion has achieved new heights of virtuosity. . . .

Societal intrusion and absorption seems effectively to forestall tendencies toward dyadic withdrawal whenever and wherever they appear.

It is perhaps for this reason that dyadic withdrawal is such a popular theme in the myths, legends, and dramas of Western Civilization. Yet even in fantasy such withdrawals are always short-lived, ending usually in dissolution or death. Apparently a permanent lifelong dyadic withdrawal is unimaginable, for to my knowledge there is no instance of such a phenomenon in the fantasy productions of any culture.

This statement, however, is somewhat misleading. In death a kind of permanent dyadic withdrawal *is* achieved, and this is the appeal that stories of tragic lovers hold. In real life, and in comedies, dyadic withdrawal usually ends in societal absorption, unless the couple separates. This does not mean, of course, that the relationship is any less satisfying—the couple may indeed "live happily ever after" as in the fairy tale. It means only that the dyad loses some of its exclusiveness and self-sufficiency and ceases to be a social threat. Some of the cathexis previously withdrawn into the dyad flows back onto larger collectivities, and some of the needs funneled into the dyad for satisfaction there now begin to seek fulfillment in a wider setting.

The great tragic lovers of fiction, however, are always set in opposition to societal forces and are always destroyed by them. But their relationship is not. They always die or are buried together, with the dyadic bond untainted by societal intrusion. The immortality of this bond and of their withdrawal is often symbolized by plants or trees growing out of their graves and entwining.

It may be recalled that we have encountered this theme before, in our discussion of the death of the narcissistic villain-hero: the crime of narcissistic withdrawal receives public punishment, i.e., death, and private reward, i.e., escape from socialization. So also with the crime of dyadic withdrawal in fiction. It is initially achieved, satisfying the desire of the spectator for libidinal contraction, and subsequently punished, relieving his social anxiety and assuaging his moral outrage. But in spite of the punishment, society is really cheated, since the withdrawal is never reversed, and both the dyad and the withdrawal remain immortally intact. A moral victory is won for the forces of regression—one in which the spectators can privately participate with secret applause, like Irishmen applauding an Irish villain in an English play.

Thus, as de Rougemont has stressed, the great tragic lovers of fiction, most notably in the Tristan and Isolde legend, actively desire and seek death. But this longing for death is a longing for an end to life in a societal context. It is a turning-away from what is felt as an over-extension, over-diffusion, over-sublimation, and over-rationalization of libido, and a desire to return to a more primitive, more simple, and more fully satisfying form of libidinal involvement. It is the association of this regressive, antisocietal impulse with the yearning for death which justifies Freud's use of the term "death-instinct." . . .

III. FAMILIAL WITHDRAWAL

A major social limitation of the withdrawn dyad is that, however self-sufficient it may appear to be, it cannot reproduce itself. This limitation is remedied when we move to the third potential product of libidinal contraction, the autonomous nuclear family. Here for the first time we encounter a true collectivity, a miniature society which is potentially immortal. In this sense it is the least regressive of the three forms we have discussed. As we move from narcissistic withdrawal through dyadic withdrawal to familial withdrawal we are tracing the waxing of the erotic instincts as defined by Freud, "which are always trying to collect living substance together into ever larger unities." . . .

Familial withdrawal occurs whenever a nuclear family becomes emotionally or libidinally sufficient unto itself, and partial expressions of this state are often seen. But it is quite obvious that such a condition can neither go very far nor persist very long without the occurrence of incest—not on the fragmentary and disruptive basis which we find in reality, but in a stable and organized manner which provides at least one sexual partner for most family members. . . .

It is therefore reasonable to ask, however, since the danger of total familial withdrawal is as hypothetical as in the case of the other forms, and since it is in fact the least regressive of the three, why the incest taboo is stronger and less often violated than the taboos surrounding more severe forms of libidinal contraction? . . .

Even if we assumed some kind of primeval normlessness, with the family structure based on power alone, we would not expect random mating, but rather a pattern reflecting the power structure. The prevailing form of incest would thus be father-daughter incest, with the other forms strongly inhibited by force. This would be the primal horde pattern described by Freud—a collectivity of normless narcissists held together and subjugated by the power of an absolutely narcissistic leader. It would cease to exist, as Mills points out, with the advent of any normative or collective action.

It would be more difficult to envision a stable family structure built upon mother-son incest, simply because the potential for dyadic withdrawal would be so high. Intimate communication is enormously facilitated between incestuous partners, due to the biological and cultural similarities between them, not to mention the great range of shared experiences. But this essentially narcissistic component is particularly strong in the relationship between mother and son, since each has at one time viewed the other as a part of or extension of the self. It is in part for this reason that mother-son incest is of all forms the most severely prohibited.

We should not leave the topic of familial withdrawal without considering the tolerated "exceptions" which we have found in the other forms of libidinal contraction. Murdock points out that institutionalized violations of the incest taboo (excluding momentary violations on special tribal occasions) are restricted to royal or aristocratic families, with the conscious purpose being to keep such families separate and impermeable. The position of these families is identical to that of the narcissistic leader, in whom libidinal contraction is encouraged so that he may bear the burdens of responsibility more easily.

But if this phenomenon appears but rarely in terrestrial royal families, it is very much the rule in mythological ones. Not only are all major deities the world over inveterate narcissists, but in all polytheistic systems the divine families are incorrigibly incestuous. In order to create a powerful and attractive nucleus which will focus libidinal diffusion for the earthly collectivity, the libido of the gods must be concentrated and intense, according to the principle that libido attracts libido. For upon these deities rests the solidarity of the community.

But it is not only as leaders and libidinal foci that the gods must hoard their libido, it is also as creators. The demiurges and progenitors of the gods are most particularly likely to be incestuous—theirs, after all, is the most "momentous constructive activity" imaginable.

41. Juliet Mitchell:
Psychoanalysis and Feminism [1940–]

The greater part of the feminist movement has identified Freud as the enemy. It is held that psychoanalysis claims women are inferior and that they can achieve true femininity only as wives and mothers. Psychoanalysis is seen as a justification for the status-quo, bourgeois and patriarchal, and Freud in his own person exemplifies these qualities. I would agree that popularized Freudianism must answer to this description; but the argument of this book is that a rejection of psychoanalysis and of Freud's works is fatal for feminism. However it may have been used, psychoanalysis is not a recommendation *for* a patriarchal society, but as analysis *of* one. If we are interested in understanding and challenging the oppression of women, we cannot afford to neglect it. . . .

Feminist critics of Freud have not only conflated his theories with those of other, often diverging, analysts and with popularizations, but, with more serious consequences still, have extrapolated his ideas about femininity from their context within the larger theories of psychoanalysis. Yet it is only this context that gives meaning to such notorious concepts as say, 'penis-envy'—without their context such notions certainly become either laughable or ideologically dangerous. In the briefest possible terms, we could say that psychoanalysis is about the material reality of ideas both within, and of, man's history; thus in 'penis-envy' we are talking not about an anatomical organ, but about the ideas of it that people hold and live by within the general culture, the order of human society. It is this last factor that also prescribes the reference point of psychoanalysis. The way we live as 'ideas' the necessary laws of human society is not so much conscious as *unconscious*—the particular task of psychoanalysis is to decipher how we acquire our heritage of the ideas and laws of human society within the unconscious mind, or, to put it another way, the unconscious mind *is* the way in which we acquire these laws. . . .

The feminist critics . . . all praise Freud for the accuracy of his *observations* on the psychological characteristics of middle-class women who are oppressed under patriarchy. They condemn, however, his *analysis* on the grounds of its biological determinism and lament that he did not see the reality of social causation that was staring him in the face. There is justification for this attack only in so far as Freud often gave up on this question when he reached the 'biological bedrock' that underlay his psychoanalytic investigation. But what Freud did, was to give up precisely because psychoanalysis has nothing to do with biology—except in the sense that our mental life also reflects, in a transformed way, what culture has already done with our biological needs and constitutions. It was with this *transformation* that Freud was concerned. What we could, and should, criticize him for is that he never makes his repeated statements to this effect forcefully enough in the context of his accounts of psychological sexual differences. To the contrary, disastrously as it turned out for the future of the psychoanalysis of femininity, it is just at these points that he most frequently turned back from the problem, leaving the reader with a nasty feeling that Freud's last word on the subject referred her to biology or anatomy.

But clearly it was just such a taste of biology that 'post'-Freudian analysts savoured. As a criticism of this aspect of *their* work, the condemnations of Freud hold good. If any analysis of feminine psychology is to take place, it is high time that a decisive break was made both with biologism in general and with the specific contribution it makes here: that a so-called biological dualism between the sexes is reflected in mental life. Psychoanalysis is about the inheritance and acquisition of the human order. The fact that it has been used to induce conformity to specific social mores is a further abuse of it that largely has been made possible on the theoretical level by the same biological preoccupation of some post-Freudians. If anatomy were indeed destiny, as Freud once disastrously remarked, then we might as well all get on with it and give up, for *nothing* would distinguish man from the animals. But Freud made this fatal remark in the context of a science concerned with exploring human social laws as they are represented in the unconscious mind.

Freud's analysis of the psychology of women takes place within a concept that it is neither socially nor biologically dualistic. It takes place within an analysis of patriarchy. His theories give us the beginnings of an explanation of the inferiorized and 'alternative' (second sex) psychology of women under patriarchy. Their concern is with how the human animal with a bisexual psychological disposition becomes the sexed social creature—the man or the woman.

In his speculative works on the origins of human culture and man's phylogenesis, in particular in *Totem and Taboo* and *Moses and Monotheism,* Freud shows quite explicitly that the psychoanalytic concept of the unconscious is a concept of mankind's transmission and inheritance of his social (cultural) laws. In each man's unconscious lie all mankind's 'ideas' of his history; a history that cannot start afresh with each individual but must be acquired and contributed to over time. Understanding the laws of the unconscious thus amounts to a start in understanding how ideology functions, how we acquire and live the ideas and laws within which we must exist. A primary aspect of the law is that we live according to our sexed identity, our ever imperfect 'masculinity' or 'femininity'.

The determining feature of Freud's reconstruction of mankind's history is the murder of the primal father in a prehistorical period. It is this dead father that is the mark of patriarchy. In an imagined pre-social epoch, the father had *all* the power and *all* rights over *all* the women of the clan; a band of sons—

all brothers, weak on their own, but strong together, murdered the father to get at his rights. Of course, they could not all have his rights and, of course, they must feel ambivalent about the deed they had committed. Totemism and exogamy are the dual signs of their response: in the totem, or symbolic substitute for the father, is guaranteed that no one else may kill him, or by then his heirs (each one of the brothers). Furthermore, not one of the brothers can inherit this father's right to all the women. For as they cannot *all* inherit, none shall. This is the start of social law and morality. The brothers identify with the father they have killed, and internalize the guilt which they feel along with the pleasure in his death. The father thus becomes far more powerful in death than in life; it is in death that he institutes human history. The dead, symbolic father is far more crucial than any actual living father who merely transmits his name. This is the story of the origins of patriarchy. It is against this symbolic mark of the dead father that boys and girls find their cultural place within the instance of the Oedipus complex.

In the situation of the Oedipus complex (which reiterates the rules of the totem and of exogamy) the little boy learns his place as the heir to this law of the father and the little girl learns her place within it. The Oedipus complex is certainly a patriarchal myth and, though he never said so, the importance of this fact was doubtless behind Freud's repudiation of a parallel myth, for women—a so-called Electra complex. Freud always opposed any idea of symmetry in the cultural 'making' of men and women. A myth for women would have to bear most dominantly the marks of the Oedipus complex because it is a man's world into which a woman enters; complementarity or parallelism are out of the question. At first both sexes want to take the place of both the mother and the father, but as they cannot take *both* places, each sex has to learn to repress the characteristics of the other sex. But both, as they learn to speak and live within society, want to take the father's place, and *only the boy will one day be allowed to do so*. Furthermore both sexes are born into the desire of the mother, and as, through cultural heritage, what the mother desires is the phallus-turned-baby, *both* children desire to be the phallus for the mother. Again, *only the boy can fully recognize himself in his mother's desire*. Thus *both* sexes repudiate the implications of femininity. Femininity is, therefore, in part a repressed condition that can only be secondarily acquired in a distorted form. It is because it is repressed that femininity is so hard to comprehend both within and without psychoanalytic investigation—it returns in symptoms, such as hysteria. In the body of the hysteric, male and female, lies the feminine protest against the law of the father. But what is repressed is both the representation of the desire and the prohibition against it: there is nothing 'pure' or 'original' about it.

The girl only acquires her secondary feminine identity within the law of patriarchy in her positive Oedipus complex when she is seduced/raped by, and/or seduces the father. As the boy becomes heir to the law with his acceptance of symbolic castration from the father, the girl learns her feminine destiny with this symbolic seduction. But it is less important than the boy's 'castration', because she has to some extent perceived her situation before it is thus confirmed by the father's intervention. She has already acquired the information that as she is not heir to the phallus she does not need to accept symbolic castration (she is already 'castrated'). But without the father's role in her positive Oedipus complex she could remain locked in pre-Oedipal dilemmas (and hence would become psychotic), for the Oedipus complex is her entry into her human heritage of femininity. Freud always said that a woman was 'more bisexual' than a man. By this he seems to have been hinting at the fact that within patriarchy her desire to take the father's place and be the phallus for the mother is as strong as is the boy's ultimate right to do so. The bisexual disposition of her pre-Oedipal moment remains strong and her Oedipus complex is a poor, secondary affair. An affair in which she learns that her subjugation to the law of the father entails her becoming the representative of 'nature' and 'sexuality', a chaos of spontaneous, intuitive creativity. As she cannot receive the 'touch' of the law, her submission to it must be in establishing herself as its opposite— as all that is loving and irrational. Such is the condition of patriarchal human history.

With the ending of his Oedipus complex and the internalizing of the 'castrating' father as his authoritative superego, the boy enters into the prospect of his future manhood. The girl, on the contrary, has almost to build her Oedipus complex out of the impossibilities of her bisexual pre-Oedipal desires. Instead of internalizing the mark of the law in a superego to which she will live up, she can only develop her narcissistic ego-ideal. She must confirm her pre-Oedipal identification (as opposed to attachment) with the mother, and instead of taking on qualities of aggression and control she acquires the art of love and conciliation. Not being heir to the law of culture, her task is to see that mankind reproduces itself within the circularity of the supposedly natural family. The family is, of course, no more 'natural' than the woman, but its place within the law is to take on 'natural' functions. For sexuality, which supposedly unites the couple, disrupts the kingdom if uncontrolled; it, too, must be contained and organized. Woman becomes, in her nineteenth-century designation, 'the sex'. Hers is the sphere of reproduction.

This is the place of all women in patriarchal culture. To put the matter in a most generalizing fashion: men enter into the class-dominated structures of history while women (as women, whatever their actual work in production) remain defined by the kinship patterns of organization. In our society the kinship system is harnessed into the family—where a woman is formed in such a way that that is where she will stay. Differences of class, historical epoch, specific social situations alter the expression of femininity; but in relation to the law of the father, women's position across the board is a comparable one. When critics condemn Freud for not taking account of social reality, their concept of that reality is too limited. The social reality that he is concerned with elucidating is the mental representation of the reality of society.

As we have seen, Freud often longed for a satisfactory biological base on which to rest his psychological theories, and yet the wish was no sooner uttered than forgotten. From the work of Ernest Jones through to that of contemporary feminist analysts such as Mary Jane Sherfy, the biological base of sexual dualism has been sought. Although there is an obvious *use* of the biological base in any social formation, it would seem dubious to stress this. For there seems little evidence of any biological priority. Quite the contrary; we are confronted with a situation that is determinately social. This situation is the initial *transformation* of biology by the exchange system expressed by kinship structures and the *social* taboos on incest that set up the differential conditions for the formation of men and women. This is not, of course, to deny that, as in all mammalian species, there is a difference between the reproductive roles of each sex, but it is to suggest that in *no* human society do these take precedence in an untransformed way. The establishment of human society relegates them to a secondary place, though their ideological reimportation may make them appear dominant.

It is not simply a question of the by-now familiar thesis that mankind, in effecting the move from nature to culture, 'chose' to preserve women within a natural ('animal') role for the sake of the propagation and nurturing of the species, for this suggestion sets up too simple a split between nature and culture and consequently too simple a division between the fate of the sexes. The very inauguration of 'culture' necessitated a different role. It is not that women are confined to a natural function but that they are given a specialized role in the formation of civilization. *It is thus not on account of their 'natural' procreative possibilities but on account of their cultural utilization as exchange-objects* (*which involves an exploitation of their role as propagators*) *that women acquire their feminine definition.* The situation, then, into which boys and girls are born is the same, the place to which they are assigned is clearly different. As it stands now, that place is in most important respects the same that it has always been: boys are to take over from fathers, girls are to want to produce babies. Any biological urge to do so is buried beneath the cultural demand that makes the way this wish is acquired coincident with human society itself. The technological conquest of the biological distinction between the sexes that Firestone and others recommend is redundant; in this instance, biology is no longer relevant. In an important sense, on this question, it has not been relevant since the foundation of human society. That foundation itself distinguished between the sexes.

In what way does this emphatic change of terrain affect the tasks of feminism? If we identify patriarchy with human history, the solution to the question of the oppression of women at first seems far less accessible than if we were to explore other theories. It has been suggested that we struggle for an 'ecological revolution'—a *humanized* brave new world of extra-uterine babies—or that in the power games of all men we locate and challenge the enemy. In the first proposition, technology conquers the biological handicap of women—their greater physical weakness and painful ability to give birth. In the second, a sociological analysis matches the perceived actuality of male superiority—men as such *do* have greater economic and political power and thus social equality should right the injustice. One or other, or a combination of both of these technological and sociological answers has held sway in all demands for change and all hopes for equity. Neither socialist practice nor Marxist theory in this field have been exempt from these essentially social-democratic visions.

It is no surprise that in these circumstances the feminist revolution has nowhere come about, and that women, in vastly differing ways and degrees remain 'oppressed'. Even if important details of these theories are correct, the posing of a biological problem and its technological solution or the sociological explanation of *male* domination and its overcoming (by consent or violence) are *both* at base misleading suggestions. It is the specific feature of patriarchy—the law of the hypothesized prehistoric murdered father—that defines the relative places of men and women in human history. This 'father' and his representatives—all fathers—are the crucial expression of patriarchal society. It is *fathers* not *men* who have the determinate power. And it is a question neither of biology nor of a specific society, but of *human* society itself.

Such a proposition possibly seems *more* generalized and its solution *less* available than the biological-technological and sociological theories. But I don't think this need be the cas . Patriarchy describes the universal culture—however, each specific economic mode of production must express this in different ideological forms. The universal aspects of patriarchy set in motion by 'the death of the father' are the exchange of women and the cultural taboo on incest, but these are rehearsed diversely in the mind of man in different societies. It would seem to me that with capitalist society something new has happened to the culture that is patriarchy.

The complexity of capitalist society makes archaic the kinship structures and incest taboos for the majority of the people and yet it preserves them through thick and thin. Freud gave the name of the Oedipus complex to the universal law by which men and women learn their place in the world, but the universal law has specific expression in the capitalist family. (Anthropological arguments that make the Oedipus complex general without demarcating its specificity are inadequate; political suggestions that it is only to be found in capitalist societies are incorrect. What Freud was deciphering was our human heritage—but he deciphered it in a particular time and place.) *The capitalist economy implies that for the masses demands of exogamy and the social taboo on incest are irrelevant; but nevertheless it must preserve both these and the patriarchal structure that they imply.* Furthermore, it would seem that the specifically capitalist ideology of a supposedly natural nuclear family would be in harsh contradiction to the kinship structure as it is articulated in the Oedipus complex, which in this instance is expressed within this nuclear family. It is, I believe, this contradiction, which is already being powerfully felt, that must be analysed and then made use of for the overthrow of patriarchy.

Under capitalism, just as the economic mode of production contains its own contradiction, so too does the ideological mode of reproduction. The social conditions of work under capitalism potentially contain the overthrow of the exploitative conditions into which they are harnessed and it is these *same* social conditions of work that make potentially redundant the laws of patriarchal culture. The working class has the power to take back to itself (for mankind) the products of the labour which are now taken from it; but no simple extension of this position can be taken to apply to patriarchal ideology. The same capitalist conditions of labour (the mass of people working together) create the conditions of change in both spheres, but because of their completely different origins, the change will come about in different ways. It is the working class as a class that has the products of its social labour privately appropriated by the capitalist class; it is women who stand at the heart of the contradiction of patriarchy under capitalism.

The controlled exchange of women that defines human culture is reproduced in the patriarchal ideology of every form of society. It goes alongside and is interlinked with class conflict, but it is not the same thing. It is not only in the ideology of their roles as mothers and procreators but above all in the very psychology of femininity that women bear witness to the patriarchal definition of human society. But today this patriarchal ideology, while it poses as the ultimate rationalization, is, in fact, in the slow death throes of its own irrationality; in this it is like the capitalist economy itself. But in both cases only a *political* struggle will bring their surcease. Neither can die a natural death; capitalism will, as it is all the time doing, intervene at a political level, to ensure their survival.

It is because it appears as the ultimate rationality, that critics mistake the Oedipus complex for the nuclear family itself. On the contrary, it is the contradiction between the internalized law of patriarchal human order described by Freud as the Oedipus complex, and its embodiment in the nuclear family, that is significant.

The patriarchal law speaks to and through each person in his unconscious; the reproduction of the ideology of human society is thus assured in the acquisition of the law by each individual. The unconscious that Freud analysed could thus be described as the domain of the reproduction of culture or ideology. The contradiction that exists between this law that is now essentially redundant but that of course still continues to speak in the unconscious, and the form of the nuclear family is therefore crucial. The bourgeois family was so to speak created to give that law a last hearing. Naturally enough, it is not very good at its job, so capitalist society offers a stop-go programme of boosting or undermining this family. It is because it is so obviously a point of weakness that so much revolutionary theory and strategy has concentrated on attacking it. But, as we have seen, its importance lies not *within* it so much as *between* it and the patriarchal law it is supposed to express. Of greater importance still is the contradiction between patriarchal law and the social organization of work—a contradiction held in check by the nuclear family.

It is at this moment, when the very structure of patriarchal culture becomes redundant, that with necessary perversity a vogue for man-as-animal comes into its own. Throughout history man has made strenuous intellectual efforts to distinguish himself from the beasts—this was always a dominant feature of his ideology; now, when the basis of his differential culture is in need of transformation, the only possible rearguard action is to consider that that culture was never in any case very significant. In the human zoo the male 'naked-ape' is naturally aggressive and the female naturally nurturative, they must regain their instinctive animal nature and forget what man has made of man. Such absurdities are a symptom of the dilemma of patriarchal human order. A symptom of a *completely different order* is the feminist movements of the nineteenth and twentieth centuries.

Under patriarchal order women are oppressed in their very psychologies of femininity; once this order is retained only in a highly contradictory manner this oppression manifests itself. Women have to organize themselves as a group to effect a change in the basic ideology of human society. To be effective, this can be no righteous challenge to the simple domination of men (though this plays a tactical part), but a struggle based on a theory of the social non-necessity at this stage of development of the laws instituted by patriarchy.

The overthrow of the capitalist economy and the political challenge that effects this, do not in themselves mean a transformation of patriarchal ideology. This is the implication of the fact that the ideological sphere has a certain autonomy. The change to a socialist economy does not by itself suggest that the end of patriarchy comfortably follows suit. A specific struggle against patriarchy—a cultural revolution—is requisite. The battles too must have their own autonomy. It seems to follow that women within revolutionary feminism can be the spearhead of general ideological change as the working class is the agent of the overthrow of the specifically capitalist mode of production. . . .

When the potentialities of the complexities of capitalism—both economic and ideological—are released by its overthrow, new structures will gradually come to be represented in the unconscious. It is the task of feminism to insist on their birth. Some other expression of the entry into culture than the implications for the unconscious of the exchange of women will have to be found in non-patriarchal society. . . . It is not a question of changing (or ending) who has or how one has babies. It is a question of overthrowing patriarchy. As the end of 'eternal' class conflict is visible within the contradictions of capitalism, so too, it would seem, is the swan-song of the 'immortal' nature of patriarchal culture to be heard.

42. Philip Rieff: *The Triumph of the Therapeutic*   [1922–]

So long as a culture maintains its vitality, whatever must be renounced disappears and is given back bettered; Freud called this process sublimation. But, as that sage among psychiatrists Harry Stack Sullivan once said, "if you tell people how they can sublimate, they can't sublimate." The dynamics of culture are in "the unwitting part of it."* Now our renunciations have failed us; less and less is given back bettered. For this reason, chiefly, I think, this culture, which once imagined itself inside a church, feels trapped in something like a zoo of separate cages. Modern men are like Rilke's panther, forever looking out from one cage into another. Because the modern sense of identity seems outraged by imprisonment in either old church or new cage, it is

* Harry Stack Sullivan, "The Illusion of Personal Individuality," *Psychiatry* (1950), Vol. 13, No. 1, p. 323.

the obligation of sociologists, so far as they remain interested in assessing the quality of our corporate life, to analyze doctrinal as well as organizational profiles of the rage to be free of the inherited morality, the better to see how these differ from what is being raged against. . . .

During the nineteenth century, when sociology helped in a major way to construct the central experience of deconversion toward an anti-creedal analytic attitude, that discipline suffered from a vast overconfidence both about its own advance and about the progress of the culture, which it understood as undergoing varieties of such deconversions. "Progress," wrote Spencer,* "is not an accident, but a necessity. Surely must evil and immorality disappear; surely must men become perfect." A basic transformation of culture appeared both inevitable and desirable.

Running parallel with and in the opposite direction from the process of deconversion was that process of conversion to a superior system of symbols—Science—which would supply the next predicate for the cultural organization of personality. Comte, for example, understood his own time as one of transition between two cultures. It was more generally proposed by students of our collective condition not merely that the old religious culture was dying but that the new scientific one had quite enough power already to be born.† Thus Comte concluded that only because of the "coexistence" of these two cultures did the "grand crisis now experienced by the most civilized nations" persist.‡ Freud was less sanguine. He believed that the crisis of coexistence was probably a permanent mode of the relation between personality and culture. . . .

Freud emphasized coercion and the renunciation of instinct

---

* Herbert Spencer, *Social Statics* (London, 1892), p. 32. Some doubts occurred to Spencer, about the pace of progress toward a culture freed from faith, but not about its inevitability or eventual terminus. (See the note he added to the passage quoted.)

† The birth pangs might be those caused by a proletariat emerging out of the womb of history, as Marx thought. But this proletariat would dominate a culture even more scientific in its substantial nature and social organization than that envisaged by Comte.

‡ Auguste Comte, "Plan of the Scientific Operations Necessary for Reorganizing Society," Frederick Harrison (ed.), *Early Essays of Comte* (London, n.d.) p. 88.

as indispensable elements in all culture. Freud was neither an eroticist nor a democrat. His theory of culture depended upon a crossing between his idea of moral authority and an elitist inclination. "It is just as impossible," he writes, "to do without control of the mass by a minority as it is to dispense with coercion in the work of civilization." By "mass" Freud means not merely the "lazy and unintelligent," but, more importantly, those who "have no love for instinctual renunciation" and who cannot be "convinced by argument of its inevitability." That such large numbers of the cultivated and intelligent have identified themselves deliberately with those who are supposed to have no *love* for instinctual renunciation, suggests to me the most elaborate act of suicide that Western intellectuals have ever staged—those intellectuals, whether of the left or right, whose historic function it has been to assert the authority of a culture organized in terms of communal purpose, through the agency of congregations of the faithful.

Of course, this suicide is intended only as an exciting pose. Renunciations of instinct, as Freud wrote, "necessarily must remain." For these renunciations, the individual must be compensated by pleasures at once higher and more realizable than the pleasure of instinctual gratification. In compensation, and in place of where faith once was, men are offered Art and/or Science. It is true that new religions are constantly being born. But modern culture is unique in having given birth to such elaborately argued anti-religions, all aiming to confirm us in our devastating illusions of individuality and freedom. I suspect the children of Israel did not spend much time elaborating a doctrine of the golden calf; they naïvely danced around it, until Moses, their first intel ectual, put a stop to the plain fun and insisted on civilizing them, by submerging their individualities within a communal purpose. Now, although there is some dancing again, the intellectuals mainly sit around and think in awe about the power and perversity of their instincts, disguising their rancorous worship of self in the religion of art. Confronted thus with a picture gallery as the new center of self-worship, civilized men must become again anti-art, in the hope of shifting attention toward modalities of worship wholly other than that of self. . . .

The religious question: How are we to be consoled for the

misery of living? may be answered by a culture, thus self-defined, in various ways; in terms of the good, the beautiful, and the true (the wordiness of Socrates); by a reference to how and by whom we are to be saved (the terseness of Christ); by tracing a line of historical development toward justice (the ponderous irony of Marx). Because Freud as a therapist refused even to ask the religious question, or proclaim a characterological ideal, he earned the polemical hatred of the best who came after him—Jung, for example, as well as Lawrence and Reich—all of whom tried to envision the next culture. The prophet in all three of Freud's most powerful successor-critics was much stronger than the scientist. Jung could not avoid finding a theology at the end of his therapy nor Reich an ideal character at the end of his analytic theory. Later on in this volume, I shall consider various struggles by Freud's successors to frame the great question in a culturally compelling way, illustrating thereby how powerfully psychotherapy may be tempted to go beyond the grim safety of diagnostic analysis to seek out the danger of creative doctrinal synthesis. All the post-Freudians treated in this volume were similarly tempted. Their psychologies became modes of consolation. Instead of raising Freud's lack of conviction into a doctrine, leaving the ruins of the old renunciatory culture by the wayside, mitigating merely its discomforts as was done by Freud, these post-Freudians tried to create a releasing conviction—a new culture, or, as in the case of Jung, a simulacrum of the old one.

Freud never felt tempted in this way. His genius was analytic, not prophetic. At its best, psychoanalytic therapy is devoted to the long and dubious task of rubbing a touch of that analytic genius into less powerful minds. Here is no large new cosset of an idea, within which Western men could comfort themselves for the inherent difficulties of living. Freud's was a severe and chill anti-doctrine, in which the awesome dichotomy with which culture imposes itself upon men—that between an ultimately meaningful and a meaningless life—must also be abandoned. This, then, was Freud's prescription to mankind as the patient, so that by the power of the analytic attitude a limit be set to the sway of culture over mankind.

With such an attitude, men could not change the dynamics of culture (which were unchangeable anyway),* but they could change at least their own relationship to these dynamics. They could become more diplomatic in their transactions with the moral demand system: not rebels but negotiators. To maintain the analytic attitude, in the everyday conduct of life, becomes the most subtle of all efforts of the ego; it is tantamount to limiting the power of the super-ego and, therewith, of culture. The analytic attitude expresses a trained capacity for entertaining tentative opinions about the inner dictates of conscience, reserving the right even to disobey the law insofar as it originates outside the individual, in the name of a gospel of a freer impulse. Not that impulse alone is to be trusted. It is merely to be respected, and a limit recognized of the ability of any culture to transform the aggressiveness of impulse, by an alchemy of .commitment, into the authority of law. Freud maintained a sober vision of man in the middle, a go-between, aware of the fact that he had little strength of his own, forever mediating between culture and instinct in an effort to gain some room for maneuver between these hostile powers. Maturity, according to Freud, lay in the trained capacity to keep the negotiations from breaking down.

Does not such a doctrine of maturity, which cannot lead beyond the difficult and unstable condition of being mature, lead instead to fresh outbursts of hope for the victory of culture or that of impulse—or, as in the case of Freud's critical successors, to the wild hope of a culture dominated by impulse? Freud's doctrine of psychological manhood has itself contributed to a resurgence of anxiety on both sides, with some accusing him of being a conservative of culture (e.g., Lawrence) and others accusing him of being a nineteenth-century radical of impulse (e.g., Jung). In time, it may become apparent that Freud and his doctrine have undergone an inexorable disciplining by the cul-

---

* "What would be the use of the most correct analysis of social neuroses, since no one possesses authority to impose such a therapy upon the group?" To change the dynamics of culture, the analytic attitude would have to become a moral demand, and thus it would cease to be analytic. Cf. Sigmund Freud, *Civilisation and Its Discontents,* Standard Edition (London, 1961), XXI, p. 144.

ture, and that the exemplary cast of Freud's mind and character is more enduring than the particulars of his doctrine. In culture it is always the example that survives; the person is the immortal idea. Psychoanalysis was the perfect vehicle for Freud's intellectual character. When, at last, Freud found himself, having searched systematically but in vain in various disciplines, he established a new discipline, first of all for himself.

Later, as psychoanalysis became more adaptable, the hidden force of Freud's character began to be effective through the discipline, detached from his person. Psychoanalysis became a transferable art, and therefore a cultural force, which, dealing as it does in moral suasion, does not distinguish between science and art.* In sociological terms, psychoanalysis became what we shall call the symbolic mode of a "negative community." It is held together by the analytic attitude, as most moderns are who think too much about themselves. Psychoanalysis is yet another method of learning how to endure the loneliness produced by culture. Psychoanalysis is its representative therapy—in contrast to classical therapies of commitment. It is characteristic of our culture that there is no longer an effective sense of communion, driving the individual out of himself, rendering the inner life serviceable to the outer. This has led to cultural artifacts like psychoanalysis, devised primarily to protect the outer life against further encroachments by the inner and to minimize the damage caused by disorders among the parts inside. When so little can be taken for granted, and when the meaningfulness of social existence no longer grants an inner life at peace with itself, every man must become something of a genius about himself. But the imagination boggles at a culture made up mainly of virtuosi of the self. It is precisely the authority of culture that limits the need for such virtuosi.

* The distinction between science and art takes on sociological importance only inasmuch as the one or the other is diagnosed as having more or less cultural force. For the rest, the distinction breaks down into pedantries about the differences of method or procedure, when in fact the creative effort differs only in its object of address and not in its ways of constituting realities not immediately available to common sense. Yet even common sense is a residue of old arts and sciences, something like a cultural deposit of perception. Every brave art or new science, however, departs from common sense and thus must appear in the beginning, before it is established, as culturally subversive.

Just this threat to the authority of culture is the reason why psychoanalysis appealed so immediately to the modern intellectual, who prides himself first of all on his independence of mind and conduct. Now, there is a curious resemblance between the futility felt by the analyst and the modern intellectual: both have the analytic attitude as the very basis and limit of their vocations. Precisely for this reason both, analyst and modern intellectual, feel the futility built in to their vocations. They are charter members of the negative community, in which membership carries precious few obligations and the corporate effort is devoted mainly to objecting to the rules. Yet, despite growing regret among its critics, the civilization of authority continues to fade into history; more accurately, it has become dysfunctional. Freud was acutely aware of this. Seen from the vantage point of membership in the negative community, all positive ones appear either fraudulent or stupid; despite a massive effort by professional psychoanalysts to remain clinical therapists rather than culture critics, there is nothing in psychoanalysis that makes them any the less so.

Since a less negative sense of vocation can be instilled only in a community blessed with both a rank order of vocations and some objective means of assigning vocations, as in a civilization of authority, the patient, when he is sent out "cured," can only make himself his own vocation. To the extent of his intellectual and emotional capacity, he joins the negative community; he settles down to limit more or less capably the power of the culture in which he lives to sink deeper into his self. A certain autonomy from the penetrative thrust of culture: this is the characteristic of the new individuality. Freud himself realized this. When Freud rejected the notion of psychoanalysis as a propaedeutic to accepting one or another religious community, he imagined an ideal patient, one so strengthened that he could tolerate a return to nothing more compelling than an environment in which the ego could fight more capably for itself in the subtle and universal war of all against all.

I have summed up, elsewhere,* Freud's attack on the moralizing function of modern culture. It was not always the case;

* "The Analytic Attitude," *Encounter*, Vol. XVII, No. 6 (June, 1962), pp. 22–28.

but nowadays, in the circumstances of modernity, to be religious is, he thought, to be sick: it is an effort to find a cure where no one can possibly survive. For Freud, religious questions induce the very symptoms they seek to cure. "The moment a man questions the meaning and value of life," Freud wrote (in a letter to Marie Bonaparte),* "he is sick, since objectively neither has any existence." The analyst, proudly, needs no synthesis. But, in scorning a synthesis, he is opposing the dynamics of culture. It is precisely as the culture fails that "not only the patient's analysis but that of the analyst himself has ceased to be terminable and become an interminable task.† The exercise of reason is transformed into a parody of that contemplative way of life which characterizes most religious representatives of the old culture. Faith develops a simulacrum in analysis: the churches break up into warring sects. Here is the first step toward trying to explain the "psychoanalytic movement," which is a subtle contradiction in terms.

* *Letters of Sigmund Freud,* ed. by Ernst L. Freud (New York, 1960), p. 436.
† "Analysis Terminable and Interminable," *Collected Papers* (London, 1950), Vol. 5, p. 353.

About the Editor

RICHARD SENNETT is the Director of the Center for Humanistic Studies and a professor of sociology at New York University. The author of *The Fall of Public Man*, *The Uses of Disorder* and *Families Against the City* and co-author of *The Hidden Injuries of Class*, he received his bachelor's degree from the University of Chicago and his Ph.D. from Harvard. Mr. Sennett now lives in New York City.

VINTAGE POLITICAL SCIENCE AND SOCIAL CRITICISM

VINTAGE WORKS OF SCIENCE AND PSYCHOLOGY